Mastering 'Metrics

Mastering 'Metrics

The Path from Cause to Effect

Joshua D. Angrist

and

Jörn-Steffen Pischke

PRINCETON UNIVERSITY PRESS ■ PRINCETON AND OXFORD

Published by Princeton University Press, 41 William Street,
Princeton, New Jersey 08540
In the United Kingdom: Princeton University Press,
6 Oxford Street, Woodstock, Oxfordshire OX20 1TW

press.princeton.edu

Jacket and illustration design by Wanda Espana
Book illustrations by Garrett Scafani

Library of Congress Cataloging-in-Publication Data

Angrist, Joshua David.
Mastering 'metrics : the path from cause to effect /
Joshua D. Angrist, Jörn-Steffen Pischke.
pages   cm
Includes index.

Summary: "Applied econometrics, known to aficionados as 'metrics, is the
original data science. 'Metrics encompasses the statistical methods economists use
to untangle cause and effect in human affairs. Through accessible discussion and
with a dose of kung fu-themed humor, *Mastering 'Metrics* presents the essential
tools of econometric research and demonstrates why econometrics is exciting and
useful. The five most valuable econometric methods, or what the authors call the
Furious Five—random assignment, regression, instrumental variables, regression
discontinuity designs, and differences in differences-are illustrated through well-
crafted real-world examples (vetted for awesomeness by *Kung Fu Panda's* Jade
Palace). Does health insurance make you healthier? Randomized experiments
provide answers. Are expensive private colleges and selective public high schools
better than more pedestrian institutions? Regression analysis and a regression
discontinuity design reveal the surprising truth. When private banks teeter, and
depositors take their money and run, should central banks step in to save them?
Differences-in-differences analysis of a Depression-era banking crisis offers a
response. Could arresting O.J. Simpson have saved his ex-wife's life? Instrumental
variables methods instruct law enforcement authorities in how best to respond to
domestic abuse. Wielding econometric tools with skill and confidence, *Mastering
'Metrics* uses data and statistics to illuminate the path from cause to effect.
Shows why econometrics is important   Explains econometric research through
humorous and accessible discussion   Outlines empirical methods central to
modern econometric practice   Works through interesting and relevant real-world
examples"—Provided by publisher.

ISBN 978-0-691-15283-7 (hardback : alk. paper)—
ISBN 978-0-691-15284-4 (paperback : alk. paper)
1. Econometrics. I. Pischke, Jörn-Steffen. II. Title.
HB139.A53984   2014
330.01'5195—dc23   2014024449

British Library Cataloging-in-Publication Data is available

This book has been composed in Sabon
with Helvetica Neue Condensed family display using ZzTEX
by Princeton Editorial Associates Inc., Scottsdale, Arizona

Printed on acid-free paper. ∞

Printed in the United States of America

9   10   8

CONTENTS

FIGURES

TABLES

INTRODUCTION

BLIND MASTER PO: Close your eyes. What do you hear?

YOUNG KWAI CHANG CAINE: I hear the water, I hear the birds.

MASTER PO: Do you hear your own heartbeat?

KWAI CHANG CAINE: No.

MASTER PO: Do you hear the grasshopper that is at your feet?

KWAI CHANG CAINE: Old man, how is it that you hear these things?

MASTER PO: Young man, how is it that you do not?
  Kung Fu, Pilot

E conomists' reputation for dismality is a bad rap. Economics is as exciting as any science can be: the world is our lab, and the many diverse people in it are our subjects.

The excitement in our work comes from the opportunity to learn about cause and effect in human affairs. The big questions of the day are *our* questions: Will loose monetary policy spark economic growth or just fan the fires of inflation? Iowa farmers and the Federal Reserve chair want to know. Will mandatory health insurance really make Americans healthier? Such policy kindling lights the fires of talk radio. We approach these questions coolly, however, armed not with passion but with data.

Economists' use of data to answer cause-and-effect questions constitutes the field of applied econometrics, known to students and masters alike as *'metrics*. The tools of the 'metrics trade are disciplined data analysis, paired with the machinery of statistical inference. There is a mystical aspect to our work as well: we're after truth, but truth is not revealed in full, and the messages the data transmit require interpretation. In this spirit, we draw inspiration from the journey

of Kwai Chang Caine, hero of the classic *Kung Fu* TV series. Caine, a mixed-race Shaolin monk, wanders in search of
his U.S.-born half-brother in the nineteenth century American
West. As he searches, Caine questions all he sees in human affairs, uncovering hidden relationships and deeper meanings.
Like Caine's journey, the Way of 'Metrics is illuminated by
questions.

Other Things Equal

In a disturbing development you may have heard of, the proportion of American college students completing their degrees
in a timely fashion has taken a sharp turn south. Politicians
and policy analysts blame falling college graduation rates on a
pernicious combination of tuition hikes and the large student
loans many students use to finance their studies. Perhaps increased student borrowing derails some who would otherwise
stay on track. The fact that the students most likely to drop
out of school often shoulder large student loans would seem
to substantiate this hypothesis.

You'd rather pay for school with inherited riches than borrowed money if you can. As we'll discuss in detail, however,
education probably boosts earnings enough to make loan re-
payment bearable for most graduates. How then should we
interpret the negative correlation between debt burden and
college graduation rates? Does indebtedness *cause* debtors to
drop out? The first question to ask in this context is who bor-
rows the most. Students who borrow heavily typically come
from middle and lower income families, since richer families
have more savings. For many reasons, students from lower income families are less likely to complete a degree than those
from higher income families, regardless of whether they've
borrowed heavily. We should therefore be skeptical of claims
that high debt burdens cause lower college completion rates
when these claims are based solely on comparisons of completion rates between those with more or less debt. By virtue of the
correlation between family background and college debt, the
contrast in graduation rates between those with and without
student loans is not an *other things equal* comparison.

As college students majoring in economics, we first learned the *other things equal* idea by its Latin name, *ceteris paribus*. Comparisons made under *ceteris paribus* conditions have a causal interpretation. Imagine two students identical in every way, so their families have the same financial resources and their parents are similarly educated. One of these virtual twins finances college by borrowing and the other from savings. Because they are otherwise equal in every way (their grandmother has treated both to a small nest egg), differences in their educational attainment can be attributed to the fact that only one has borrowed. To this day, we wonder why so many economics students first encounter this central idea in Latin; maybe it's a conspiracy to keep them from thinking about it. Because, as this hypothetical comparison suggests, real *other things equal* comparisons are hard to engineer, some would even say *impossibile* (that's Italian not Latin, but at least people still speak it).

Hard to engineer, maybe, but not necessarily impossible. The 'metrics craft uses data to get to *other things equal* in spite of the obstacles—called selection bias or omitted variables bias—found on the path running from raw numbers to reliable causal knowledge. The path to causal understanding is rough and shadowed as it snakes around the boulders of selection bias. And yet, masters of 'metrics walk this path with confidence as well as humility, successfully linking cause and effect.

Our first line of attack on the causality problem is a randomized experiment, often called a randomized trial. In a randomized trial, researchers change the causal variables of interest (say, the availability of college financial aid) for a group selected using something like a coin toss. By changing circumstances randomly, we make it highly likely that the variable of interest is unrelated to the many other factors determining the outcomes we mean to study. Random assignment isn't the same as holding everything else fixed, but it has the same effect. Random manipulation makes *other things equal* hold on average across the groups that did and did not experience manipulation. As we explain in Chapter 1, "on average" is usually good enough.

Randomized trials take pride of place in our 'metrics toolkit. Alas, randomized social experiments are expensive to field and may be slow to bear fruit, while research funds are scarce and life is short. Often, therefore, masters of 'metrics turn to less powerful but more accessible research designs. Even when we can't practicably randomize, however, we still dream of the trials we'd like to do. The notion of an ideal experiment disciplines our approach to econometric research. *Mastering 'Metrics* shows how wise application of our five favorite econometric tools brings us as close as possible to the causality-revealing power of a real experiment.

Our favorite econometric tools are illustrated here through a series of well-crafted and important econometric studies. Vetted by Grand Master Oogway of *Kung Fu Panda*'s Jade Palace, these investigations of causal effects are distinguished by their awesomeness. The methods they use—random assignment, regression, instrumental variables, regression discontinuity designs, and differences-in-differences—are the Furious Five of econometric research. For starters, motivated by the contemporary American debate over health care, the first chapter describes two social experiments that reveal whether, as many policymakers believe, health insurance indeed helps those who have it stay healthy. Chapters 2–5 put our other tools to work, crafting answers to important questions ranging from the benefits of attending private colleges and selective high schools to the costs of teen drinking and the effects of central bank injections of liquidity.

Our final chapter puts the Furious Five to the test by returning to the education arena. On average, college graduates earn about twice as much as high school graduates, an earnings gap that only seems to be growing. Chapter 6 asks whether this gap is evidence of a large causal return to schooling or merely a reflection of the many other advantages those with more education might have (such as more educated parents). Can the relationship between schooling and earnings ever be evaluated on a *ceteris paribus* basis, or must the boulders of selection bias forever block our way? The challenge of quantifying the causal link between schooling and earnings provides a gripping test match for 'metrics tools and the masters who wield them.

Mastering 'Metrics

Chapter 1

Randomized Trials

||||||||||||||||||||||||||||||||||||||||||||||||||||❦||||||||||||||||||||||||||||||||||||||||||||||||||||

KWAI CHANG CAINE: What happens in a man's life is already written. A man must move through life as his destiny wills.

OLD MAN: Yet each is free to live as he chooses. Though they seem opposite, both are true.
Kung Fu, Pilot

Our Path

Our path begins with experimental *random assignment,* both as a framework for causal questions and a benchmark by which the results from other methods are judged. We illustrate the awesome power of random assignment through two randomized evaluations of the effects of health insurance. The appendix to this chapter also uses the experimental framework to review the concepts and methods of statistical inference.

1.1   In Sickness and in Health (Insurance)

The Affordable Care Act (ACA) has proven to be one of the most controversial and interesting policy innovations we've seen. The ACA requires Americans to buy health insurance, with a tax penalty for those who don't voluntarily buy in. The question of the proper role of government in the market for health care has many angles. One is the causal effect of health insurance on health. The United States spends more of its GDP on health care than do other developed nations, yet Americans are surprisingly unhealthy. For example, Americans are more likely to be overweight and die sooner than their Canadian cousins, who spend only about two-thirds as much on care.

America is also unusual among developed countries in having no universal health insurance scheme. Perhaps there's a causal connection here.

Elderly Americans are covered by a federal program called Medicare, while some poor Americans (including most single mothers, their children, and many other poor children) are covered by Medicaid. Many of the working, prime-age poor, however, have long been uninsured. In fact, many uninsured Americans have chosen not to participate in an employer-provided insurance plan.[1] These workers, perhaps correctly, count on hospital emergency departments, which cannot turn them away, to address their health-care needs. But the emergency department might not be the best place to treat, say, the flu, or to manage chronic conditions like diabetes and hypertension that are so pervasive among poor Americans. The emergency department is not required to provide long-term care. It therefore stands to reason that government-mandated health insurance might yield a health dividend. The push for subsidized universal health insurance stems in part from the belief that it does.

The *ceteris paribus* question in this context contrasts the health of someone with insurance coverage to the health of the same person were they without insurance (other than an emergency department backstop). This contrast highlights a fundamental empirical conundrum: people are either insured or not. We don't get to see them both ways, at least not at the same time in exactly the same circumstances.

In his celebrated poem, "The Road Not Taken," Robert Frost used the metaphor of a crossroads to describe the causal effects of personal choice:

> Two roads diverged in a yellow wood,
> And sorry I could not travel both
> And be one traveler, long I stood
> And looked down one as far as I could
> To where it bent in the undergrowth;

---

[1] For more on this surprising fact, see Jonathan Gruber, "Covering the Uninsured in the United States," *Journal of Economic Literature*, vol. 46, no. 3, September 2008, pages 571–606.

Frost's traveler concludes:

> Two roads diverged in a wood, and I—
> I took the one less traveled by,
> And that has made all the difference.

The traveler claims his choice has mattered, but, being only one person, he can't be sure. A later trip or a report by other travelers won't nail it down for him, either. Our narrator might be older and wiser the second time around, while other travelers might have different experiences on the same road. So it is with any choice, including those related to health insurance: would uninsured men with heart disease be disease-free if they had insurance? In the novel *Light Years,* James Salter's irresolute narrator observes: "Acts demolish their alternatives, that is the paradox." We can't know what lies at the end of the road not taken.

We can't know, but evidence can be brought to bear on the question. This chapter takes you through some of the evidence related to paths involving health insurance. The starting point is the National Health Interview Survey (NHIS), an annual survey of the U.S. population with detailed information on health and health insurance. Among many other things, the NHIS asks: "Would you say your health in general is excellent, very good, good, fair, or poor?" We used this question to code an index that assigns 5 to excellent health and 1 to poor health in a sample of married 2009 NHIS respondents who may or may not be insured.[2] This index is our *outcome:* a measure we're interested in studying. The causal relation of interest here is determined by a variable that indicates coverage by private health insurance. We call this variable the *treatment,* borrowing from the literature on medical trials, although the treatments we're interested in need not be medical treatments like drugs or surgery. In this context, those with insurance can be thought of as the *treatment group;* those without insurance make up the *comparison* or *control group.* A good control group reveals the fate of the treated in a counterfactual world where they are not treated.

---

[2] Our sample is aged 26–59 and therefore does not yet qualify for Medicare.

The first row of Table 1.1 compares the average health index of insured and uninsured Americans, with statistics tabulated separately for husbands and wives.[3] Those with health insurance are indeed healthier than those without, a gap of about .3 in the index for men and .4 in the index for women. These are large differences when measured against the standard deviation of the health index, which is about 1. (Standard deviations, reported in square brackets in Table 1.1, measure variability in data. The chapter appendix reviews the relevant formula.) These large gaps might be the health dividend we're looking for.

Fruitless and Fruitful Comparisons

Simple comparisons, such as those at the top of Table 1.1, are often cited as evidence of causal effects. More often than not, however, such comparisons are misleading. Once again the problem is *other things equal,* or lack thereof. Comparisons of people with and without health insurance are not apples to apples; such contrasts are apples to oranges, or worse.

Among other differences, those with health insurance are better educated, have higher income, and are more likely to be working than the uninsured. This can be seen in panel B of Table 1.1, which reports the average characteristics of NHIS respondents who do and don't have health insurance. Many of the differences in the table are large (for example, a nearly 3-year schooling gap); most are statistically precise enough to rule out the hypothesis that these discrepancies are merely chance findings (see the chapter appendix for a refresher on statistical significance). It won't surprise you to learn that most variables tabulated here are highly correlated with health as well as with health insurance status. More-educated people, for example, tend to be healthier as well as being overrepresented in the insured group. This may be because more-educated people exercise more, smoke less, and are more likely to wear seat belts. It stands to reason that the difference in health between insured and uninsured NHIS

[3] An Empirical Notes section after the last chapter gives detailed notes for this table and most of the other tables and figures in the book.

TABLE 1.1
Health and demographic characteristics of insured and uninsured
couples in the NHIS

	Husbands			Wives		
	Some HI (1)	No HI (2)	Difference (3)	Some HI (4)	No HI (5)	Difference (6)
A. Health						
Health index	4.01 [.93]	3.70 [1.01]	.31 (.03)	4.02 [.92]	3.62 [1.01]	.39 (.04)
B. Characteristics						
Nonwhite	.16	.17	−.01 (.01)	.15	.17	−.02 (.01)
Age	43.98	41.26	2.71 (.29)	42.24	39.62	2.62 (.30)
Education	14.31	11.56	2.74 (.10)	14.44	11.80	2.64 (.11)
Family size	3.50	3.98	−.47 (.05)	3.49	3.93	−.43 (.05)
Employed	.92	.85	.07 (.01)	.77	.56	.21 (.02)
Family income	106,467	45,656	60,810 (1,355)	106,212	46,385	59,828 (1,406)
Sample size	8,114	1,281		8,264	1,131	

Notes: This table reports average characteristics for insured and uninsured married couples in the 2009 National Health Interview Survey (NHIS). Columns (1), (2), (4), and (5) show average characteristics of the group of individuals specified by the column heading. Columns (3) and (6) report the difference between the average characteristic for individuals with and without health insurance (HI). Standard deviations are in brackets; standard errors are reported in parentheses.

respondents at least partly reflects the extra schooling of the insured.

Our effort to understand the causal connection between insurance and health is aided by fleshing out Frost's two-roads metaphor. We use the letter Y as shorthand for health, the outcome variable of interest. To make it clear when we're talking about specific people, we use subscripts as a stand-in for names: Y_i is the health of individual i. The outcome Y_i is recorded in our data. But, facing the choice of whether to pay for health insurance, person i has two *potential outcomes*, only one of which is observed. To distinguish one potential outcome from another, we add a second subscript: The road taken without health insurance leads to Y_{0i} (read this as "y-zero-i") for person i, while the road with health insurance leads to Y_{1i} (read this as "y-one–i") for person i. Potential outcomes lie at the end of each road one *might* take. The causal effect of insurance on health is the difference between them, written $Y_{1i} - Y_{0i}$.[4]

To nail this down further, consider the story of visiting Massachusetts Institute of Technology (MIT) student Khuzdar Khalat, recently arrived from Kazakhstan. Kazakhstan has a national health insurance system that covers all its citizens automatically (though you wouldn't go there just for the health insurance). Arriving in Cambridge, Massachusetts, Khuzdar is surprised to learn that MIT students must decide whether to opt in to the university's health insurance plan, for which MIT levies a hefty fee. Upon reflection, Khuzdar judges the MIT insurance worth paying for, since he fears upper respiratory infections in chilly New England. Let's say that $Y_{0i} = 3$ and $Y_{1i} = 4$ for $i =$ Khuzdar. For him, the causal effect of insurance is one step up on the NHIS scale:

$$Y_{1,\text{Khuzdar}} - Y_{0,\text{Khuzdar}} = 1.$$

Table 1.2 summarizes this information.

---

[4] Robert Frost's insights notwithstanding, econometrics isn't poetry. A modicum of mathematical notation allows us to describe and discuss subtle relationships precisely. We also use italics to introduce repeatedly used terms, such as *potential outcomes*, that have special meaning for masters of 'metrics.

TABLE 1.2
Outcomes and treatments for Khuzdar and Maria

	Khuzdar Khalat	Maria Moreño
Potential outcome without insurance: Y_{0i}	3	5
Potential outcome with insurance: Y_{1i}	4	5
Treatment (insurance status chosen): D_i	1	0
Actual health outcome: Y_i	4	5
Treatment effect: $Y_{1i} - Y_{0i}$	1	0

It's worth emphasizing that Table 1.2 is an imaginary table: some of the information it describes must remain hidden. Khuzdar will either buy insurance, revealing his value of Y_{1i}, or he won't, in which case his Y_{0i} is revealed. Khuzdar has walked many a long and dusty road in Kazakhstan, but even he cannot be sure what lies at the end of those not taken.

Maria Moreño is also coming to MIT this year; she hails from Chile's Andean highlands. Little concerned by Boston winters, hearty Maria is not the type to fall sick easily. She therefore passes up the MIT insurance, planning to use her money for travel instead. Because Maria has $Y_{0,\text{Maria}} = Y_{1,\text{Maria}} = 5$, the causal effect of insurance on her health is

$$Y_{1,\text{Maria}} - Y_{0,\text{Maria}} = 0.$$

Maria's numbers likewise appear in Table 1.2.

Since Khuzdar and Maria make different insurance choices, they offer an interesting comparison. Khuzdar's health is $Y_{\text{Khuzdar}} = Y_{1,\text{Khuzdar}} = 4$, while Maria's is $Y_{\text{Maria}} = Y_{0,\text{Maria}} = 5$. The difference between them is

$$Y_{\text{Khuzdar}} - Y_{\text{Maria}} = -1.$$

Taken at face value, this quantity—which we observe— suggests Khuzdar's decision to buy insurance is counter-productive. His MIT insurance coverage notwithstanding, in-sured Khuzdar's health is worse than uninsured Maria's.

In fact, the comparison between frail Khuzdar and hearty Maria tells us little about the causal effects of their choices. This can be seen by linking observed and potential outcomes as follows:

$$Y_{\text{Khuzdar}} - Y_{\text{Maria}} = Y_{1,\text{Khuzdar}} - Y_{0,\text{Maria}}$$

$$= \underbrace{Y_{1,\text{Khuzdar}} - Y_{0,\text{Khuzdar}}}_{1} + \underbrace{\{Y_{0,\text{Khuzdar}} - Y_{0,\text{Maria}}\}}_{-2}.$$

The second line in this equation is derived by adding and subtracting $Y_{0,\text{Khuzdar}}$, thereby generating two hidden comparisons that determine the one we see. The first comparison, $Y_{1,\text{Khuzdar}} - Y_{0,\text{Khuzdar}}$, is the causal effect of health insurance on Khuzdar, which is equal to 1. The second, $Y_{0,\text{Khuzdar}} - Y_{0,\text{Maria}}$, is the difference between the two students' health status were both to decide against insurance. This term, equal to -2, reflects Khuzdar's relative frailty. In the context of our effort to uncover causal effects, the lack of comparability captured by the second term is called *selection bias*.

You might think that selection bias has something to do with our focus on particular individuals instead of on groups, where, perhaps, extraneous differences can be expected to "average out." But the difficult problem of selection bias carries over to comparisons of groups, though, instead of individual causal effects, our attention shifts to *average causal effects*. In a group of n people, average causal effects are written $Avg_n[Y_{1i} - Y_{0i}]$, where averaging is done in the usual way (that is, we sum individual outcomes and divide by n):

$$Avg_n[Y_{1i} - Y_{0i}] = \frac{1}{n} \sum_{i=1}^{n} [Y_{1i} - Y_{0i}]$$

$$= \frac{1}{n} \sum_{i=1}^{n} Y_{1i} - \frac{1}{n} \sum_{i=1}^{n} Y_{0i}. \quad (1.1)$$

The symbol $\sum_{i=1}^{n}$ indicates a sum over everyone from $i = 1$ to n, where n is the size of the group over which we are averaging. Note that both summations in equation (1.1) are taken over everybody in the group of interest. The average causal effect of health insurance compares average health in hypothetical scenarios where everybody in the group does and does not have health insurance. As a computational matter, this is the average of individual causal effects like $Y_{1,\text{Khuzdar}} - Y_{0,\text{Khuzdar}}$ and $Y_{1,\text{Maria}} - Y_{0,\text{Maria}}$ for each student in our data.

An investigation of the average causal effect of insurance naturally begins by comparing the average health of groups of insured and uninsured people, as in Table 1.1. This comparison is facilitated by the construction of a *dummy variable*, D_i, which takes on the values 0 and 1 to indicate insurance status:

$$D_i = \begin{cases} 1 & \text{if } i \text{ is insured} \\ 0 & \text{otherwise.} \end{cases}$$

We can now write $Avg_n[Y_i | D_i = 1]$ for the average among the insured and $Avg_n[Y_i | D_i = 0]$ for the average among the uninsured. These quantities are averages *conditional* on insurance status.[5]

The average Y_i for the insured is necessarily an average of outcome Y_{1i}, but contains no information about Y_{0i}. Likewise, the average Y_i among the uninsured is an average of outcome Y_{0i}, but this average is devoid of information about the corresponding Y_{1i}. In other words, the road taken by those with insurance ends with Y_{1i}, while the road taken by those without insurance leads to Y_{0i}. This in turn leads to a simple but important conclusion about the difference in average health by insurance status:

Difference in group means

$$= Avg_n[Y_i | D_i = 1] - Avg_n[Y_i | D_i = 0]$$

$$= Avg_n[Y_{1i} | D_i = 1] - Avg_n[Y_{0i} | D_i = 0], \quad (1.2)$$

---

[5] Order the n observations on Y_i so that the n_0 observations from the group indicated by $D_i = 0$ precede the n_1 observations from the $D_i = 1$ group. The conditional average

$$Avg_n[Y_i | D_i = 0] = \frac{1}{n_0} \sum_{i=1}^{n_0} Y_i$$

is the sample average for the n_0 observations in the $D_i = 0$ group. The term $Avg_n[Y_i | D_i = 1]$ is calculated analogously from the remaining n_1 observations.

an expression highlighting the fact that the comparisons in Table 1.1 tell us something about potential outcomes, though not necessarily what we want to know. We're after $Avg_n[Y_{1i} - Y_{0i}]$, an average causal effect involving everyone's Y_{1i} and everyone's Y_{0i}, but we see average Y_{1i} only for the insured and average Y_{0i} only for the uninsured.

To sharpen our understanding of equation (1.2), it helps to imagine that health insurance makes everyone healthier by a constant amount, κ. As is the custom among our people, we use Greek letters to label such *parameters*, so as to distinguish them from variables or data; this one is the letter "kappa." The *constant-effects assumption* allows us to write:

$$Y_{1i} = Y_{0i} + \kappa, \qquad (1.3)$$

or, equivalently, $Y_{1i} - Y_{0i} = \kappa$. In other words, κ is both the individual and average causal effect of insurance on health. The question at hand is how comparisons such as those at the top of Table 1.1 relate to κ.

Using the constant-effects model (equation (1.3)) to substitute for $Avg_n[Y_{1i}|D_i = 1]$ in equation (1.2), we have:

$$Avg_n[Y_{1i}|D_i = 1] - Avg_n[Y_{0i}|D_i = 0]$$
$$= \{\kappa + Avg_n[Y_{0i}|D_i = 1]\} - Avg_n[Y_{0i}|D_i = 0]$$
$$= \kappa + \{Avg_n[Y_{0i}|D_i = 1] - Avg_n[Y_{0i}|D_i = 0]\}. \quad (1.4)$$

This equation reveals that health comparisons between those with and without insurance equal the causal effect of interest (κ) plus the difference in average Y_{0i} between the insured and the uninsured. As in the parable of Khuzdar and Maria, this second term describes selection bias. Specifically, the difference in average health by insurance status can be written:

> *Difference in group means*
> $= Average\ causal\ effect + Selection\ bias,$

where selection bias is defined as the difference in average Y_{0i} between the groups being compared.

How do we know that the difference in means by insurance status is contaminated by selection bias? We know because Y_{0i} is shorthand for everything about person i related to health, other than insurance status. The lower part of Table 1.1 documents important noninsurance differences between the insured and uninsured, showing that *ceteris* isn't *paribus* here in many ways. The insured in the NHIS are healthier for all sorts of reasons, including, perhaps, the causal effects of insurance. But the insured are also healthier because they are more educated, among other things. To see why this matters, imagine a world in which the causal effect of insurance is zero (that is, $\kappa = 0$). Even in such a world, we should expect insured NHIS respondents to be healthier, simply because they are more educated, richer, and so on. This positive selection bias runs counter to the negative selection bias we imagined in the parable of frail, insured Khuzdar and hearty, uninsured Maria; in fact it's relatively healthy people who opt for insurance in the NHIS. Either way, however, comparisons of the insured and uninsured are not apples-to-apples.

We wrap up this discussion by pointing out the subtle role played by information like that reported in panel B of Table 1.1. This panel shows that the groups being compared differ in ways that we can observe. As we'll see in the next chapter, if the only source of selection bias is a set of differences in characteristics that we can observe and measure, selection bias is (relatively) easy to fix. Suppose, for example, that the only source of selection bias in the insurance comparison is education. This bias is eliminated by focusing on samples of people with the same schooling, say, college graduates. Education is the same for insured and uninsured people in such a sample, because it's the same for everyone in the sample.

The subtlety in Table 1.1 arises because when observed differences proliferate, so should our suspicions about unobserved differences. The fact that people with and without health insurance differ in many visible ways suggests that even were we to hold observed characteristics fixed, the uninsured would likely differ from the insured in ways we don't see (after all, the list of variables we can see is partly fortuitous). In other words, even in a sample consisting of insured and uninsured people with the same education, income, and employment status, the insured might have higher values of Y_{0i}. The principal challenge facing masters of 'metrics is elimination of the selection bias that arises from such unobserved differences.

Breaking the Deadlock: Just RANDomize

My doctor gave me 6 months to live . . . but when I couldn't pay
the bill, he gave me 6 months more.
  Walter Matthau

Experimental random assignment eliminates selection bias.
The logistics of a randomized experiment, sometimes called
a *randomized trial*, can be complex, but the logic is simple. To
study the effects of health insurance in a randomized trial, we'd
start with a sample of people who are currently uninsured.
We'd then provide health insurance to a randomly chosen
subset of this sample, and let the rest go to the emergency
department if the need arises. Later, the health of the insured
and uninsured groups can be compared. Random assignment
makes this comparison *ceteris paribus*: groups insured and
uninsured by random assignment differ only in their insurance
status and any consequences that follow from it.

Suppose the MIT Health Service elects to forgo payment and tosses a coin to determine the insurance status of new students Ashish and Zandile (just this once, as a favor to their distinguished Economics Department). Zandile is insured if the toss comes up heads; otherwise, Ashish gets the coverage. A good start, but not good enough, since random assignment of two experimental subjects does not produce insured and uninsured apples. For one thing, Ashish is male and Zandile female. Women, as a rule, are healthier than men. If Zandile winds up healthier, it might be due to her good luck in having been born a woman and unrelated to her lucky draw in the insurance lottery. The problem here is that two is not enough to tango when it comes to random assignment. We must randomly assign treatment in a sample that's large enough to ensure that differences in individual characteristics like sex wash out.

Two randomly chosen groups, when large enough, are indeed comparable. This fact is due to a powerful statistical property known as the *Law of Large Numbers* (LLN). The LLN characterizes the behavior of sample averages in relation to sample size. Specifically, the LLN says that a sample average can be brought as close as we like to the average in the population from which it is drawn (say, the population of American college students) simply by enlarging the sample.

To see the LLN in action, play dice.[6] Specifically, roll a fair die once and save the result. Then roll again and average these two results. Keep on rolling and averaging. The numbers 1 to 6 are equally likely (that's why the die is said to be "fair"), so we can expect to see each value an equal number of times if we play long enough. Since there are six possibilities here, and all are equally likely, the expected outcome is an equally weighted average of each possibility, with weights equal to 1/6:

$$\left(1 \times \tfrac{1}{6}\right) + \left(2 \times \tfrac{1}{6}\right) + \left(3 \times \tfrac{1}{6}\right) + \left(4 \times \tfrac{1}{6}\right) + \left(5 \times \tfrac{1}{6}\right) + \left(6 \times \tfrac{1}{6}\right)$$
$$= \frac{1+2+3+4+5+6}{6} = 3.5.$$

[6] Six-sided cubes with one to six dots engraved on each side. There's an app for 'em on your smartphone.

This average value of 3.5 is called a *mathematical expectation;* in this case, it's the average value we'd get in infinitely many rolls of a fair die. The expectation concept is important to our work, so we define it formally here.

MATHEMATICAL EXPECTATION   The mathematical expectation of a variable, Y_i, written $E[Y_i]$, is the population average of this variable. If Y_i is a variable generated by a random process, such as throwing a die, $E[Y_i]$ is the average in infinitely many repetitions of this process. If Y_i is a variable that comes from a sample survey, $E[Y_i]$ is the average obtained if everyone in the population from which the sample is drawn were to be enumerated.

Rolling a die only a few times, the average toss may be far from the corresponding mathematical expectation. Roll two times, for example, and you might get boxcars or snake eyes (two sixes or two ones). These average to values well away from the expected value of 3.5. But as the number of tosses goes up, the average across tosses reliably tends to 3.5. This is the LLN in action (and it's how casinos make a profit: in most gambling games, you can't beat the house in the long run, because the expected payout for players is negative). More remarkably, it needn't take too many rolls or too large a sample for a sample average to approach the expected value. The chapter appendix addresses the question of how the number of rolls or the size of a sample survey determines statistical accuracy.

In randomized trials, experimental samples are created by sampling from a population we'd like to study rather than by repeating a game, but the LLN works just the same. When sampled subjects are randomly divided (as if by a coin toss) into treatment and control groups, they come from the same underlying population. The LLN therefore promises that those in randomly assigned treatment and control samples will be similar if the samples are large enough. For example, we expect to see similar proportions of men and women in randomly assigned treatment and control groups. Random assignment also produces groups of about the same age and with similar schooling levels. In fact, randomly assigned groups should be similar in every way, including in ways that we cannot easily measure or observe. This is the root of random assignment's awesome power to eliminate selection bias.

The power of random assignment can be described precisely using the following definition, which is closely related to the definition of mathematical expectation.

CONDITIONAL EXPECTATION   The conditional expectation of a variable, Y_i, given a dummy variable, $D_i = 1$, is written $E[Y_i|D_i = 1]$. This is the average of Y_i in the population that has D_i equal to 1. Likewise, the conditional expectation of a variable, Y_i, given $D_i = 0$, written $E[Y_i|D_i = 0]$, is the average of Y_i in the population that has D_i equal to 0. If Y_i and D_i are variables generated by a random process, such as throwing a die under different circumstances, $E[Y_i|D_i = d]$ is the average of infinitely many repetitions of this process while holding the circumstances indicated by D_i fixed at d. If Y_i and D_i come from a sample survey, $E[Y_i|D_i = d]$ is the average computed when everyone in the population who has $D_i = d$ is sampled.

Because randomly assigned treatment and control groups come from the same underlying population, they are the same in every way, including their expected Y_{0i}. In other words, the conditional expectations, $E[Y_{0i}|D_i = 1]$ and $E[Y_{0i}|D_i = 0]$, are the same. This in turn means that:

RANDOM ASSIGNMENT ELIMINATES SELECTION BIAS   When D_i is randomly assigned, $E[Y_{0i}|D_i = 1] = E[Y_{0i}|D_i = 0]$, and the difference in expectations by treatment status captures the causal effect of treatment:

$$E[Y_i|D_i = 1] - E[Y_i|D_i = 0]$$
$$= E[Y_{1i}|D_i = 1] - E[Y_{0i}|D_i = 0]$$
$$= E[Y_{0i} + \kappa|D_i = 1] - E[Y_{0i}|D_i = 0]$$
$$= \kappa + E[Y_{0i}|D_i = 1] - E[Y_{0i}|D_i = 0]$$
$$= \kappa.$$

Provided the sample at hand is large enough for the LLN to work its magic (so we can replace the conditional averages in equation (1.4) with conditional expectations), selection bias disappears in a randomized experiment. Random assignment works not by eliminating individual differences but rather by ensuring that the mix of individuals being compared is the same. Think of this as comparing barrels that include equal proportions of apples and oranges. As we explain in the chapters that follow, randomization isn't the only way to generate such *ceteris paribus* comparisons, but most masters believe it's the best.

When analyzing data from a randomized trial or any other research design, masters almost always begin with a check on whether treatment and control groups indeed look similar. This process, called *checking for balance,* amounts to a comparison of sample averages as in panel B of Table 1.1. The average characteristics in panel B appear dissimilar or unbalanced, underlining the fact that the data in this table don't come from anything like an experiment. It's worth checking for balance in this manner any time you find yourself estimating causal effects.

Random assignment of health insurance seems like a fanciful proposition. Yet health insurance coverage has twice been randomly assigned to large representative samples of Americans. The RAND Health Insurance Experiment (HIE), which ran from 1974 to 1982, was one of the most influential social experiments in research history. The HIE enrolled 3,958 people aged 14 to 61 from six areas of the country. The HIE sample excluded Medicare participants and most Medicaid and military health insurance subscribers. HIE participants were randomly assigned to one of 14 insurance plans. Participants did not have to pay insurance premiums, but the plans had a variety of provisions related to cost sharing, leading to large differences in the amount of insurance they offered.

The most generous HIE plan offered comprehensive care for free. At the other end of the insurance spectrum, three "catastrophic coverage" plans required families to pay 95% of their health-care costs, though these costs were capped as a proportion of income (or capped at $1,000 per family, if that was lower). The catastrophic plans approximate a no-insurance condition. A second insurance scheme (the "individual deductible" plan) also required families to pay 95% of outpatient charges, but only up to $150 per person or $450 per family. A group of nine other plans had a variety of coinsurance provisions, requiring participants to cover anywhere from 25% to 50% of charges, but always capped at a proportion of income or $1,000, whichever was lower. Participating families enrolled in the experimental plans for 3 or 5 years and agreed to give up any earlier insurance coverage in return for a fixed monthly payment unrelated to their use of medical care.[7]

The HIE was motivated primarily by an interest in what economists call the price elasticity of demand for health care. Specifically, the RAND investigators wanted to know whether and by how much health-care use falls when the price of health care goes up. Families in the free care plan faced a price of zero, while coinsurance plans cut prices to 25% or 50% of costs incurred, and families in the catastrophic coverage and deductible plans paid something close to the sticker price for care, at least until they hit the spending cap. But the investigators also wanted to know whether more comprehensive and more generous health insurance coverage indeed leads to better health. The answer to the first question was a clear "yes": health-care consumption is highly responsive to the price of care. The answer to the second question is murkier.

Randomized Results

Randomized field experiments are more elaborate than a coin toss, sometimes regrettably so. The HIE was complicated by

[7] Our description of the HIE follows Robert H. Brook et al., "Does Free Care Improve Adults' Health? Results from a Randomized Controlled Trial," *New England Journal of Medicine*, vol. 309, no. 23, December 8, 1983, pages 1426–1434. See also Aviva Aron-Dine, Liran Einav, and Amy Finkelstein, "The RAND Health Insurance Experiment, Three Decades Later," *Journal of Economic Perspectives*, vol. 27, Winter 2013, pages 197–222, for a recent assessment.

having many small treatment groups, spread over more than a dozen insurance plans. The treatment groups associated with each plan are mostly too small for comparisons between them to be statistically meaningful. Most analyses of the HIE data therefore start by grouping subjects who were assigned to similar HIE plans together. We do that here as well.[8]

A natural grouping scheme combines plans by the amount of cost sharing they require. The three catastrophic coverage plans, with subscribers shouldering almost all of their medical expenses up to a fairly high cap, approximate a no-insurance state. The individual deductible plan provided more coverage, but only by reducing the cap on total expenses that plan participants were required to shoulder. The nine coinsurance plans provided more substantial coverage by splitting subscribers' health-care costs with the insurer, starting with the first dollar of costs incurred. Finally, the free plan constituted a radical intervention that might be expected to generate the largest increase in health-care usage and, perhaps, health. This categorization leads us to four groups of plans: catastrophic, deductible, coinsurance, and free, instead of the 14 original plans. The catastrophic plans provide the (approximate) no-

---

[8] Other HIE complications include the fact that instead of simply tossing a coin (or the computer equivalent), RAND investigators implemented a complex assignment scheme that potentially affects the statistical properties of the resulting analyses (for details, see Carl Morris, "A Finite Selection Model for Experimental Design of the Health Insurance Study," *Journal of Econometrics*, vol. 11, no. 1, September 1979, pages 43–61). Intentions here were good, in that the experimenters hoped to insure themselves against chance deviation from perfect balance across treatment groups. Most HIE analysts ignore the resulting statistical complications, though many probably join us in regretting this attempt to gild the random assignment lily. A more serious problem arises from the large number of HIE subjects who dropped out of the experiment and the large differences in attrition rates across treatment groups (fewer left the free plan, for example). As noted by Aron-Dine, Einav, and Finkelstein, "The RAND Experiment," *Journal of Economic Perspectives*, 2013, differential attrition may have compromised the experiment's validity. Today's "randomistas" do better on such nuts-and-bolts design issues (see, for example, the experiments described in Abhijit Banerjee and Esther Duflo, *Poor Economics: A Radical Rethinking of the Way to Fight Global Poverty*, Public Affairs, 2011).

insurance control, while the deductible, coinsurance, and free plans are characterized by increasing levels of coverage.

As with nonexperimental comparisons, a first step in our experimental analysis is to check for balance. Do subjects randomly assigned to treatment and control groups—in this case, to health insurance schemes ranging from little to complete coverage—indeed look similar? We gauge this by comparing demographic characteristics and health data collected before the experiment began. Because demographic characteristics are unchanging, while the health variables in question were measured before random assignment, we expect to see only small differences in these variables across the groups assigned to different plans.

In contrast with our comparison of NHIS respondents' characteristics by insurance status in Table 1.1, a comparison of characteristics across randomly assigned treatment groups in the RAND experiment shows the people assigned to different HIE plans to be similar. This can be seen in panel A of Table 1.3. Column (1) in this table reports averages for the catastrophic plan group, while the remaining columns compare the groups assigned more generous insurance coverage with the catastrophic control group. As a summary measure, column (5) compares a sample combining subjects in the deductible, coinsurance, and free plans with subjects in the catastrophic plans. Individuals assigned to the plans with more generous coverage are a little less likely to be female and a little less educated than those in the catastrophic plans. We also see some variation in income, but differences between plan groups are mostly small and are as likely to go one way as another. This pattern contrasts with the large and systematic demographic differences between insured and uninsured people seen in the NHIS data summarized in Table 1.1.

The small differences across groups seen in panel A of Table 1.3 seem likely to reflect chance variation that emerges naturally as part of the sampling process. In any statistical sample, chance differences arise because we're looking at one of many possible draws from the underlying population from which we've sampled. A new sample of similar size from the same population can be expected to produce comparisons that are similar—though not identical—to those in the table.

TABLE 1.3
Demographic characteristics and baseline health in the RAND HIE

	Means	Differences between plan groups			
	Catastrophic plan (1)	Deductible − catastrophic (2)	Coinsurance − catastrophic (3)	Free − catastrophic (4)	Any insurance − catastrophic (5)
A. Demographic characteristics					
Female	.560	−.023 (.016)	−.025 (.015)	−.038 (.015)	−.030 (.013)
Nonwhite	.172	−.019 (.027)	−.027 (.025)	−.028 (.025)	−.025 (.022)
Age	32.4 [12.9]	.56 (.68)	.97 (.65)	.43 (.61)	.64 (.54)
Education	12.1 [2.9]	−.16 (.19)	−.06 (.19)	−.26 (.18)	−.17 (.16)
Family income	31,603 [18,148]	−2,104 (1,384)	970 (1,389)	−976 (1,345)	−654 (1,181)
Hospitalized last year	.115	.004 (.016)	−.002 (.015)	.001 (.015)	.001 (.013)
B. Baseline health variables					
General health index	70.9 [14.9]	−1.44 (.95)	.21 (.92)	−1.31 (.87)	−.93 (.77)
Cholesterol (mg/dl)	207 [40]	−1.42 (2.99)	−1.93 (2.76)	−5.25 (2.70)	−3.19 (2.29)
Systolic blood pressure (mm Hg)	122 [17]	2.32 (1.15)	.91 (1.08)	1.12 (1.01)	1.39 (.90)
Mental health index	73.8 [14.3]	−.12 (.82)	1.19 (.81)	.89 (.77)	.71 (.68)
Number enrolled	759	881	1,022	1,295	3,198

Notes: This table describes the demographic characteristics and baseline health of subjects in the RAND Health Insurance Experiment (HIE). Column (1) shows the average for the group assigned catastrophic coverage. Columns (2)–(5) compare averages in the deductible, cost-sharing, free care, and any insurance groups with the average in column (1). Standard errors are reported in parentheses in columns (2)–(5); standard deviations are reported in brackets in column (1).

The question of how much variation we should expect from one sample to another is addressed by the tools of statistical inference.

The appendix to this chapter briefly explains how to quantify sampling variation with formal statistical tests. Such tests amount to the juxtaposition of differences in sample averages with their *standard errors*, the numbers in parentheses reported below the differences in averages listed in columns (2)–(5) of Table 1.3. The standard error of a difference in averages is a measure of its statistical precision: when a difference in sample averages is smaller than about two standard errors, the difference is typically judged to be a chance finding compatible with the hypothesis that the populations from which these samples were drawn are, in fact, the same.

Differences that are larger than about two standard errors are said to be *statistically significant:* in such cases, it is highly unlikely (though not impossible) that these differences arose purely by chance. Differences that are not statistically significant are probably due to the vagaries of the sampling process. The notion of statistical significance helps us interpret comparisons like those in Table 1.3. Not only are the differences in this table mostly small, only two (for proportion female in columns (4) and (5)) are more than twice as large as the associated standard errors. In tables with many comparisons, the presence of a few isolated statistically significant differences is usually also attributable to chance. We also take comfort from the fact that the standard errors in this table are not very big, indicating differences across groups are measured reasonably precisely.

Panel B of Table 1.3 complements the contrasts in panel A with evidence for reasonably good balance in *pre-treatment outcomes* across treatment groups. This panel shows no statistically significant differences in a pre-treatment index of general health. Likewise, pre-treatment cholesterol, blood pressure, and mental health appear largely unrelated to treatment assignment, with only a couple of contrasts close to statistical significance. In addition, although lower cholesterol in the

free group suggests somewhat better health than in the catastrophic group, differences in the general health index between
these two groups go the other way (since lower index values
indicate worse health). Lack of a consistent pattern reinforces
the notion that these gaps are due to chance.

The first important finding to emerge from the HIE was
that subjects assigned to more generous insurance plans used
substantially more health care. This finding, which vindicates
economists' view that demand for a good should go up when
it gets cheaper, can be seen in panel A of Table 1.4.[9] As
might be expected, hospital inpatient admissions were less
sensitive to price than was outpatient care, probably because
admissions decisions are usually made by doctors. On the
other hand, assignment to the free care plan raised outpatient
spending by two-thirds (169/248) relative to spending by those
in catastrophic plans, while total medical expenses increased
by 45%. These large gaps are economically important as well
as statistically significant.

Subjects who didn't have to worry about the cost of health
care clearly consumed quite a bit more of it. Did this extra care
and expense make them healthier? Panel B in Table 1.4, which
compares health indicators across HIE treatment groups, suggests not. Cholesterol levels, blood pressure, and summary
indices of overall health and mental health are remarkably
similar across groups (these outcomes were mostly measured
3 or 5 years after random assignment). Formal statistical tests
show no statistically significant differences, as can be seen in
the group-specific contrasts (reported in columns (2)–(4)) and
in the differences in health between those in a catastrophic plan
and everyone in the more generous insurance groups (reported
in column (5)).

These HIE findings convinced many economists that generous health insurance can have unintended and undesirable

[9] The RAND results reported here are based on our own tabulations from
the HIE public use file, as described in the Empirical Notes section at the end of
the book. The original RAND results are summarized in Joseph P. Newhouse
et al., *Free for All? Lessons from the RAND Health Insurance Experiment*,
Harvard University Press, 1994.

TABLE 1.4
Health expenditure and health outcomes in the RAND HIE

	Means	Differences between plan groups			
	Catastrophic plan (1)	Deductible − catastrophic (2)	Coinsurance − catastrophic (3)	Free − catastrophic (4)	Any insurance − catastrophic (5)
A. Health-care use					
Face-to-face visits	2.78 [5.50]	.19 (.25)	.48 (.24)	1.66 (.25)	.90 (.20)
Outpatient expenses	248 [488]	42 (21)	60 (21)	169 (20)	101 (17)
Hospital admissions	.099 [.379]	.016 (.011)	.002 (.011)	.029 (.010)	.017 (.009)
Inpatient expenses	388 [2,308]	72 (69)	93 (73)	116 (60)	97 (53)
Total expenses	636 [2,535]	114 (79)	152 (85)	285 (72)	198 (63)
B. Health outcomes					
General health index	68.5 [15.9]	−.87 (.96)	.61 (.90)	−.78 (.87)	−.36 (.77)
Cholesterol (mg/dl)	203 [42]	.69 (2.57)	−2.31 (2.47)	−1.83 (2.39)	−1.32 (2.08)
Systolic blood pressure (mm Hg)	122 [19]	1.17 (1.06)	−1.39 (.99)	−.52 (.93)	−.36 (.85)
Mental health index	75.5 [14.8]	.45 (.91)	1.07 (.87)	.43 (.83)	.64 (.75)
Number enrolled	759	881	1,022	1,295	3,198

Notes: This table reports means and treatment effects for health expenditure and health outcomes in the RAND Health Insurance Experiment (HIE). Column (1) shows the average for the group assigned catastrophic coverage. Columns (2)–(5) compare averages in the deductible, cost-sharing, free care, and any insurance groups with the average in column (1). Standard errors are reported in parentheses in columns (2)–(5); standard deviations are reported in brackets in column (1).

consequences, increasing health-care usage and costs, without generating a dividend in the form of better health.[10]

1.2   The Oregon Trail

MASTER KAN: Truth is hard to understand.

KWAI CHANG CAINE: It is a fact, it is not the truth. Truth is often hidden, like a shadow in darkness.
   Kung Fu, Season 1, Episode 14

The HIE was an ambitious attempt to assess the impact of health insurance on health-care costs and health. And yet, as far as the contemporary debate over health insurance goes, the HIE might have missed the mark. For one thing, each HIE treatment group had at least catastrophic coverage, so financial liability for health-care costs was limited under every treatment. More importantly, today's uninsured Americans differ considerably from the HIE population: most of the uninsured are younger, less educated, poorer, and less likely to be working. The value of extra health care in such a group might be very different than for the middle class families that participated in the HIE.

One of the most controversial ideas in the contemporary health policy arena is the expansion of Medicaid to cover the currently uninsured (interestingly, on the eve of the RAND experiment, talk was of expanding Medicare, the public insurance program for America's elderly). Medicaid now covers families on welfare, some of the disabled, other poor children, and poor pregnant women. Suppose we were to expand Medicaid to cover those who don't qualify under current rules. How would such an expansion affect health-care spending? Would it shift treatment from costly and crowded emergency departments to possibly more effective primary care? Would Medicaid expansion improve health?

---

[10] Participants in the free plan had slightly better corrected vision than those in the other plans; see Brook et al., "Does Free Care Improve Health?" *New England Journal of Medicine,* 1983, for details.

Many American states have begun to "experiment" with Medicaid expansion in the sense that they've agreed to broaden eligibility, with the federal government footing most of the bill. Alas, these aren't real experiments, since everyone who is eligible for expanded Medicaid coverage gets it. The most convincing way to learn about the consequences of Medicaid expansion is to randomly offer Medicaid coverage to people in currently ineligible groups. Random assignment of Medicaid seems too much to hope for. Yet, in an awesome social experiment, the state of Oregon recently offered Medicaid to thousands of randomly chosen people in a publicly announced health insurance lottery.

We can think of Oregon's health insurance lottery as randomly selecting winners and losers from a pool of registrants, though coverage was not automatic, even for lottery winners. Winners won the opportunity to apply for the state-run Oregon Health Plan (OHP), the Oregon version of Medicaid. The state then reviewed these applications, awarding coverage to Oregon residents who were U.S. citizens or legal immigrants aged 19–64, not otherwise eligible for Medicaid, uninsured for at least 6 months, with income below the federal poverty level, and few financial assets. To initiate coverage, lottery winners had to document their poverty status and submit the required paperwork within 45 days.

The rationale for the 2008 OHP lottery was fairness and not research, but it's no less awesome for that. The Oregon health insurance lottery provides some of the best evidence we can hope to find on the costs and benefits of insurance coverage for the currently uninsured, a fact that motivated research on OHP by MIT master Amy Finkelstein and her coauthors.[11]

---

[11] See Amy Finkelstein et al., "The Oregon Health Insurance Experiment: Evidence from the First Year," *Quarterly Journal of Economics*, vol. 127, no. 3, August 2012, pages 1057–1106; Katherine Baicker et al., "The Oregon Experiment—Effects of Medicaid on Clinical Outcomes," *New England Journal of Medicine*, vol. 368, no. 18, May 2, 2013, pages 1713–1722; and Sarah Taubman et al., "Medicaid Increases Emergency Department Use: Evidence from Oregon's Health Insurance Experiment," *Science*, vol. 343, no. 6168, January 17, 2014, pages 263–268.

Roughly 75,000 lottery applicants registered for expanded coverage through the OHP. Of these, almost 30,000 were randomly selected and invited to apply for OHP; these winners constitute the OHP treatment group. The other 45,000 constitute the OHP control sample.

The first question that arises in this context is whether OHP lottery winners were more likely to end up insured as a result of winning. This question is motivated by the fact that some applicants qualified for regular Medicaid even without the lottery. Panel A of Table 1.5 shows that about 14% of controls (lottery losers) were covered by Medicaid in the year following the first OHP lottery. At the same time, the second column, which reports differences between the treatment and control groups, shows that the probability of Medicaid coverage increased by 26 percentage points for lottery winners. Column (4) shows a similar increase for the subsample living in and around Portland, Oregon's largest city. The upshot is that OHP lottery winners were insured at much higher rates than were lottery losers, a difference that might have affected their use of health care and their health.[12]

The OHP treatment group (that is, lottery winners) used more health-care services than they otherwise would have. This can also be seen in Table 1.5, which shows estimates of changes in service use in the rows below the estimate of the OHP effect on Medicaid coverage. The hospitalization rate increased by about half a percentage point, a modest though statistically significant effect. Emergency department visits, outpatient visits, and prescription drug use all increased markedly. The fact that the number of emergency department visits rose about 10%, a precisely estimated effect (the standard error associated with this estimate, reported in column (4), is .029), is especially noteworthy. Many policymakers hoped and expected health insurance to shift formerly uninsured patients

---

[12] Why weren't all OHP lottery winners insured? Some failed to submit the required paperwork on time, while about half of those who did complete the necessary forms in a timely fashion turned out to be ineligible on further review.

TABLE 1.5
OHP effects on insurance coverage and health-care use

	Oregon		Portland area	
	Control mean	Treatment effect	Control mean	Treatment effect
Outcome	(1)	(2)	(3)	(4)
A. Administrative data				
Ever on Medicaid	.141	.256 (.004)	.151	.247 (.006)
Any hospital admissions	.067	.005 (.002)		
Any emergency department visit			.345	.017 (.006)
Number of emergency department visits			1.02	.101 (.029)
Sample size	74,922		24,646	
B. Survey data				
Outpatient visits (in the past 6 months)	1.91	.314 (.054)		
Any prescriptions?	.637	.025 (.008)		
Sample size	23,741			

Notes: This table reports estimates of the effect of winning the Oregon Health Plan (OHP) lottery on insurance coverage and use of health care. Odd-numbered columns show control group averages. Even-numbered columns report the regression coefficient on a dummy for lottery winners. Standard errors are reported in parentheses.

away from hospital emergency departments toward less costly sources of care.

Finally, the proof of the health insurance pudding appears in Table 1.6: lottery winners in the statewide sample report a modest improvement in the probability they assess their health as being good or better (an effect of .039, which can be

TABLE 1.6
OHP effects on health indicators and financial health

Outcome	Oregon		Portland area	
	Control mean (1)	Treatment effect (2)	Control mean (3)	Treatment effect (4)
A. Health indicators				
Health is good	.548	.039 (.008)		
Physical health index			45.5	.29 (.21)
Mental health index			44.4	.47 (.24)
Cholesterol			204	.53 (.69)
Systolic blood pressure (mm Hg)			119	−.13 (.30)
B. Financial health				
Medical expenditures >30% of income			.055	−.011 (.005)
Any medical debt?			.568	−.032 (.010)
Sample size	23,741		12,229	

Notes: This table reports estimates of the effect of winning the Oregon Health Plan (OHP) lottery on health indicators and financial health. Odd-numbered columns show control group averages. Even-numbered columns report the regression coefficient on a dummy for lottery winners. Standard errors are reported in parentheses.

compared with a control mean of .55; the Health is Good variable is a dummy). Results from in-person interviews conducted in Portland suggest these gains stem more from improved mental rather than physical health, as can be seen in the second and third rows in column (4) (the health variables in the Portland sample are indices ranging from 0 to 100). As in the RAND experiment, results from Portland suggest physical health indicators like cholesterol and blood pressure were largely unchanged by increased access to OHP insurance.

The weak health effects of the OHP lottery disappointed policymakers who looked to publicly provided insurance to generate a health dividend for low-income Americans. The fact that health insurance increased rather than decreased expensive emergency department use is especially frustrating. At the same time, panel B of Table 1.6 reveals that health insurance provided the sort of financial safety net for which it was designed. Specifically, households winning the lottery were less likely to have incurred large medical expenses or to have accumulated debt generated by the need to pay for health care. It may be this improvement in financial health that accounts for improved mental health in the treatment group.

It also bears emphasizing that the financial and health effects seen in Table 1.6 most likely come from the 25% of the sample who obtained insurance as a result of the lottery. Adjusting for the fact that insurance status was unchanged for many winners shows that gains in financial security and mental health for the one-quarter of applicants who were insured as a result of the lottery were considerably larger than simple comparisons of winners and losers would suggest. Chapter 3, on instrumental variables methods, details the nature of such adjustments. As you'll soon see, the appropriate adjustment here amounts to the division of win/loss differences in outcomes by win/loss differences in the probability of insurance. This implies that the effect of being insured is as much as four times larger than the effect of winning the OHP lottery (statistical significance is unchanged by this adjustment).

The RAND and Oregon findings are remarkably similar. Two ambitious experiments targeting substantially different populations show that the use of health-care services increases sharply in response to insurance coverage, while neither experiment reveals much of an insurance effect on physical health. In 2008, OHP lottery winners enjoyed small but noticeable improvements in mental health. Importantly, and not coincidentally, OHP also succeeded in insulating many lottery winners from the financial consequences of poor health, just as a good insurance policy should. At the same time, these studies suggest that subsidized public health insurance should not be expected to yield a dramatic health dividend.

MASTER JOSHWAY: In a nutshell, please, Grasshopper.

GRASSHOPPER: Causal inference compares potential outcomes, descriptions of the world when alternative roads are taken.

MASTER JOSHWAY: Do we compare those who took one road with those who took another?

GRASSHOPPER: Such comparisons are often contaminated by selection bias, that is, differences between treated and control subjects that exist even in the absence of a treatment effect.

MASTER JOSHWAY: Can selection bias be eliminated?

GRASSHOPPER: Random assignment to treatment and control conditions eliminates selection bias. Yet even in randomized trials, we check for balance.

MASTER JOSHWAY: Is there a single causal truth, which all randomized investigations are sure to reveal?

GRASSHOPPER: I see now that there can be many truths, Master, some compatible, some in contradiction. We therefore take special note when findings from two or more experiments are similar.

Masters of 'Metrics: From Daniel to R. A. Fisher

The value of a control group was revealed in the Old Testament. The Book of Daniel recounts how Babylonian King Nebuchadnezzar decided to groom Daniel and other Israelite captives for his royal service. As slavery goes, this wasn't a bad gig, since the king ordered his captives be fed "food and wine from the king's table." Daniel was uneasy about the rich diet, however, preferring modest vegetarian fare. The king's chamberlains initially refused Daniel's special meals request, fearing that his diet would prove inadequate for one called on to serve the king. Daniel, not without chutzpah, proposed a controlled experiment: "Test your servants for ten days. Give us nothing but vegetables to eat and water to drink. Then compare our appearance with that of the young men who eat the royal food, and treat your servants in accordance with what you see" (Daniel 1, 12–13). The Bible recounts how this experiment supported Daniel's conjecture regarding the relative healthfulness of a vegetarian diet, though as far as we know Daniel himself didn't get an academic paper out of it.

Nutrition is a recurring theme in the quest for balance. Scurvy, a debilitating disease caused by vitamin C deficiency, was the scourge of the British Navy. In 1742, James Lind, a surgeon on HMS *Salisbury*, experimented with a cure for scurvy. Lind chose 12 seamen with scurvy and started them on an identical diet. He then formed six pairs and treated each of the pairs with a different supplement to their daily food ration. One of the additions was an extra two oranges and one lemon (Lind believed an acidic diet might cure scurvy). Though Lind did not use random assignment, and his sample was small by our standards, he was a pioneer in that he chose his 12 study members so they were "as similar as I could have them." The citrus eaters—Britain's first limeys—were quickly and incontrovertibly cured, a life-changing empirical finding that emerged from Lind's data even though his theory was wrong.[13]

Almost 150 years passed between Lind and the first recorded use of experimental random assignment. This was by Charles Peirce, an American philosopher and scientist, who experimented with subjects' ability to detect small differences in weight. In a less-than-fascinating but methodologically significant 1885 publication, Peirce and his student Joseph Jastrow explained how they varied experimental conditions according to draws from a pile of playing cards.[14]

---

[13] Lind's experiment is described in Duncan P. Thomas, "Sailors, Scurvy, and Science," *Journal of the Royal Society of Medicine,* vol. 90, no. 1, January 1997, pages 50–54.

[14] Charles S. Peirce and Joseph Jastrow, "On Small Differences in Sensation," *Memoirs of the National Academy of Sciences,* vol. 3, 1885, pages 75–83.

Sir Ronald Aylmer Fisher's devotion to scientific truth being literally passionate, he was an implacable enemy of those whom he judged guilty of propagating error (John Aldrich)

The idea of a randomized controlled trial emerged in earnest only at the beginning of the twentieth century, in the work of statistician and geneticist Sir Ronald Aylmer Fisher, who analyzed data from agricultural experiments. Experimental random assignment features in Fisher's 1925 *Statistical Methods for Research Workers* and is detailed in his landmark *The Design of Experiments,* published in 1935.[15]

Fisher had many fantastically good ideas and a few bad ones. In addition to explaining the value of random assignment, he developed the statistical method of maximum likelihood. Along with 'metrics master Sewall Wright (and J.B.S. Haldane), Fisher launched the field of theoretical population genetics. But he was also a committed eugenicist and a proponent of forced sterilization (as was regression master Sir Francis Galton, who coined the term "eugenics"). Fisher, a

[15] Ronald A. Fisher, *Statistical Methods for Research Workers,* Oliver and Boyd, 1925, and Ronald A. Fisher, *The Design of Experiments,* Oliver and Boyd, 1935.

lifelong pipe smoker, was also on the wrong side of the debate over smoking and health, due in part to his strongly held belief that smoking and lung cancer share a common genetic origin. The negative effect of smoking on health now seems well established, though Fisher was right to worry about selection bias in health research. Many lifestyle choices, such as low-fat diets and vitamins, have been shown to be unrelated to health outcomes when evaluated with random assignment.

Appendix: Mastering Inference

YOUNG CAINE: I am puzzled.

MASTER PO: That is the beginning of wisdom.
  Kung Fu, Season 2, Episode 25

This is the first of a number of appendices that fill in key econometric and statistical details. You can spend your life studying statistical inference; many masters do. Here we offer a brief sketch of essential ideas and basic statistical tools, enough to understand tables like those in this chapter.

The HIE is based on a sample of participants drawn (more or less) at random from the population eligible for the experiment. Drawing another sample from the same population, we'd get somewhat different results, but the general picture should be similar if the sample is large enough for the LLN to kick in. How can we decide whether statistical results constitute strong evidence or merely a lucky draw, unlikely to be replicated in repeated samples? How much sampling variance should we expect? The tools of formal statistical inference answer these questions. These tools work for all of the econometric strategies of concern to us. Quantifying sampling uncertainty is a necessary step in any empirical project and on the road to understanding statistical claims made by others. We explain the basic inference idea here in the context of HIE treatment effects.

The task at hand is the quantification of the uncertainty associated with a particular sample average and, especially, groups of averages and the differences among them. For example, we'd like to know if the large differences in health-care expenditure across HIE treatment groups can be discounted as a chance finding. The HIE samples were drawn from a much larger data set that we think of as covering the population of interest. The HIE population consists of all families eligible for the experiment (too young for Medicare and so on). Instead of studying the many millions of such families, a much smaller group of about 2,000 families (containing about 4,000 people) was selected at random and then randomly allocated to one of 14 plans or treatment groups. Note that there are two sorts of randomness at work here: the first pertains to the construction of the study sample and the second to how treatment was allocated to those who were sampled. *Random sampling* and *random assignment* are closely related but distinct ideas.

A World without Bias

We first quantify the uncertainty induced by random sampling, beginning with a single sample average, say, the average health of everyone in the sample at hand, as measured by a health index. Our target is the corresponding population average health index, that is, the mean over everyone in the population of interest. As we noted on p. 14, the population mean of a variable is called its *mathematical expectation,* or just *expectation* for short. For the expectation of a variable, Y_i, we write $E[Y_i]$. Expectation is intimately related to formal notions of *probability.* Expectations can be written as a weighted average of all possible values that the variable Y_i can take on, with weights given by the probability these values appear in the population. In our dice-throwing example, these weights are equal and given by 1/6 (see Section 1.1).

Unlike our notation for averages, the symbol for expectation does not reference the sample size. That's because expectations are population quantities, defined without reference to a particular sample of individuals. For a given population, there is only one $E[Y_i]$, while there are many $Avg_n[Y_i]$, depending on how we choose n and just who ends up in our sample. Because $E[Y_i]$ is a fixed feature of a particular population, we call it a *parameter.* Quantities that vary from one sample to another, such as the sample average, are called *sample statistics.*

At this point, it's helpful to switch from $Avg_n[Y_i]$ to a more compact notation for averages, $\bar{Y}$. Note that we're dispensing with the subscript n to avoid clutter—henceforth, it's on you to remember that sample averages are computed in a sample of a particular size. The sample average, $\bar{Y}$, is a good estimator of $E[Y_i]$ (in statistics, an *estimator* is any function of sample data used to estimate parameters). For one thing, the LLN tells us that in large samples, the sample average is likely to be very close to the corresponding population mean. A related property is that the expectation of $\bar{Y}$ is also $E[Y_i]$. In other words, if we were to draw infinitely many random samples, the average of the resulting $\bar{Y}$ across draws would be the underlying population mean. When a sample statistic has expectation equal to the corresponding population parameter, it's said to be an *unbiased estimator* of that parameter. Here's the sample mean's unbiasedness property stated formally:

UNBIASEDNESS OF THE SAMPLE MEAN $E[\bar{Y}] = E[Y_i]$

The sample mean should not be expected to be bang on the corresponding population mean: the sample average in one sample might be too big, while in other samples it will be too small. Unbiasedness tells us that these deviations are not systematically up or down; rather, in repeated samples they average out to zero. This unbiasedness property is distinct from the LLN, which says that the sample mean gets closer and closer to the population mean as the sample size grows. Unbiasedness of the sample mean holds for samples of any size. Unbiasedness of the sample mean is also distinct from selection bias. The latter sort of bias concerns the *interpretation* of differences in means rather than the statistical properties of particular estimators.

Measuring Variability

In addition to averages, we're interested in variability. To gauge variability, it's customary to look at average squared deviations from the mean, in which positive and negative gaps get equal weight. The resulting summary of variability is called *variance.*

The *sample variance of Y_i in a sample of size n* is defined as

$$S(Y_i)^2 = \frac{1}{n} \sum_{i=1}^{n} \left(Y_i - \bar{Y}\right)^2 .$$

The corresponding *population variance* replaces averages with expectations, giving:

$$V(Y_i) = E\left[\left(Y_i - E[Y_i]\right)^2\right].$$

Like $E[Y_i]$, the quantity $V(Y_i)$ is a fixed feature of a population —a parameter. It's therefore customary to christen it in Greek: $V(Y_i) = \sigma_Y^2$, which is read as "sigma-squared-y."[16]

Because variances square the data they can be very large. Multiply a variable by 10 and its variance goes up by 100. Therefore, we often describe variability using the square root of the variance: this is called the *standard deviation*, written σ_Y. Multiply a variable by 10 and its standard deviation increases by 10. As always, the population standard deviation, σ_Y, has a sample counterpart $S(Y_i)$, the square root of $S(Y_i)^2$.

Variance is a descriptive fact about the distribution of Y_i. (Reminder: the *distribution* of a variable is the set of values the variable takes on and the relative frequency that each value is observed in the population or generated by a random process.) Some variables take on a narrow set of values (like a dummy variable indicating families with health insurance), while others (like income) tend to be spread out with some very high values mixed in with many smaller ones.

It's important to document the variability of the variables you're working with. Our goal here, however, goes beyond

---

[16] Sample variances tend to underestimate population variances. Sample variance is therefore sometimes defined as

$$S(Y_i)^2 = \frac{1}{n-1} \sum_{i=1}^{n} \left(Y_i - \bar{Y}\right)^2 ,$$

that is, dividing by $n-1$ instead of by n. This modified formula provides an unbiased estimate of the corresponding population variance.

this. We're interested in quantifying the variance of the sample mean in repeated samples. Since the expectation of the sample mean is $E[Y_i]$ (from the unbiasedness property), the population variance of the sample mean can be written as

$$V(\bar{Y}) = E\left[\left(\bar{Y} - E[\bar{Y}]\right)^2\right] = E\left[\left(\bar{Y} - E[Y_i]\right)^2\right].$$

The variance of a statistic like the sample mean is distinct from the variance used for descriptive purposes. We write $V(\bar{Y})$ for the variance of the sample mean, while $V(Y_i)$ (or σ_Y^2) denotes the variance of the underlying data. Because the quantity $V(\bar{Y})$ measures the variability of a sample statistic in repeated samples, as opposed to the dispersion of raw data, $V(\bar{Y})$ has a special name: *sampling variance.*

Sampling variance is related to descriptive variance, but, unlike descriptive variance, sampling variance is also determined by sample size. We show this by simplifying the formula for $V(\bar{Y})$. Start by substituting the formula for $\bar{Y}$ inside the notation for variance:

$$V(\bar{Y}) = V\left(\left[\frac{1}{n} \sum_{i=1}^{n} Y_i\right]\right).$$

To simplify this expression, we first note that random sampling ensures the individual observations in a sample are not systematically related to one another; in other words, they are statistically independent. This important property allows us to take advantage of the fact that the variance of a sum of statistically independent observations, each drawn randomly from the same population, is the sum of their variances. Moreover, because each Y_i is sampled from the same population, each draw has the same variance, σ_Y^2. Finally, we use the property that the variance of a constant (like $1/n$) times Y_i is the square of this constant times the variance of Y_i. From these considerations, we get

$$V(\bar{Y}) = V\left(\left[\frac{1}{n}\sum_{i=1}^{n}Y_i\right]\right) = \frac{1}{n^2}\sum_{i=1}^{n}\sigma_Y^2.$$

Simplifying further, we have

$$V(\bar{Y}) = \frac{1}{n^2}\sum_{i=1}^{n}\sigma_Y^2 = \frac{n\sigma_Y^2}{n^2} = \frac{\sigma_Y^2}{n}. \tag{1.5}$$

We've shown that the sampling variance of a sample average depends on the variance of the underlying observations, σ_Y^2, and the sample size, n. As you might have guessed, more data means less dispersion of sample averages in repeated samples. In fact, when the sample size is very large, there's almost no dispersion at all, because when n is large, σ_Y^2/n is small. This is the LLN at work: as n approaches infinity, the sample average approaches the population mean, and sampling variance disappears.

In practice, we often work with the standard deviation of the sample mean rather than its variance. The standard deviation of a statistic like the sample average is called its *standard error*. The standard error of the sample mean can be written as

$$SE(\bar{Y}) = \frac{\sigma_Y}{\sqrt{n}}. \tag{1.6}$$

Every estimate discussed in this book has an associated standard error. This includes sample means (for which the standard error formula appears in equation (1.6)), differences in sample means (discussed later in this appendix), regression coefficients (discussed in Chapter 2), and instrumental variables and other more sophisticated estimates. Formulas for standard errors can get complicated, but the idea remains simple. The standard error summarizes the variability in an estimate due to random sampling. Again, it's important to avoid confusing standard errors with the standard deviations of the underlying variables; the two quantities are intimately related yet measure different things.

One last step on the road to standard errors: most population quantities, including the standard deviation in the numerator of (1.6), are unknown and must be estimated. In practice, therefore, when quantifying the sampling variance of a sample mean, we work with an *estimated standard error.* This is obtained by replacing σ_Y with $S(Y_i)$ in the formula for $SE(\bar{Y})$. Specifically, the estimated standard error of the sample mean can be written as

$$\hat{SE}(\bar{Y}) = \frac{S(Y_i)}{\sqrt{n}}.$$

We often forget the qualifier "estimated" when discussing statistics and their standard errors, but that's still what we have in mind. For example, the numbers in parentheses in Table 1.4 are estimated standard errors for the relevant differences in means.

The t-Statistic and the Central Limit Theorem

Having laid out a simple scheme to measure variability using standard errors, it remains to interpret this measure. The simplest interpretation uses a *t-statistic.* Suppose the data at hand come from a distribution for which we believe the population mean, $E[Y_i]$, takes on a particular value, μ (read this Greek letter as "mu"). This value constitutes a working *hypothesis.* A t-statistic for the sample mean under the working hypothesis that $E[Y_i] = \mu$ is constructed as

$$t(\mu) = \frac{\bar{Y} - \mu}{\hat{SE}(\bar{Y})}.$$

The working hypothesis is a reference point that is often called the *null hypothesis.* When the null hypothesis is $\mu = 0$, the t-statistic is the ratio of the sample mean to its estimated standard error.

Many people think the science of statistical inference is boring, but in fact it's nothing short of miraculous. One miraculous statistical fact is that if $E[Y_i]$ is indeed equal to μ, then—as long as the sample is large enough—the quantity $t(\mu)$ has a sampling distribution that is very close to a bell-shaped standard normal distribution, sketched in Figure 1.1. This property, which applies regardless of whether Y_i itself is normally distributed, is called the *Central Limit Theorem* (CLT). The

FIGURE 1.1
A standard normal distribution

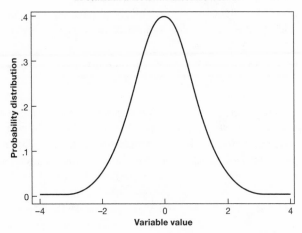

CLT allows us to make an empirically informed decision as to whether the available data support or cast doubt on the hypothesis that $E[Y_i]$ equals μ.

The CLT is an astonishing and powerful result. Among other things, it implies that the (large-sample) distribution of a t-statistic is independent of the distribution of the underlying data used to calculate it. For example, suppose we measure health status with a dummy variable distinguishing healthy people from sick and that 20% of the population is sick. The distribution of this dummy variable has two spikes, one of height .8 at the value 1 and one of height .2 at the value 0. The CLT tells us that with enough data, the distribution of the t-statistic is smooth and bell-shaped even though the distribution of the underlying data has only two values.

We can see the CLT in action through a sampling experiment. In sampling experiments, we use the random number generator in our computer to draw random samples of different sizes over and over again. We did this for a dummy variable that equals one 80% of the time and for samples of size 10, 40, and 100. For each sample size, we calculated the t-statistic in half a million random samples using .8 as our value of μ.

Figures 1.2–1.4 plot the distribution of 500,000 *t*-statistics calculated for each of the three sample sizes in our experiment, with the standard normal distribution superimposed. With only 10 observations, the sampling distribution is spiky, though the outlines of a bell-shaped curve also emerge. As the sample size increases, the fit to a normal distribution improves. With 100 observations, the standard normal is just about bang on.

The standard normal distribution has a mean of 0 and standard deviation of 1. With any standard normal variable, values larger than ±2 are highly unlikely. In fact, realizations larger than 2 in absolute value appear only about 5% of the time. Because the *t*-statistic is close to normally distributed, we similarly expect it to fall between about ±2 most of the time. Therefore, it's customary to judge any *t*-statistic larger than about 2 (in absolute value) as too unlikely to be consistent with the null hypothesis used to construct it. When the null hypothesis is $\mu = 0$ and the *t*-statistic exceeds 2 in absolute value, we say the sample mean is *significantly different from*

FIGURE 1.2

The distribution of the *t*-statistic for the mean in a sample of size 10

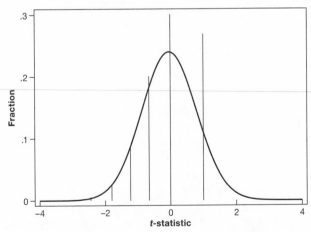

Note: This figure shows the distribution of the sample mean of a dummy variable that equals 1 with probability .8.

FIGURE 1.3

The distribution of the *t*-statistic for the mean in a sample of size 40

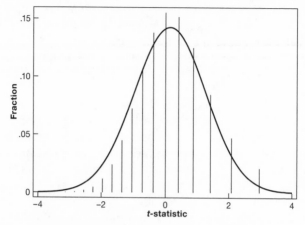

Note: This figure shows the distribution of the sample mean of a dummy variable that equals 1 with probability .8.

FIGURE 1.4

The distribution of the *t*-statistic for the mean in a sample of size 100

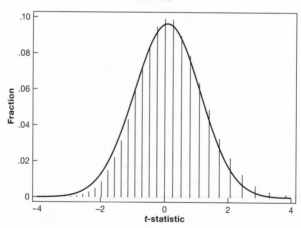

Note: This figure shows the distribution of the sample mean of a dummy variable that equals 1 with probability .8.

zero. Otherwise, it's not. Similar language is used for other values of μ as well.

We might also turn the question of statistical significance on its side: instead of checking whether the sample is consistent with a specific value of μ, we can construct the set of all values of μ that are consistent with the data. The set of such values is called a *confidence interval* for $E[Y_i]$. When calculated in repeated samples, the interval

$$\left[\bar{Y} - 2 \times \hat{SE}(\bar{Y}), \bar{Y} + 2 \times \hat{SE}(\bar{Y}) \right]$$

should contain $E[Y_i]$ about 95% of the time. This interval is therefore said to be a *95% confidence interval* for the population mean. By describing the set of parameter values consistent with our data, confidence intervals provide a compact summary of the information these data contain about the population from which they were sampled.

Pairing Off

One sample average is the loneliest number that you'll ever do. Luckily, we're usually concerned with two. We're especially keen to compare averages for subjects in experimental treatment and control groups. We reference these averages with a compact notation, writing $\bar{Y}^1$ for $Avg_n[Y_i|D_i = 1]$ and $\bar{Y}^0$ for $Avg_n[Y_i|D_i = 0]$. The treatment group mean, $\bar{Y}^1$, is the average for the n_1 observations belonging to the treatment group, with $\bar{Y}^0$ defined similarly. The total sample size is $n = n_0 + n_1$.

For our purposes, the difference between $\bar{Y}^1$ and $\bar{Y}^0$ is either an estimate of the causal effect of treatment (if Y_i is an outcome), or a check on balance (if Y_i is a covariate). To keep the discussion focused, we'll assume the former. The most important null hypothesis in this context is that treatment has no effect, in which case the two samples used to construct treatment and control averages come from the same population. On the other hand, if treatment changes outcomes, the populations from which treatment and control observations are drawn are necessarily different. In particular, they have different means, which we denote μ^1 and μ^0.

We decide whether the evidence favors the hypothesis that $\mu^1 = \mu^0$ by looking for statistically significant differences in the corresponding sample averages. Statistically significant results provide strong evidence of a treatment effect, while results that fall short of statistical significance are consistent with the notion that the observed difference in treatment and control means is a chance finding. The expression "chance finding" in this context means that in a hypothetical experiment involving very large samples—so large that any sampling variance is effectively eliminated—we'd find treatment and control means to be the same.

Statistical significance is determined by the appropriate t-statistic. A key ingredient in any t recipe is the standard error that lives downstairs in the t ratio. The standard error for a comparison of means is the square root of the sampling variance of $\bar{Y}^1 - \bar{Y}^0$. Using the fact that the variance of a difference between two statistically independent variables is the sum of their variances, we have

$$
V\left(\bar{Y}^1 - \bar{Y}^0\right) = V\left(\bar{Y}^1\right) + V\left(\bar{Y}^0\right)
$$

$$
= \frac{\sigma_Y^2}{n_1} + \frac{\sigma_Y^2}{n_0} = \sigma_Y^2 \left[\frac{1}{n_1} + \frac{1}{n_0}\right].
$$

The second equality here uses equation (1.5), which gives the sampling variance of a single average. The standard error we need is therefore

$$
SE\left(\bar{Y}^1 - \bar{Y}^0\right) = \sigma_Y \sqrt{\frac{1}{n_1} + \frac{1}{n_0}}.
$$

In deriving this expression, we've assumed that the variances of individual observations are the same in treatment and control groups. This assumption allows us to use one symbol, σ_Y^2, for the common variance. A slightly more complicated formula allows variances to differ across groups even if the means are the same (an idea taken up again in the discussion of robust regression standard errors in the appendix to Chapter 2).[17]

Recognizing that σ_Y^2 must be estimated, in practice we work with the estimated standard error

$$\hat{SE}\left(\bar{Y}^1 - \bar{Y}^0\right) = S(Y_i)\sqrt{\frac{1}{n_1} + \frac{1}{n_0}}, \qquad (1.7)$$

where $S(Y_i)$ is the *pooled sample standard deviation*. This is the sample standard deviation calculated using data from both treatment and control groups combined.

Under the null hypothesis that $\mu^1 - \mu^0$ is equal to the value μ, the t-statistic for a difference in means is

$$t(\mu) = \frac{\bar{Y}^1 - \bar{Y}^0 - \mu}{\hat{SE}(\bar{Y}^1 - \bar{Y}^0)}.$$

We use this t-statistic to test working hypotheses about $\mu_1 - \mu_0$ and to construct confidence intervals for this difference. When the null hypothesis is one of equal means ($\mu = 0$), the statistic $t(\mu)$ equals the difference in sample means divided by the estimated standard error of this difference. When the t-statistic is large enough to reject a difference of zero, we say the estimated difference is statistically significant. The confidence interval for a difference in means is the difference in sample means plus or minus two standard errors.

Bear in mind that t-statistics and confidence intervals have little to say about whether findings are substantively large or small. A large t-statistic arises when the estimated effect of interest is large but also when the associated standard error is small (as happens when you're blessed with a large sample). Likewise, the width of a confidence interval is determined by

---

[17] Using separate variances for treatment and control observations, we have

$$SE\left(\bar{Y}^1 - \bar{Y}^0\right) = \sqrt{\frac{V^1(Y_i)}{n_1} + \frac{V^0(Y_i)}{n_0}},$$

where $V^1(Y_i)$ is the variance of treated observations, and $V^0(Y_i)$ is the variance of control observations.

statistical precision as reflected in standard errors and not by the magnitude of the relationships you're trying to uncover. Conversely, t-statistics may be small either because the difference in the estimated averages is small or because the standard error of this difference is large. The fact that an estimated difference is not significantly different from zero need not imply that the relationship under investigation is small or unimportant. Lack of statistical significance often reflects lack of statistical precision, that is, high sampling variance. Masters are mindful of this fact when discussing econometric results.

Chapter 2

Regression

IIIIIIIIIIIIIIIIIIIIIIIIIIIIIIIIIIIIIIIIIIIIIIIIIIII 🕉 IIIIIIIIIIIIIIIIIIIIIIIIIIIIIIIIIIIIIIIIIIIIIIIIIII

KWAI CHANG CAINE: A worker is known by his tools. A shovel for a man who digs. An ax for a woodsman. The econometrician runs regressions.
Kung Fu, Season 1, Episode 8

Our Path

When the path to random assignment is blocked, we look for alternate routes to causal knowledge. Wielded skillfully, 'metrics tools other than random assignment can have much of the causality-revealing power of a real experiment. The most basic of these tools is *regression*, which compares treatment and control subjects who have the same observed characteristics. Regression concepts are foundational, paving the way for the more elaborate tools used in the chapters that follow. Regression-based causal inference is predicated on the assumption that when key observed variables have been made equal across treatment and control groups, selection bias from the things we can't see is also mostly eliminated. We illustrate this idea with an empirical investigation of the economic returns to attendance at elite private colleges.

2.1   A Tale of Two Colleges

Students who attended a private four-year college in America paid an average of about $29,000 in tuition and fees in the 2012–2013 school year. Those who went to a public university in their home state paid less than $9,000. An elite private education might be better in many ways: the classes smaller, the athletic facilities newer, the faculty more distinguished, and the students smarter. But $20,000 per year of study is a big difference. It makes you wonder whether the difference is worth it.

The apples-to-apples question in this case asks how much a 40-year-old Massachusetts-born graduate of, say, Harvard, would have earned if he or she had gone to the University of Massachusetts (U-Mass) instead. Money isn't everything, but, as Groucho Marx observed: "Money frees you from doing things you dislike. Since I dislike doing nearly everything, money is handy." So when we ask whether the private school tuition premium is worth paying, we focus on the possible earnings gain enjoyed by those who attend elite private universities. Higher earnings aren't the only reason you might prefer an elite private institution over your local state school. Many college students meet a future spouse and make lasting friendships while in college. Still, when families invest an additional $100,000 or more in human capital, a higher anticipated earnings payoff seems likely to be part of the story.

Comparisons of earnings between those who attend different sorts of schools invariably reveal large gaps in favor of elite-college alumni. Thinking this through, however, it's easy to see why comparisons of the earnings of students who attended Harvard and U-Mass are unlikely to reveal the payoff to a Harvard degree. This comparison reflects the fact that Harvard grads typically have better high school grades and higher SAT scores, are more motivated, and perhaps have other skills and talents. No disrespect intended for the many good students who go to U-Mass, but it's damn hard to get into Harvard, and those who do are a special and select group. In contrast, U-Mass accepts and even awards scholarship money to almost every Massachusetts applicant with decent tenth-grade test scores. We should therefore expect earnings comparisons across alma maters to be contaminated by selection bias, just like the comparisons of health by insurance status discussed in the previous chapter. We've also seen that this sort of selection bias is eliminated by random assignment. Regrettably, the Harvard admissions office is not yet prepared to turn their admissions decisions over to a random number generator.

The question of whether college selectivity matters must be answered using the data generated by the routine application, admission, and matriculation decisions made by students and universities of various types. Can we use these data to mimic the randomized trial we'd like to run in this context? Not to perfection, surely, but we may be able to come close. The key to this undertaking is the fact that many decisions and choices, including those related to college attendance, involve a certain amount of serendipitous variation generated by financial considerations, personal circumstances, and timing.

Serendipity can be exploited in a sample of applicants on the cusp, who could easily go one way or the other. Does anyone admitted to Harvard really go to their local state school instead? Our friend and former MIT PhD student, Nancy, did just that. Nancy grew up in Texas, so the University of Texas (UT) was her state school. UT's flagship Austin campus is rated "Highly Competitive" in Barron's rankings, but it's not Harvard. UT is, however, much less expensive than Harvard (*The Princeton Review* recently named UT Austin a "Best Value College"). Admitted to both Harvard and UT, Nancy chose UT over Harvard because the UT admissions office, anxious to boost average SAT scores on campus, offered Nancy and a few other outstanding applicants an especially generous financial aid package, which Nancy gladly accepted.

What are the consequences of Nancy's decision to accept UT's offer and decline Harvard's? Things worked out pretty well for Nancy in spite of her choice of UT over Harvard: today she's an economics professor at another Ivy League school in New England. But that's only one example. Well, actually, it's two: Our friend Mandy got her bachelor's from the University of Virginia, her home state school, declining offers from Duke, Harvard, Princeton, and Stanford. Today, Mandy teaches at Harvard.

A sample of two is still too small for reliable causal inference. We'd like to compare many people like Mandy and Nancy to many other similar people who chose private colleges and universities. From larger group comparisons, we can hope to draw general lessons. Access to a large sample is not enough, however. The first and most important step in our effort to isolate the serendipitous component of school choice is to hold constant the most obvious and important differences between students who go to private and state schools. In this manner, we hope (though cannot promise) to make *other things equal.*

Here's a small-sample numerical example to illustrate the *ceteris paribus* idea (we'll have more data when the time comes for real empirical work). Suppose the only things that matter in life, at least as far as your earnings go, are your SAT scores and where you go to school. Consider Uma and Harvey, both of whom have a combined reading and math score of 1,400 on the SAT.[1] Uma went to U-Mass, while Harvey went to Harvard. We start by comparing Uma's and Harvey's earnings. Because we've assumed that all that matters for earnings besides college choice is the combined SAT score, Uma vs. Harvey is a *ceteris paribus* comparison.

In practice, of course, life is more complicated. This simple example suggests one significant complication: Uma is a young woman, and Harvey is a young man. Women with similar educational qualifications often earn less than men, perhaps due to discrimination or time spent out of the labor market to have children. The fact that Harvey earns 20% more than Uma may be the effect of a superior Harvard education, but it might just as well reflect a male-female wage gap generated by other things.

We'd like to disentangle the pure Harvard effect from these other things. This is easy if the only other thing that matters is gender: replace Harvey with a female Harvard student, Hannah, who also has a combined SAT of 1,400, comparing Uma and Hannah. Finally, because we're after general conclusions that go beyond individual stories, we look for many similar same-sex and same-SAT contrasts across the two schools. That is, we compute the average earnings difference among Harvard and U-Mass students with the same gender and SAT score. The

---

[1] SAT scores here are from the pre-2005 SAT. Pre-2005 total scores add math and verbal scores, each of which range from 0 to 800, so the combined maximum is 1,600.

average of all such group-specific Harvard versus U-Mass differences is our first shot at estimating the causal effect of a Harvard education. This is an econometric *matching* estimator that *controls for*—that is, holds fixed—sex and SAT scores. Assuming that, conditional on sex and SAT scores, the students who attend Harvard and U-Mass have similar earnings potential, this estimator captures the average causal effect of a Harvard degree on earnings.

Matchmaker, Matchmaker

Alas, there's more to earnings than sex, schools, and SAT scores. Since college attendance decisions aren't randomly assigned, we must control for *all* factors that determine both attendance decisions and later earnings. These factors include student characteristics, like writing ability, diligence, family connections, and more. Control for such a wide range of factors seems daunting: the possibilities are virtually infinite, and many characteristics are hard to quantify. But Stacy Berg Dale and Alan Krueger came up with a clever and compelling shortcut.[2] Instead of identifying everything that might matter for college choice and earnings, they work with a key summary measure: the characteristics of colleges to which students applied and were admitted.

Consider again the tale of Uma and Harvey: both applied to, and were admitted to, U-Mass and Harvard. The fact that Uma applied to Harvard suggests she has the motivation to go there, while her admission to Harvard suggests she has the ability to succeed there, just like Harvey. At least that's what the Harvard admissions office thinks, and they are not easily fooled.[3] Uma

---

[2] Stacy Berg Dale and Alan B. Krueger, "Estimating the Payoff to Attending a More Selective College: An Application of Selection on Observables and Unobservables," *Quarterly Journal of Economics,* vol. 117, no. 4, November 2002, pages 1491–1527.

[3] Which isn't to say they are never fooled. Adam Wheeler faked his way into Harvard with doctored transcripts and board scores in 2007. His fakery notwithstanding, Adam managed to earn mostly As and Bs at Harvard before his scheme was uncovered (John R. Ellement and Tracy Jan, "Ex-Harvard Student Accused of Living a Lie," *The Boston Globe,* May 18, 2010).

nevertheless opts for a cheaper U-Mass education. Her choice might be attributable to factors that are not closely related to Uma's earnings potential, such as a successful uncle who went to U-Mass, a best friend who chose U-Mass, or the fact that Uma missed the deadline for that easily won Rotary Club scholarship that would have funded an Ivy League education. If such serendipitous events were decisive for Uma and Harvey, then the two of them make a good match.

Dale and Krueger analyzed a large data set called College and Beyond (C&B). The C&B data set contains information on thousands of students who enrolled in a group of moderately to highly selective U.S. colleges and universities, together with survey information collected from the students at the time they took the SAT, about a year before college entry, and information collected in 1996, long after most had graduated from college. The analysis here focuses on students who enrolled in 1976 and who were working in 1995 (most adult college graduates are working). The colleges include prestigious private universities, like the University of Pennsylvania, Princeton, and Yale; a number of smaller private colleges, like Swarthmore, Williams, and Oberlin; and four public universities (Michigan, The University of North Carolina, Penn State, and Miami University in Ohio). The average (1978) SAT scores at these schools ranged from a low of 1,020 at Tulane to a high of 1,370 at Bryn Mawr. In 1976, tuition rates were as low as $540 at the University of North Carolina and as high as $3,850 at Tufts (those were the days).

Table 2.1 details a stripped-down version of the Dale and Krueger matching strategy, in a setup we call the "college matching matrix." This table lists applications, admissions, and matriculation decisions for a (made-up) list of nine students, each of whom applied to as many as three schools chosen from an imaginary list of six. Three out of the six schools listed in the table are public (All State, Tall State, and Altered State) and three are private (Ivy, Leafy, and Smart). Five of our nine students (numbers 1, 2, 4, 6, and 7) attended private schools. Average earnings in this group are $92,000. The other four, with average earnings of $72,500, went to a public school. The almost $20,000 gap between these two groups suggests a large private school advantage.

TABLE 2.1
The college matching matrix

Applicant group	Student	Private			Public			1996 earnings
		Ivy	Leafy	Smart	All State	Tall State	Altered State	
A	1		Reject	Admit		Admit		110,000
	2		Reject	Admit		Admit		100,000
	3		Reject	Admit			Admit	110,000
B	4	Admit			Admit		Admit	60,000
	5	Admit			Admit		Admit	30,000
C	6		Admit					115,000
	7		Admit					75,000
D	8	Reject			Admit	Admit		90,000
	9	Reject			Admit	Admit		60,000

Note: Enrollment decisions are highlighted in gray.

The students in Table 2.1 are organized in four groups defined by the set of schools to which they applied and were admitted. Within each group, students are likely to have similar career ambitions, while they were also judged to be of similar ability by admissions staff at the schools to which they applied. Within-group comparisons should therefore be considerably more apples-to-apples than uncontrolled comparisons involving all students.

The three group A students applied to two private schools, Leafy and Smart, and one public school, Tall State. Although these students were rejected at Leafy, they were admitted to Smart and Tall State. Students 1 and 2 went to Smart, while student 3 opted for Tall State. The students in group A have high earnings, and probably come from upper middle class families (a signal here is that they applied to more private schools than public). Student 3, though admitted to Smart, opted for cheaper Tall State, perhaps to save her family money (like our friends Nancy and Mandy). Although the students in group A have done well, with high average earnings and a high rate of private school attendance, within group A, the private school differential is negative: $(110 + 100)/2 - 110 = -5$, in other words, a gap of $-\$5,000$.

The comparison in group A is one of a number of possible matched comparisons in the table. Group B includes two students, each of whom applied to one private and two public schools (Ivy, All State, and Altered State). The students in group B have lower average earnings than those in group A. Both were admitted to all three schools to which they applied. Number 4 enrolled at Ivy, while number 5 chose Altered State. The earnings differential here is $30,000 ($60 - 30 = 30$). This gap suggests a substantial private school advantage.

Group C includes two students who applied to a single school (Leafy), where they were admitted and enrolled. Group C earnings reveal nothing about the effects of private school attendance, because both students in this group attended private school. The two students in group D applied to three schools, were admitted to two, and made different choices. But these two students chose All State and Tall State, both public schools, so their earnings also reveal nothing about the value of a private education. Groups C and D are uninformative, because, from the perspective of our effort to estimate a private school treatment effect, each is composed of either all-treated or all-control individuals.

Groups A and B are where the action is in our example, since these groups include public and private school students who applied to and were admitted to the same set of schools. To generate a single estimate that uses all available data, we average the group-specific estimates. The average of $-\$5,000$ for group A and $30,000 for group B is $12,500. This is a good estimate of the effect of private school attendance on average earnings, because, to a large degree, it controls for applicants' choices and abilities.

The simple average of treatment-control differences in groups A and B isn't the only well-controlled comparison that can be computed from these two groups. For example, we might construct a weighted average which reflects the fact that group B includes two students and group A includes three. The weighted average in this case is calculated as

$$\left(\frac{3}{5} \times -5,000\right) + \left(\frac{2}{5} \times 30,000\right) = 9,000.$$

By emphasizing larger groups, this weighting scheme uses the data more efficiently and may therefore generate a statistically more precise summary of the private-public earnings differential.

The most important point in this context is the apples-to-apples and oranges-to-oranges nature of the underlying matched comparisons. Apples in group A are compared to other group A apples, while oranges in group B are compared only with other oranges in group B. In the language of Chapter 1, we can say that within groups A and B, private and public school alumni are likely to have similar average Y_0. In contrast, naive comparisons that simply compare the earnings of private and public school students generate a much larger gap of $19,500 when computed using all nine students in the table. Even when limited to the five students in groups A and B, the uncontrolled comparison generates a gap of $20,000 (20 = (110 + 100 + 60)/3 − (110 + 30)/2). These much larger uncontrolled comparisons reflect selection bias: students who apply to and are admitted to private schools have higher earnings wherever they ultimately chose to go.

Evidence of selection bias emerges from a comparison of average earnings across (instead of within) groups A and B. Average earnings in group A, where two-thirds apply to private schools, are around $107,000. Average earnings in group B, where two-thirds apply to public schools, are only $45,000. Our within-group comparisons reveal that much of this shortfall is unrelated to students' college attendance decisions. Rather, the cross-group differential is explained by a combination of ambition and ability, as reflected in application decisions and the set of schools to which students were admitted.

2.2 Make Me a Match, Run Me a Regression

Regression is the tool that masters pick up first, if only to provide a benchmark for more elaborate empirical strategies.

Although regression is a many-splendored thing, we think of it as an automated matchmaker. Specifically, regression estimates are weighted averages of multiple matched comparisons of the sort constructed for the groups in our stylized matching matrix (the appendix to this chapter discusses a closely related connection between regression and mathematical expectation).

The key ingredients in the regression recipe are

- the *dependent variable,* in this case, student i's earnings later in life, also called the *outcome variable* (denoted by Y_i);
- the *treatment variable,* in this case, a dummy variable that indicates students who attended a private college or university (denoted by P_i); and
- a set of *control variables,* in this case, variables that identify sets of schools to which students applied and were admitted.

In our matching matrix, the five students in groups A and B (Table 2.1) contribute useful data, while students in groups C and D can be discarded. In a data set containing those left after discarding groups C and D, a single variable indicating the students in group A tells us which of the two groups the remaining students are in, because those not in group A are in group B. This variable, which we'll call A_i, is our sole control. Note that both P_i and A_i are dummy variables, that is, they equal 1 to indicate observations in a specific state or condition, and 0 otherwise. Dummies, as they are called (no reference to ability here), classify data into simple yes-or-no categories. Even so, by coding many dummies, we get a set of control variables that's as detailed as we like.[4]

The regression model in this context is an equation linking the treatment variable to the dependent variable while holding control variables fixed by including them in the model. With only one control variable, A_i, the regression of interest can be written as

$$Y_i = \alpha + \beta P_i + \gamma A_i + e_i. \qquad (2.1)$$

The distinction between the treatment variable, P_i, and the control variable, A_i, in equation (2.1) is conceptual, not formal: there is nothing in equation (2.1) to indicate which is which. Your research question and empirical strategy justify the choice of variables and determine the roles they play.

As in the previous chapter, here we also use Greek letters for parameters to distinguish them from the variables in the model. The regression parameters—called *regression coefficients*—are

- the intercept, α ("alpha");
- the causal effect of treatment, β ("beta"); and
- the effect of being a group A student, γ ("gamma").

---

[4] When data fall into one of J groups, we need $J - 1$ dummies for a full description of the groups. The category for which no dummy is coded is called the *reference group*.

The last component of equation (2.1) is the *residual, e_i* (also called an error term). Residuals are defined as the difference between the observed Y_i and the *fitted values* generated by the specific regression model we have in mind. These fitted values are written as

$$\hat{Y}_i = \alpha + \beta P_i + \gamma A_i,$$

and the corresponding residuals are given by

$$e_i = Y_i - \hat{Y}_i = Y_i - (\alpha + \beta P_i + \gamma A_i).$$

Regression analysis assigns values to model parameters (α, β, and γ) so as to make $\hat{Y}_i$ as close as possible to Y_i. This is accomplished by choosing values that minimize the sum of squared residuals, leading to the moniker *ordinary least squares* (OLS) for the resulting estimates.[5] Executing this minimization in a particular sample, we are said to be *estimating* regression parameters. 'Metrics masters, who estimate regression models every day, are sometimes said to "run regressions," though often it seems that regressions run us rather than the other way around. The formalities of regression estimation and the statistical theory that goes with it are sketched in the appendix to this chapter.

Running regression (2.1) on data for the five students in groups A and B generates the following estimates (these estimates can be computed using a hand calculator, but for real empirical work, we use professional regression software):

$$\alpha = 40,000$$
$$\beta = 10,000$$
$$\gamma = 60,000.$$

The private school coefficient in this case is 10,000, implying a private-public earnings differential of \$10,000. This is indeed a weighted average of our two group-specific effects (recall the group A effect is $-5,000$ and the group B effect is 30,000).

---

[5] "Ordinary-ness" here refers to the fact that OLS weights each observation in this sum of squares equally. We discuss weighted least squares estimation in Chapter 5.

While this is neither the simple unweighted average (12,500) nor the group-size weighted average (9,000), it's not too far from either of them. In this case, regression assigns a weight of 4/7 to group A and 3/7 to group B. As with these other averages, the regression-weighted average is considerably smaller than the uncontrolled earnings gap between private and public school alumni.[6]

Regression estimates (and the associated standard errors used to quantify their sampling variance) are readily constructed using computers and econometric software. Computational simplicity and the conceptual interpretation of regression estimates as a weighted average of group-specific differences are two of the reasons we regress. Regression also has two more things going for it. First, it's a convention among masters to report regression estimates in almost every econometric investigation of causal effects, including those involving treatment variables that take on more than two values. Regression estimates provide a simple benchmark for fancier techniques. Second, under some circumstances, regression estimates are efficient in the sense of providing the most statistically precise estimates of average causal effects that we can hope to obtain from a given sample. This technical point is reviewed briefly in the chapter appendix.

Public-Private Face-Off

The C&B data set includes more than 14,000 former students. These students were admitted and rejected at many different combinations of schools (C&B asked for the names of at least three schools students considered seriously, besides the one attended). Many of the possible application/acceptance sets in this data set are represented by only a single student. Moreover, in some sets with more than one student, all schools are either public or private. Just as with groups C and D in Table 2.1, these perfectly homogeneous groups provide no guidance as to the value of a private education.

---

[6] Our book, *Mostly Harmless Econometrics* (Princeton University Press, 2009), discusses regression-weighting schemes in more detail.

We can increase the number of useful comparisons by deeming schools to be matched if they are equally selective instead of insisting on identical matches. To fatten up the groups this scheme produces, we'll call schools comparable if they fall into the same Barron's selectivity categories.[7] Returning to our stylized matching matrix, suppose All State and Tall State are rated as Competitive, Altered State and Smart are rated Highly Competitive, and Ivy and Leafy are Most Competitive. In the Barron's scheme, those who applied to Tall State, Smart, and Leafy, and were admitted to Tall State and Smart can be compared with students who applied to All State, Smart, and Ivy, and were admitted to All State and Smart. Students in both groups applied to one Competitive, one Highly Competitive, and one Most Competitive school, and they were admitted to one Competitive and one Highly Competitive school.

In the C&B data, 9,202 students can be matched in this way. But because we're interested in public-private comparisons, our Barron's matched sample is also limited to matched applicant groups that contain both public and private school students. This leaves 5,583 matched students for analysis. These matched students fall into 151 similar-selectivity groups containing both public and private students.

Our operational regression model for the Barron's selectivity-matched sample differs from regression (2.1), used to analyze the matching matrix in Table 2.1, in a number of ways. First, the operational model puts the natural log of earnings on the left-hand side instead of earnings itself. As explained in the chapter appendix, use of a logged dependent variable allows regression estimates to be interpreted as a percent change. For example, an estimated β of .05 implies that private school alumni earn about 5% more than public school alumni, conditional on whatever controls were included in the model.

Another important difference between our operational empirical model and the Table 2.1 example is that the former in-

---

[7] Barron's classifies colleges as Most Competitive, Highly Competitive, Very Competitive, Competitive, Less Competitive, and Noncompetitive, according to the class rank of enrolled students and the proportion of applicants admitted.

cludes many control variables, while the example controls only for the dummy variable A_i, indicating students in group A. The key controls in the operational model are a set of many dummy variables indicating all Barron's matches represented in the sample (with one group left out as a reference category). These controls capture the relative selectivity of the schools to which students applied and were admitted in the real world, where many combinations of schools are possible. The resulting regression model looks like

$$\ln Y_i = \alpha + \beta P_i + \sum_{j=1}^{150} \gamma_j GROUP_{ji} + \delta_1 SAT_i + \delta_2 \ln PI_i + e_i.$$

$$(2.2)$$

The parameter β in this model is still the treatment effect of interest, an estimate of the causal effect of attendance at a private school. But this model controls for 151 groups instead of the two groups in our example. The parameters γ_j, for $j = 1$ to 150, are the coefficients on 150 selectivity-group dummies, denoted $GROUP_{ji}$.

It's worth unpacking the notation in equation (2.2), since we'll use it again. The dummy variable $GROUP_{ji}$ equals 1 when student i is in group j and is 0 otherwise. For example, the first of these dummies, denoted $GROUP_{1i}$, might indicate students who applied and were admitted to three Highly Competitive schools. The second, $GROUP_{2i}$, might indicate students who applied to two Highly Competitive schools and one Most Competitive school, and were admitted to one of each type. The order in which the categories are coded doesn't matter as long as we code dummies for all possible combinations, with one group omitted as a reference group. Although we've gone from one group dummy to 150, the idea is as before: controlling for the sets of schools to which students applied and were admitted brings us one giant step closer to a *ceteris paribus* comparison between private and public school students.

A final modification for operational purposes is the addition of two further control variables: individual SAT scores (SAT_i) and the log of parental income (PI_i), plus a few variables we'll relegate to a footnote.[8] The individual SAT and log parental income controls appear in the model with coefficients δ_1 and δ_2 (read as "delta-1" and "delta-2"), respectively. Controls for a direct measure of individual aptitude, like students' SAT scores, and a measure of family background, like parental income, may help make the public-private comparisons at the heart of our model more apples-to-apples and oranges-to-oranges than they otherwise would be. At the same time, conditional on selectivity-group dummies, such controls may no longer matter, a point explored in detail below.

Regressions Run

We start with regression estimates of the private school earnings advantage from models with no controls. The coefficient from a regression of log earnings (in 1995) on a dummy for private school attendance, with no other regressors (right-hand side variables) in the model, gives the raw difference in log earnings between those who attended a private school and everyone else (the chapter appendix explains why regression on a single dummy variable produces a difference in means across groups defined by the dummy). Not surprisingly, this raw gap, reported in the first column of Table 2.2, shows a substantial private school premium. Specifically, private school students are estimated to have earnings about 14% higher than the earnings of other students.

The numbers that appear in parentheses below the regression estimates in Table 2.2 are the estimated standard errors that go with these estimates. Like the standard errors for a difference in means discussed in the appendix to Chapter 1, these standard errors quantify the statistical precision of the regression estimates reported here. The standard error associated with the estimate in column (1) is .055. The fact that .135 is more than twice the size of the associated standard error of .055 makes it very unlikely the positive estimated private-

---

[8] Other controls in the empirical model include dummies for female students, student race, athletes, and a dummy for those who graduated in the top 10% of their high school class. These variables are not written out in equation (2.2).

TABLE 2.2
Private school effects: Barron's matches

	No selection controls			Selection controls		
	(1)	(2)	(3)	(4)	(5)	(6)
Private school	.135	.095	.086	.007	.003	.013
	(.055)	(.052)	(.034)	(.038)	(.039)	(.025)
Own SAT score ÷ 100		.048	.016		.033	.001
		(.009)	(.007)		(.007)	(.007)
Log parental income			.219			.190
			(.022)			(.023)
Female			−.403			−.395
			(.018)			(.021)
Black			.005			−.040
			(.041)			(.042)
Hispanic			.062			.032
			(.072)			(.070)
Asian			.170			.145
			(.074)			(.068)
Other/missing race			−.074			−.079
			(.157)			(.156)
High school top 10%			.095			.082
			(.027)			(.028)
High school rank missing			.019			.015
			(.033)			(.037)
Athlete			.123			.115
			(.025)			(.027)
Selectivity-group dummies	No	No	No	Yes	Yes	Yes

Notes: This table reports estimates of the effect of attending a private college or university on earnings. Each column reports coefficients from a regression of log earnings on a dummy for attending a private institution and controls. The results in columns (4)–(6) are from models that include applicant selectivity-group dummies. The sample size is 5,583. Standard errors are reported in parentheses.

school gap is merely a chance finding. The private school coefficient is statistically significant.

The large private school premium reported in column (1) of Table 2.2 is an interesting descriptive fact, but, as in our example calculation, some of this gap is almost certainly due to selection bias. As we show below, private school students have higher SAT scores and come from wealthier families than do public school students, and so might be expected to earn more regardless of where they went to college. We therefore control for measures of ability and family background when estimating the private school premium. An estimate of the private school premium from a regression model that includes an individual SAT control is reported in column (2) of Table 2.2. Every 100 points of SAT achievement are associated with about a 5 percentage point earnings gain. Controlling for students' SAT scores reduces the measured private school premium to about .1. Adding controls for parental income, as well as for demographic characteristics related to race and sex, high school rank, and whether the graduate was a college athlete brings the private school premium down a little further, to a still substantial and statistically significant .086, reported in column (3) of the table.

A substantial effect indeed, but probably still too big, that is, contaminated by positive selection bias. Column (4) reports estimates from a model with no controls for ability, family background, or demographic characteristics. Importantly, however, the regression model used to construct the estimate reported in this column includes a dummy for each matched college selectivity group in the sample. That is, the model used to construct this estimate includes the dummy variables $GROUP_{ji}$, for $j = 1, \ldots, 150$ (the table omits the many estimated γ_j this model produces, but indicates their inclusion in the row labeled "selection controls"). The estimated private school premium with selectivity-group controls included is almost bang on 0, with a standard error of about .04. And that's not all: having killed the private school premium with selectivity-group dummies, columns (5) and (6) show that the premium moves little when controls for ability and family background are added to the model. This suggests that control for college application and admissions selectivity groups takes us a long way toward the apples-to-apples and oranges-to-oranges comparisons at the heart of any credible regression strategy for causal inference.

The results in columns (4)–(6) of Table 2.2 are generated by the subsample of 5,583 students for whom we can construct Barron's matches and generate within-group comparisons of public and private school students. Perhaps there's something special about this limited sample, which contains less than half of the full complement of C&B respondents. This concern motivates a less demanding control scheme that includes only the average SAT score in the set of schools students applied to plus dummies for the number of schools applied to (that is, a dummy for students who applied to two schools, a dummy for students who applied to three schools, and so on), instead of a full set of 150 selectivity-group dummies. This regression, which can be estimated in the full C&B sample, is christened the "self-revelation model" because it's motivated by the notion that applicants have a pretty good idea of their ability and where they're likely to be admitted. This self-assessment is reflected in the number and average selectivity of the schools to which they apply. As a rule, weaker applicants apply to fewer and to less-selective schools than do stronger applicants.

The self-revelation model generates results remarkably similar to those generated by Barron's matches. The self-revelation estimates, computed in a sample of 14,238 students, can be seen in Table 2.3. As before, the first three columns of the table show that the raw private school premium falls markedly, but remains substantial, when controls for ability and family background are added to the model (falling in this case, from .21 to .14). At the same time, columns (4)–(6) show that models controlling for the number and average selectivity of the schools students apply to generate small and statistically insignificant effects on the order of .03. Moreover, as with the models that control for Barron's matches, models with average selectivity controls generate estimates that are largely insensitive to the inclusion of controls for ability and family background.

Private university attendance seems unrelated to future earnings once we control for selection bias. But perhaps our focus on public-private comparisons misses the point. Students may benefit from attending schools like Ivy, Leafy, or Smart simply because their classmates at such schools are so much better. The synergy generated by a strong peer group may be the feature that justifies the private school price tag.

We can explore this hypothesis by replacing the private school dummy in the self-revelation model with a measure of

TABLE 2.3
Private school effects: Average SAT score controls

	No selection controls			Selection controls		
	(1)	(2)	(3)	(4)	(5)	(6)
Private school	.212	.152	.139	.034	.031	.037
	(.060)	(.057)	(.043)	(.062)	(.062)	(.039)
Own SAT score ÷ 100		.051	.024		.036	.009
		(.008)	(.006)		(.006)	(.006)
Log parental income			.181			.159
			(.026)			(.025)
Female			−.398			−.396
			(.012)			(.014)
Black			−.003			−.037
			(.031)			(.035)
Hispanic			.027			.001
			(.052)			(.054)
Asian			.189			.155
			(.035)			(.037)
Other/missing race			−.166			−.189
			(.118)			(.117)
High school top 10%			.067			.064
			(.020)			(.020)
High school rank missing			.003			−.008
			(.025)			(.023)
Athlete			.107			.092
			(.027)			(.024)
Average SAT score of schools applied to ÷ 100				.110	.082	.077
				(.024)	(.022)	(.012)
Sent two applications				.071	.062	.058
				(.013)	(.011)	(.010)
Sent three applications				.093	.079	.066
				(.021)	(.019)	(.017)
Sent four or more applications				.139	.127	.098
				(.024)	(.023)	(.020)

Notes: This table reports estimates of the effect of attending a private college or university on earnings. Each column shows coefficients from a regression of log earnings on a dummy for attending a private institution and controls. The sample size is 14,238. Standard errors are reported in parentheses.

TABLE 2.4
School selectivity effects: Average SAT score controls

	No selection controls			Selection controls		
	(1)	(2)	(3)	(4)	(5)	(6)
School average SAT score ÷ 100	.109	.071	.076	−.021	−.031	.000
	(.026)	(.025)	(.016)	(.026)	(.026)	(.018)
Own SAT score ÷ 100		.049	.018		.037	.009
		(.007)	(.006)		(.006)	(.006)
Log parental income			.187			.161
			(.024)			(.025)
Female			−.403			−.396
			(.015)			(.014)
Black			−.023			−.034
			(.035)			(.035)
Hispanic			.015			.006
			(.052)			(.053)
Asian			.173			.155
			(.036)			(.037)
Other/missing race			−.188			−.193
			(.119)			(.116)
High school top 10%			.061			.063
			(.018)			(.019)
High school rank missing			.001			−.009
			(.024)			(.022)
Athlete			.102			.094
			(.025)			(.024)
Average SAT score of schools applied to ÷ 100				.138	.116	.089
				(.017)	(.015)	(.013)
Sent two applications				.082	.075	.063
				(.015)	(.014)	(.011)
Sent three applications				.107	.096	.074
				(.026)	(.024)	(.022)
Sent four or more applications				.153	.143	.106
				(.031)	(.030)	(.025)

Notes: This table reports estimates of the effect of alma mater selectivity on earnings. Each column shows coefficients from a regression of log earnings on the average SAT score at the institution attended and controls. The sample size is 14,238. Standard errors are reported in parentheses.

peer quality. Specifically, as in the original Dale and Krueger study that inspires our analysis, we replace P_i in equation (2.2) with the average SAT score of classmates at the school attended.[9] Columns (1)–(3) of Table 2.4 show that students who attended more selective schools do markedly better in the labor market, with an estimated college selectivity effect on the order of 8% higher earnings for every 100 points of average selectivity increase. Yet, this effect too appears to be an artifact of selection bias due to the greater ambition and ability of those who attend selective schools. Estimates from models with self-revelation controls, reported in columns (4)–(6) of the table, show average college selectivity to be essentially unrelated to earnings.

2.3   Ceteris Paribus?

TOPIC: Briefly describe experiences, challenges, and accomplishments that define you as a person.

ESSAY: I am a dynamic figure, often seen scaling walls and crushing ice. I cook Thirty-Minute Brownies in twenty minutes. I am an expert in stucco, a veteran in love, and an outlaw in Peru. On Wednesdays, after school, I repair electrical appliances free of charge.

I am an abstract artist, a concrete analyst, and a ruthless bookie. I wave, dodge, and frolic, yet my bills are all paid. I have won bullfights in San Juan, cliff-diving competitions in Sri Lanka, and spelling bees at the Kremlin. I have played Hamlet, I have performed open-heart surgery, and I have spoken with Elvis.

But I have not yet gone to college.

From an essay by Hugh Gallagher, age 19.

(Hugh later went to New York University.)

Imagine Harvey and Uma on the day admissions letters go out. Both are delighted to get into Harvard (it must be those

[9] Dale and Krueger, "Estimating the Payoff to Attending a More Selective College," *Quarterly Journal of Economics*, 2002.

20-minute brownies). Harvey immediately accepts Harvard's offer—wouldn't you? But Uma makes a difficult choice and goes to U-Mass instead. What's up with Uma? Is her *ceteris* really *paribus?*

Uma might have good reasons to opt for less-prestigious U-Mass over Harvard. Price is an obvious consideration (Uma won a Massachusetts Adams Scholarship, which pays state school tuition for good students like her but cannot be used at private schools). If price matters more to Uma than to Harvey, it's possible that Uma's circumstances differ from Harvey's in other ways. Perhaps she's poorer. Some of our regression models control for parental income, but this is an imperfect measure of family living standards. Among other things, we don't know how many brothers and sisters the students in the C&B sample had. A larger family at the same income level may find it harder to pay for each child's education. If family size is also related to later earnings (see Chapter 3 for more on this point), our regression estimates of private college premia may not be apples-to-apples after all.

This is more than a campfire story. Regression is a way to make other things equal, but equality is generated only for variables included as controls on the right-hand side of the model. Failure to include enough controls or the right controls still leaves us with selection bias. The regression version of the selection bias generated by inadequate controls is called *omitted variables bias* (OVB), and it's one of the most important ideas in the 'metrics canon.

To illustrate OVB, we return to our five-student example and the bias from omitting control for membership in applicant group A. The "long regression" here includes the dummy variable, A_i, which indicates those in group A. We write the regression model that includes A_i as

$$Y_i = \alpha^l + \beta^l P_i + \gamma A_i + e_i^l. \tag{2.3}$$

This is equation (2.1) rewritten with superscript l on parameters and the residual to remind us that the intercept and private school coefficient are from the long model, and to facilitate comparisons with the short model to come.

Does the inclusion of A_i matter for estimates of the private school effect in the regression above? Suppose we make do with a short regression with no controls. This can be written as

$$Y_i = \alpha^s + \beta^s P_i + e_i^s.$$

Because the single regressor here is a dummy variable, the slope coefficient in this model is the difference in average Y_i between those with P_i switched on and those with P_i switched off. As we noted in Section 2.1, $\beta^s = 20{,}000$ in the short regression, while the long regression parameter, β^l, is only 10,000. The difference between β^s and β^l is the OVB due to omission of A_i in the short regression. Here, OVB amounts to $10,000, a figure worth worrying about.

Why does the omission of the group A dummy change the private college effect so much? Recall that the average earnings of students in group A exceeds the average earnings of those in group B. Moreover, two-thirds of the students in high-earning group A attended a private school, while lower-earning group B is only half private. Differences in earnings between private and public alumni come in part from the fact that the mostly private students in group A have higher earnings anyway, regardless of where they enrolled. Inclusion of the group A dummy in the long regression controls for this difference.

As this discussion suggests, the formal connection between short and long regression coefficients has two components:

(i) The relationship between the omitted variable (A_i) and the treatment variable (P_i); we'll soon see how to quantify this with an additional regression.
(ii) The relationship between the omitted variable (A_i) and the outcome variable (Y_i). This is given by the coefficient on the omitted variable in the long regression, in this case, the parameter γ in equation (2.3).

Together, these pieces produce the *OVB formula*. We start with the fact that

Effect of P_i in short = Effect of P_i in long

    + (\{Relationship between omitted and included\}

        × \{Effect of omitted in long\}).

To be specific, when the omitted variable is A_i and the treatment variable is P_i, we have

Effect of P_i in short = Effect of P_i in long

    + (\{Relationship between A_i and P_i\}

        × \{Effect of A_i in long\}).

Omitted variables bias, defined as the difference between the coefficient on P_i in the short and long models, is a simple rearrangement of this equation:

OVB = \{Relationship between A_i and P_i\}

    × \{Effect of A_i in long\}.

We can refine the OVB formula using the fact that both terms in the formula are themselves regression coefficients. The first term is the coefficient from a regression of the omitted variable A_i on the private school dummy. In other words, this term is the coefficient π_1 (read "pi-1") in the regression model

$$A_i = \pi_0 + \pi_1 P_i + u_i,$$

where u_i is a residual. We can now write the OVB formula compactly in Greek:

OVB = Effect of P_i in short − Effect of P_i in long

$$= \beta^s - \beta^l = \pi_1 \times \gamma,$$

where γ is the coefficient on A_i in the long regression. This important formula is derived in the chapter appendix.

Among students who attended private school, two are in group A and one in group B, while among those who went to public school, one is in group A and one in group B.

The coefficient π_1 in our five-student example is therefore $2/3 - 1/2 = .1667$. As noted in Section 2.2, the coefficient γ is 60,000, reflecting the higher earnings of group A. Putting the pieces together, we have

$$OVB = Short - Long$$
$$= \beta^s - \beta^l$$
$$= 20{,}000 - 10{,}000 = 10{,}000$$

and

$$OVB = \{Regression\ of\ omitted\ on\ included\}$$
$$\times \{Effect\ of\ omitted\ in\ long\}$$
$$= \pi_1 \times \gamma = .1667 \times 60{,}000 = 10{,}000.$$

Phew! The calculation suggested by the OVB formula indeed matches the direct comparison of short and long regression coefficients.

The OVB formula is a mathematical result that explains differences between regression coefficients in any short-versus-long scenario, irrespective of the causal interpretation of the regression parameters. The labels "short" and "long" are purely relative: The short regression need not be particularly short, but the long regression is always longer, since it includes the same regressors plus at least one more. Often, the additional variables that make the long regression long are hypothetical, that is, unavailable in our data. The OVB formula is a tool that allows us to consider the impact of control for variables we *wish* we had. This in turn helps us assess whether *ceteris* is indeed *paribus*. Which brings us back to Uma and Harvey.

Suppose an omitted variable in equation (2.2) is family size, FS_i. We've included parental income as a control variable, but not the number of brothers and sisters who might also go to college, which is not available in the C&B data set. When the omitted variable is FS_i, we have

$$OVB = Short - Long$$
$$= \{Relationship \ between \ FS_i \ and \ P_i\}$$
$$\times \{Effect \ of \ FS_i \ in \ long\}.$$

Why might the omission of family size bias regression estimates of the private college effect? Because differences in earnings between Harvard and U-Mass graduates arise in part from differences in family size between the two groups of students (this is the relationship between FS_i and P_i) *and* from the fact that smaller families are associated with higher earnings, even after controlling for the variables included in the short regression (this is the effect of FS_i in the long regression, which includes these same controls as well). The long regression controls for the fact that students who go to Harvard come from smaller families (on average) than do students who went to U-Mass, while the short regression that omits FS_i does not.

The first term in this application of the OVB formula is the coefficient in a regression of omitted (FS_i) on included (P_i) variables and everything else that appears on the right-hand side of equation (2.2). This regression—which is sometimes said to be "auxiliary" because it helps us interpret the regression we care about—can be written as

$$FS_i = \pi_0 + \pi_1 P_i + \sum_j \theta_j GROUP_{ji} + \pi_2 SAT_i + \pi_3 \ln PI_i + u_i. \tag{2.4}$$

Most of the coefficients in equation (2.4) are of little interest. What matters here is π_1, since this captures the relationship between the omitted variable, FS_i, and the variable whose effect we're after, P_i, after controlling for other variables that appear in both the short and long regression models.[10]

To complete the OVB formula for this case, we write the long regression as

$$\ln Y_i = \alpha^l + \beta^l P_i + \sum_j \gamma_j^l GROUP_{ji}$$
$$+ \delta_1^l SAT_i + \delta_2^l \ln PI_i + \lambda FS_i + e_i^l, \tag{2.5}$$

[10] The group dummies in (2.4), θ_j, are read "theta-j."

again using superscript l for "long." The regressor FS_i appears here with coefficient λ.[11] The OVB formula is therefore

$$OVB = Short - Long = \beta - \beta^l = \pi_1 \times \lambda,$$

where β is from equation (2.2).

Continuing to think of equation (2.2) as the short regression, while the long regression includes the control variables that appear in this model plus family size, we see that OVB here is probably positive. Private school students tend to come from smaller families on average, even after conditioning on family income. If so, the regression coefficient linking family size and private college attendance is negative ($\pi_1 < 0$ in equation (2.4)). Students from smaller families are also likely to earn more no matter where they go to school, so the effect of omitting family size controls in a long regression is also negative ($\lambda < 0$ in equation (2.5)). The product of these two negative terms is positive.

Careful reasoning about OVB is an essential part of the 'metrics game. We can't use data to check the consequences of omitting variables that we don't observe, but we can use the OVB formula to make an educated guess as to the likely consequences of their omission. Most of the control variables that might be omitted from equation (2.2) are similar to family size in that the sign of the OVB from their omission is probably positive. From this we conclude that, as small as the estimates of the effects of private school attendance in columns (4)–(6) of Tables 2.2–2.3 are, they could well be too big. These estimates therefore weigh strongly against the hypothesis of a substantial private school earnings advantage.

Regression Sensitivity Analysis

Because we can never be sure whether a given set of controls is enough to eliminate selection bias, it's important to ask how sensitive regression results are to changes in the list

---

[11] This coefficient is read "lambda."

of controls. Our confidence in regression estimates of causal effects grows when treatment effects are insensitive—masters say "robust"—to whether a particular variable is added or dropped as long as a few core controls are always included in the model. This desirable pattern is illustrated by columns (4)–(6) in Tables 2.2–2.3, which show that estimates of the private school premium are insensitive to the inclusion of students' ability (as measured by own SAT scores), parental income, and a few other control variables, once we control for the nature of the schools to which students applied.

The OVB formula explains this remarkable finding. Start with Table 2.5, which reports coefficients from regressions like equation (2.4), except that instead of FS_i, we put SAT_i on the left-hand side to produce the estimates in columns (1)–(3) while $\ln PI_i$ on the left-hand side generates columns (4)–(6). These auxiliary regressions assess the relationship between private school attendance and two of our controls, SAT_i and $\ln PI_i$, conditional on other controls in the model. Not surprisingly, private school attendance is a strong predictor of students' own SAT scores and family income, relationships documented in columns (1) and (4) in the table. The addition of demographic controls, high school rank, and a dummy for athletic participation does little to change this, as can be seen in columns (2) and (5). But control for the number of applications and the average SAT score of schools applied to, as in the self-revelation model, effectively eliminates the relationship between private school attendance and these important background variables. This explains why the estimated private school coefficients in columns (4), (5), and (6) of Table 2.3 are essentially the same.

The OVB formula is the Prime Directive of applied econometrics, so let's rock it with our numbers and see how it works out. For illustration, we'll take the short model to be a regression of log wages on P_i with no controls and the long model to be the regression that adds individual SAT scores. The short (no controls) coefficient on P_i in column (1) of Table 2.3 is .212, while the corresponding long coefficient (controlling for SAT_i) in column (2) is .152. As can also be seen in column (2) of

TABLE 2.5
Private school effects: Omitted variables bias

	Dependent variable					
	Own SAT score ÷ 100			Log parental income		
	(1)	(2)	(3)	(4)	(5)	(6)
Private school	1.165 (.196)	1.130 (.188)	.066 (.112)	.128 (.035)	.138 (.037)	.028 (.037)
Female		−.367 (.076)			.016 (.013)	
Black		−1.947 (.079)			−.359 (.019)	
Hispanic		−1.185 (.168)			−.259 (.050)	
Asian		−.014 (.116)			−.060 (.031)	
Other/missing race		−.521 (.293)			−.082 (.061)	
High school top 10%		.948 (.107)			−.066 (.011)	
High school rank missing		.556 (.102)			−.030 (.023)	
Athlete		−.318 (.147)			.037 (.016)	
Average SAT score of schools applied to ÷ 100			.777 (.058)			.063 (.014)
Sent two applications			.252 (.077)			.020 (.010)
Sent three applications			.375 (.106)			.042 (.013)
Sent four or more applications			.330 (.093)			.079 (.014)

Notes: This table describes the relationship between private school attendance and personal characteristics. Dependent variables are the respondent's SAT score (divided by 100) in columns (1)–(3) and log parental income in columns (4)–(6). Each column shows the coefficient from a regression of the dependent variable on a dummy for attending a private institution and controls. The sample size is 14,238. Standard errors are reported in parentheses.

the table, the effect of SAT_i in the long regression is .051. The first column in Table 2.5 shows that the regression of omitted SAT_i on included P_i produces a coefficient of 1.165. Putting these together, we have OVB, two ways:

$$OVB = Short - Long = .212 - .152 = .06$$

$$OVB = \{Regression\ of\ omitted\ on\ included\}$$
$$\times \{Effect\ of\ omitted\ in\ long\}$$
$$= 1.165 \times .051 = .06.$$

Compare this with the parallel calculation taking us from column (4) to column (5) in Table 2.3. These columns report results from models that include self-revelation controls. Here, $Short - Long$ is small: $.034 - .031 = .003$, to be precise. Both the short and long regressions include selectivity controls from the self-revelation model, as does the relevant auxiliary regression of own SAT scores on P_i. With self-revelation controls included in both models, we have

$$OVB = \{Regression\ of\ omitted\ on\ included\}$$
$$\times \{Effect\ of\ omitted\ in\ long\}$$
$$= .066 \times .036 = .0024.$$

(Rounding error with small numbers pushes us off of the target of .003.) The effect of the omitted SAT_i in the long regression falls here from .051 to .036, while the regression of omitted on included goes from a hefty 1.165 to something an order of magnitude smaller at .066 (shown in column (3) of Table 2.5). This shows that, conditional on the number and average selectivity of schools applied to, students who chose private and public schools aren't very different, at least as far as their own SAT scores go. Consequently, the gap between short and long estimates disappears.

Because our estimated private school effect is insensitive to the inclusion of the available ability and family background variables once the self-revelation controls are included, other control variables, including those for which we have no data, might matter little as well. In other words, any remaining

OVB due to uncontrolled differences is probably modest.[12] This circumstantial evidence for modest OVB doesn't guarantee that the regression results discussed in this chapter have the same causal force as results from a randomized trial—we'd still rather have a real experiment. At a minimum, however, these findings call into question claims for a substantial earnings advantage due to attendance at expensive private colleges.

MASTER STEVEFU: In a nutshell, please, Grasshopper.

GRASSHOPPER: Causal comparisons compare like with like. In assessing the effects of college choice, we focus on students with similar characteristics.

MASTER STEVEFU: Each is different in a thousand ways. Must all ways be similar?

GRASSHOPPER: Good comparisons eliminate systematic differences between those who chose one path and those who choose another, when such differences are associated with outcomes.

MASTER STEVEFU: How is this accomplished?

GRASSHOPPER: The method of matching sorts individuals into groups with the same values of control variables, like measures of ability and family background. Matched comparisons within these groups are then averaged to get a single overall effect.

MASTER STEVEFU: And regression?

---

[12] Joseph Altonji, Todd Elder, and Christopher Taber formalize the notion that the OVB associated with the regressors you have at hand provides a guide to the OVB generated by those you don't. For details, see their study "Selection on Observed and Unobserved Variables: Assessing the Effectiveness of Catholic Schools," *Journal of Political Economy*, vol. 113, no. 1, February 2005, pages 151–184.

GRASSHOPPER: Regression is an automated matchmaker. The regression estimate of a causal effect is also an average of within-group comparisons.

MASTER STEVEFU: What is the Tao of OVB?

GRASSHOPPER: OVB is the difference between short and long regression coefficients. The long regression includes additional controls, those omitted from the short. Short equals long plus the effect of omitted in long times the regression of omitted on included.

MASTER JOSHWAY: Nothing omitted here, Grasshopper.

Masters of 'Metrics: Galton and Yule

The term "regression" was coined by Sir Francis Galton, Charles Darwin's half-cousin, in 1886. Galton had many interests, but he was gripped by Darwin's masterpiece, *The Origin of Species*. Galton hoped to apply Darwin's theory of evolution to variation in human traits. In the course of his research,

Sir Francis Galton,
Fellow of the Royal Geographical Society,
Author of The Art of Travel

Galton studied attributes ranging from fingerprints to beauty. He was also one of many British intellectuals to use Darwin in the sinister service of eugenics. This regrettable diversion notwithstanding, his work in theoretical statistics had a lasting and salutary effect on social science. Galton laid the statistical foundations for quantitative social science of the sort that grips us.

Galton discovered that the average heights of fathers and sons are linked by a regression equation. He also uncovered an interesting implication of this particular regression model: the average height of sons is a weighted average of their fathers' height and the average height in the population from which the fathers and sons were sampled. Thus, parents who are taller than average will have children who are not quite as tall, while parents who are shorter than average will have children who are a bit taller. To be specific, Master Stevefu, who is 6'3", can expect his children to be tall, though not as tall as he is. Thankfully, however, Master Joshway, who is 5'6" on a good day, can expect his children to attain somewhat grander stature.

Galton explained this averaging phenomenon in his celebrated 1886 paper "Regression towards Mediocrity in Hereditary Stature."[13] Today, we call this property "regression to the mean." Regression to the mean is not a causal relationship. Rather, it's a statistical property of correlated pairs of variables like the heights of fathers and sons. Although fathers' and sons' heights are never exactly the same, their frequency distributions are essentially unchanging. This distributional stability generates the Galton regression.

We see regression as a statistical procedure with the power to make comparisons more equal through the inclusion of control variables in models for treatment effects. Galton seems to have been uninterested in regression as a control strategy. The use of regression for statistical control was pioneered by George Udny Yule, a student of statistician Karl Pearson, who

---

[13] Francis Galton, "Regression towards Mediocrity in Hereditary Stature," *Journal of the Anthropological Institute of Great Britain and Ireland*, vol. 15, 1886, pages 246–263.

George Udny Yule,
Fellow and president of the
Royal Statistical Society and
winner of its highest honors in 1911,
qualified for his pilot's license in 1931

was Galton's protégé. Yule realized that Galton's regression method could be extended to include many variables. In an 1899 paper, Yule used this extension to link the administration of the English Poor Laws in different counties to the likelihood county residents were poor, while controlling for population growth and the age distribution in the county.[14] The poor laws provided subsistence for the indigent, usually by offering shelter and employment in institutions called workhouses. Yule was particularly interested in whether the practice of outdoor relief, which provided income support for poor people without requiring them to move to a workhouse, increased poverty rates by making pauperism less onerous. This is a well-defined causal question much like those that occupy social scientists today.

[14] George Udny Yule, "An Investigation into the Causes of Changes in Pauperism in England, Chiefly during the Last Two Intercensal Decades," *Journal of the Royal Statistical Society*, vol. 62, no. 2, June 1899, pages 249–295.

Appendix: Regression Theory

Conditional Expectation Functions

Chapter 1 introduces the notion of mathematical expectation, called "expectation" for short. We write $E[Y_i]$ for the expectation of a variable, Y_i. We're also concerned with *conditional expectations,* that is, the expectation of a variable in groups (also called "cells") defined by a second variable. Sometimes this second variable is a dummy, taking on only two values, but it need not be. Often, as in this chapter, we're interested in conditional expectations in groups defined by the values of variables that aren't dummies, for example, the expected earnings for people who have completed 16 years of schooling. This sort of conditional expectation can be written as

$$E[Y_i|X_i = x],$$

and it's read as "The conditional expectation of Y_i given that X_i equals the particular value x."

Conditional expectations tell us how the population average of one variable changes as we move the conditioning variable over the values this variable might assume. For every value of the conditioning variable, we might get a different average of the dependent variable, Y_i. The collection of all such averages is called the *conditional expectation function* (CEF for short). $E[Y_i|X_i]$ is the CEF of Y_i given X_i, without specifying a value for X_i, while $E[Y_i|X_i = x]$ is one point in the range of this function.

A favorite CEF of ours appears in Figure 2.1. The dots in this figure show the average log weekly wage for men with different levels of schooling (measured by highest grade completed), with schooling levels arrayed on the X-axis (data here come from the 1980 U.S. Census). Though it bobs up and down, the earnings-schooling CEF is strongly upward-sloping, with an average slope of about .1. In other words, each year of schooling is associated with wages that are about 10% higher on average.

Many of the CEFs we're interested in involve more than one conditioning variable, each of which takes on two or more

FIGURE 2.1
The CEF and the regression line

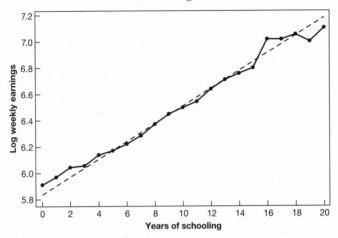

Notes: This figure shows the conditional expectation function (CEF) of log weekly wages given years of education, and the line generated by regressing log weekly wages on years of education (plotted as a broken line).

values. We write

$$E[Y_i | X_{1i}, \ldots, X_{Ki}]$$

for a CEF with K conditioning variables. With many conditioning variables, the CEF is harder to plot, but the idea is the same. $E[Y_i | X_{1i} = x_1, \ldots, X_{Ki} = x_K]$ gives the population average of Y_i with these K other variables held fixed. Instead of looking at average wages conditional only on schooling, for example, we might also condition on cells defined by age, race, and sex.

Regression and the CEF

Table 2.1 illustrates the matchmaking idea by comparing students who attended public and private colleges, after sorting students into cells on the basis of the colleges to which they applied and were admitted. The body of the chapter explains how we see regression as a quick and easy way of automating such matched comparisons. Here, we use the CEF to make this interpretation of regression more rigorous.[15]

The regression estimates of equation (2.2) reported in Table 2.3 suggest that private school attendance is unrelated to average earnings once individual SAT scores, parental income, and the selectivity of colleges applied and admitted to are held fixed. As a simplification, suppose that the CEF of log wages is a linear function of these conditioning variables. Specifically, assume that

$$E[\ln Y_i | P_i, GROUP_i, SAT_i, \ln PI_i] \tag{2.6}$$
$$= \alpha + \beta P_i + \sum_j \gamma_j GROUP_{ji} + \delta_1 SAT_i + \delta_2 \ln PI_i,$$

where Greek letters, as always, are parameters. When the CEF of $\ln Y_i$ is a linear function of the conditioning variables as in equation (2.6), the regression of $\ln Y_i$ on these same conditioning variables recovers this linear function. (We skip a detailed proof of this fact, though it's not hard to show.) In particular, given linearity, the coefficient on P_i in equation (2.2) will be equal to the coefficient on P_i in equation (2.6).

With a linear CEF, regression estimates of private school effects based on equation (2.2) are also identical to those we'd get from a strategy that (i) matches students by values of $GROUP_i$, SAT_i, and $\ln PI_i$; (ii) compares the average earnings of matched students who went to private ($P_i = 1$) and public ($P_i = 0$) schools for each possible combination of the conditioning variables; and (iii) produces a single average by averaging all of these cell-specific contrasts. To see this, it's enough to use equation (2.6) to write cell-specific comparisons as

$$E[\ln Y_i | P_i = 1, GROUP_i, SAT_i, \ln PI_i]$$
$$- E[\ln Y_i | P_i = 0, GROUP_i, SAT_i, \ln PI_i] = \beta.$$

---

[15] For a more detailed explanation, see Chapter 3 of Angrist and Pischke, *Mostly Harmless Econometrics*, 2009.

Because our linear model for the CEF assumes that the effect of private school attendance is equal to the constant β in every cell, any weighted average of cell-specific private-attendance contrasts is also equal to β.

Linear models help us understand regression, but regression is a wonderfully flexible tool, useful regardless of whether the underlying CEF is linear. Regression inherits this flexibility from the following pair of closely related theoretical properties:

- If $E[Y_i|X_{1i}, \ldots, X_{Ki}] = a + \sum_{k=1}^{K} b_k X_{ki}$ for some constants a and $b_1, \ldots, b_K$, then the regression of Y_i on $X_{1i}, \ldots, X_{Ki}$ has intercept a and slopes $b_1, \ldots, b_K$. In other words, if the CEF of Y_i on $X_{1i}, \ldots, X_{Ki}$ is linear, then the regression of Y_i on $X_{1i}, \ldots, X_{Ki}$ is it.
- If $E[Y_i|X_{1i}, \ldots, X_{Ki}]$ is a nonlinear function of the conditioning variables, then the regression of Y_i on $X_{1i}, \ldots, X_{Ki}$ gives the best linear approximation to this nonlinear CEF in the sense of minimizing the expected squared deviation between the fitted values from a linear model and the CEF.

To summarize: if the CEF is linear, regression finds it; if not linear, regression finds a good approximation to it. We've just used the first theoretical property to interpret regression estimates of private school effects when the CEF is linear. The second property tells us that we can expect regression estimates of a treatment effect to be close to those we'd get by matching on covariates and then averaging within-cell treatment-control differences, even if the CEF isn't linear.

Figure 2.1 documents the manner in which regression approximates the nonlinear CEF of log wages conditional on schooling. Although the CEF bounces around the regression line, this line captures the strong positive relationship between schooling and wages. Moreover, the regression slope is close to $E\{E[Y_i|X_i] - E[Y_i|X_i - 1]\}$; that is, the regression slope also comes close to the expected effect of a one-unit change in X_i on $E[Y_i|X_i]$.[16]

---

[16] The thing inside braces here, $E[Y_i|X_i] - E[Y_i|X_i - 1]$, is a function of X_i, and so, like the variable X_i, it has an expectation.

Bivariate Regression and Covariance

Regression is closely related to the statistical concept of *covariance*. The covariance between two variables, X_i and Y_i, is defined as

$$C(X_i, Y_i) = E\big[\big(X_i - E[X_i]\big)\big(Y_i - E[Y_i]\big)\big].$$

Covariance has three important properties:

(i) The covariance of a variable with itself is its variance; $C(X_i, X_i) = \sigma_X^2$.

(ii) If the expectation of either X_i or Y_i is 0, the covariance between them is the expectation of their product; $C(X_i, Y_i) = E[X_i Y_i]$.

(iii) The covariance between linear functions of variables X_i and Y_i—written $W_i = a + bX_i$ and $Z_i = c + dY_i$ for constants a, b, c, d—is given by

$$C(W_i, Z_i) = bd\, C(X_i, Y_i).$$

The intimate connection between regression and covariance can be seen in a *bivariate regression model,* that is, a regression with one regressor, X_i, plus an intercept.[17] The bivariate regression slope and intercept are the values of a and b that minimize the associated *residual sum of squares,* which we write as

$$RSS(a, b) = E[Y_i - a - bX_i]^2.$$

The term *RSS* references a *sum* of squares because, carrying out this minimization in a particular sample, we replace expectation with a sample average or sum. The solution for the bivariate case is

$$b = \beta = \frac{C(Y_i, X_i)}{V(X_i)} \tag{2.7}$$

$$a = \alpha = E[Y_i] - \beta E[X_i].$$

---

[17] The term "bivariate" comes from the fact that two variables are involved, one dependent, on the left-hand side, and one regressor, on the right. *Multivariate* regression models add regressors to this basic setup.

An implication of equation (2.7) is that when two variables are *uncorrelated* (have a covariance of 0), the regression of either one on the other generates a slope coefficient of 0. Likewise, a bivariate regression slope of 0 implies the two variables involved are uncorrelated.

Fits and Residuals

Regression breaks any dependent variable into two pieces. Specifically, for dependent variable Y_i, we can write

$$Y_i = \hat{Y}_i + e_i.$$

The first term is the fitted value, $\hat{Y}_i$, sometimes said to be the part of Y_i that's "explained" by the model. The second part, the residual, e_i, is what's left over.

Regression residuals and the regressors included in the model that produced them are uncorrelated. In other words, if e_i is the residual from a regression on $X_{1i}, \ldots, X_{Ki}$, then the regression of e_i on these same variables produces coefficients that are all 0. Because fitted values are a linear combination of regressors, they're also uncorrelated with residuals. We summarize these important properties here.

PROPERTIES OF RESIDUALS   Suppose that α and $\beta_1, \ldots, \beta_K$ are the intercept and slope coefficients from a regression of Y_i on $X_{1i}, \ldots, X_{Ki}$. The *fitted values* from this regression are

$$\hat{Y}_i = \alpha + \sum_{k=1}^{K} \beta_k X_{ki},$$

and the associated regression *residuals* are

$$e_i = Y_i - \hat{Y}_i = Y_i - \alpha - \sum_{k=1}^{K} \beta_k X_{ki}.$$

Regression residuals

(i) have expectation 0: $E[e_i] = 0$;

(ii) are uncorrelated with all the regressors that made them and with the corresponding fitted values. That is, for each regressor, X_{ki},

$$E[X_{ki}e_i] = 0 \quad \text{and} \quad E[\hat{Y}_i e_i] = 0.$$

You can take these properties on faith, but for those who know a little calculus, they're easy to establish. Start with the fact that regression parameters minimize the residual sum of squares. The first-order conditions for this minimization problem amount to statements equivalent to (i) and (ii). By the same logic, replacing expectations with sample averages and replacing parameters with parameter estimates, we get versions of properties (i) and (ii), stated above for populations, that hold in samples as well.

Regression for Dummies

An important regression special case is bivariate regression with a dummy regressor. The conditional expectation of Y_i given a dummy variable, Z_i, takes on two values. Write them in Greek, like this:

$$E[Y_i | Z_i = 0] = \alpha$$
$$E[Y_i | Z_i = 1] = \alpha + \beta,$$

so that

$$\beta = E[Y_i | Z_i = 1] - E[Y_i | Z_i = 0]$$

is the difference in expected Y_i with the dummy regressor, Z_i, switched on and off.

Using this notation, we can write

$$E[Y_i | Z_i] = E[Y_i | Z_i = 0] + \big(E[Y_i | Z_i = 1] - E[Y_i | Z_i = 0]\big) Z_i$$

$$= \alpha + \beta Z_i. \tag{2.8}$$

This shows that $E[Y_i | Z_i]$ is a linear function of Z_i, with slope β and intercept α. Because the CEF with a single dummy variable is linear, regression fits this CEF perfectly. As a result, the regression slope must also be $\beta = E[Y_i | Z_i = 1] - E[Y_i | Z_i = 0]$, the difference in expected Y_i with Z_i switched on and off.

Regression for dummies is important because dummy regressors crop up often, as in our analyses of health insurance and types of college attended.

Regression Anatomy and the OVB Formula

The most interesting regressions are multiple; that is, they include a causal variable of interest, plus one or more control variables. Equation (2.2), for example, regresses log earnings on a dummy for private college attendance in a model that controls for ability, family background, and the selectivity of schools that students have applied to and been admitted to. We've argued that control for covariates in a regression model is much like matching. That is, the regression coefficient on a private school dummy in a model with controls is similar to what we'd get if we divided students into cells based on these controls, compared public school and private school students within these cells, and then took an average of the resulting set of conditional comparisons. Here, we offer a more detailed "regression anatomy" lesson.

Suppose the causal variable of interest is X_{1i} (say, a dummy for private school) and the control variable is X_{2i} (say, SAT scores). With a little work, the coefficient on X_{1i} in a regression controlling for X_{2i} can be written as

$$\beta_1 = \frac{C(Y_i, \tilde{X}_{1i})}{V(\tilde{X}_{1i})},$$

where $\tilde{X}_{1i}$ is the residual from a regression of X_{1i} on X_{2i}:

$$X_{1i} = \pi_0 + \pi_1 X_{2i} + \tilde{X}_{1i}.$$

As always, residuals are uncorrelated with the regressors that made them, and so it is for the residual $\tilde{X}_{1i}$. It's not surprising, therefore, that the coefficient on X_{1i} in a multivariate regression that controls for X_{2i} is the bivariate coefficient from a model that includes only the part of X_{1i} that is uncorrelated with X_{2i}. This important regression anatomy formula shapes our understanding of regression coefficients from around the world.

The regression anatomy idea extends to models with more than two regressors. The multivariate coefficient on a given regressor can be written as the coefficient from a bivariate regression on the residual from regressing this regressor on all others. Here's the anatomy of the kth coefficient in a model with K regressors:

REGRESSION ANATOMY

$$\beta_k = \frac{C(Y_i, \tilde{X}_{ki})}{V(\tilde{X}_{ki})},$$

where $\tilde{X}_{ki}$ is the residual from a regression of X_{ki} on the $K - 1$ other covariates included in the model.

Regression anatomy is especially revealing when the controls consist of dummy variables, as in equation (2.2). For the purposes of this discussion, we simplify the model of interest to have only dummy controls, that is,

$$\ln Y_i = \alpha + \beta P_i + \sum_{j=1}^{150} \gamma_j GROUP_{ji} + e_i. \qquad (2.9)$$

Regression anatomy tells us that the coefficient on P_i controlling for the set of 150 $GROUP_{ji}$ dummies is the bivariate coefficient from a regression on $\tilde{P}_i$, where this is the residual from a regression of P_i on a constant and the set of 150 $GROUP_{ji}$ dummies.

It's helpful here to add a second subscript to index groups as well as individuals. In this scheme, $\ln Y_{ij}$ is the log earnings of college graduate i in selectivity group j, while P_{ij} is this graduate's private school enrollment status. What is the residual, $\tilde{P}_{ij}$, from the auxiliary regression of P_{ij} on the set of 150 selectivity-group dummies? Because the auxiliary regression that generates $\tilde{P}_{ij}$ has a parameter for every possible value of the underlying CEF, this regression captures the CEF of P_{ij} conditional on selectivity group perfectly. (Here we're extending the dummy-variable result described by equation (2.8) to regression on dummies describing a categorical variable that takes on many values instead of just two.) Consequently, the fitted value from a regression of P_{ij} on the full set of selectivity-group dummies is the mean private school attendance rate in each group. For applicant i in group j, the auxiliary regression residual is therefore $\tilde{P}_{ij} = P_{ij} - \bar{P}_j$, where $\bar{P}_j$ is shorthand for the mean private school enrollment rate in the selectivity group to which i belongs.

Finally, putting the pieces together, regression anatomy tells us that the multivariate β in the model described by equation (2.9) is

$$\beta = \frac{C\left(\ln Y_{ij}, \tilde{P}_{ij}\right)}{V\left(\tilde{P}_{ij}\right)} = \frac{C\left(\ln Y_{ij}, P_{ij} - \bar{P}_j\right)}{V\left(P_{ij} - \bar{P}_j\right)}. \quad (2.10)$$

This expression reveals that, just as if we were to manually sort students into groups and compare public and private students within each group, regression on private school attendance with control for selectivity-group dummies is also a within-group procedure: variation across groups is removed by subtracting $\bar{P}_j$ to construct the residual, $\tilde{P}_{ij}$. Moreover, as for groups C and D in Table 2.1, equation (2.10) implies that applicant groups in which everyone attends either a public or private institution are uninformative about the effects of private school attendance because $P_{ij} - \bar{P}_j$ is 0 for everyone in such groups.

The OVB formula, used at the end of this chapter (in Section 2.3) to interpret estimates from models with different sets of controls, provides another revealing take on regression anatomy. Call the coefficient on X_{1i} in a multivariate regression model controlling for X_{2i} the long regression coefficient, β^l:

$$Y_i = \alpha^l + \beta^l X_{1i} + \gamma X_{2i} + e_i^l.$$

Call the coefficient on X_{1i} in a bivariate regression (that is, without X_{2i}) the short regression coefficient, β^s:

$$Y_i = \alpha^s + \beta^s X_{1i} + e_i^s.$$

The OVB formula describes the relationship between short and long coefficients as follows.

OMITTED VARIABLES BIAS (OVB) FORMULA

$$\beta^s = \beta^l + \pi_{21}\gamma,$$

where γ is the coefficient on X_{2i} in the long regression, and π_{21} is the coefficient on X_{1i} in a regression of X_{2i} on X_{1i}. In words: *short equals long plus the effect of omitted times the regression of omitted on included.*

This central formula is worth deriving. The slope coefficient in the short model is

$$\beta^s = \frac{C(Y_i, X_{1i})}{V(X_{1i})}. \tag{2.11}$$

Substituting the long model for Y_i in equation (2.11) gives

$$\frac{C\left(\alpha^l + \beta^l_1 X_{1i} + \gamma X_{2i} + e^l_i, X_{1i}\right)}{V(X_{1i})}$$

$$= \frac{\beta^l_1 V(X_{1i}) + \gamma C(X_{2i}, X_{1i}) + C(e^l_i, X_{1i})}{V(X_{1i})}$$

$$= \beta^l_1 + \frac{C(X_{2i}, X_{1i})}{V(X_{1i})}\gamma = \beta^l_1 + \pi_{21}\gamma.$$

The first equals sign comes from the fact that the covariance of a linear combination of variables is the corresponding linear combination of covariances after distributing terms. Also, the covariance of a constant with anything else is 0, and the covariance of a variable with itself is the variance of that variable. The second equals sign comes from the fact that $C(e^l_i, X_{1i}) = 0$, because residuals are uncorrelated with the regressors that made them (e^l_i is the residual from a regression that includes X_{1i}). The third equals sign defines π_{21} to be the coefficient on X_{1i} in a regression of X_{2i} on X_{1i}.[18]

Often, as in the discussion of equations (2.2) and (2.5), we're interested in short vs. long comparisons across regression models that include a set of controls common to both models. The OVB formula for this scenario is a straightforward extension of the one above. Call the coefficient on X_{1i} in a multivariate regression controlling for X_{2i} and X_{3i} the long regression coefficient, β^l; call the coefficient on X_{1i} in a multivariate regression controlling only for X_{3i} (that is, without X_{2i}) the short regression coefficient, β^s. The OVB formula in this

---

[18] The regression anatomy formula is derived similarly, hence we show the steps only for OVB.

case can still be written

$$\beta^s = \beta^l + \pi_{21}\gamma, \qquad (2.12)$$

where γ is the coefficient on X_{2i} in the long regression, but that regression now includes X_{3i} as well as X_{2i}, and π_{21} is the coefficient on X_{1i} in a regression of X_{2i} on both X_{1i} and X_{3i}. Once again, we can say: *short equals long plus the effect of omitted times the regression of omitted on included.* We leave it to the reader to derive equation (2.12); this derivation tests your understanding (and makes an awesome exam question).

Building Models with Logs

The regressions discussed in this chapter look like

$$\ln Y_i = \alpha + \beta P_i + \sum_j \gamma_j GROUP_{ji} + \delta_1 SAT_i + \delta_2 \ln PI_i + e_i,$$

a repeat of equation (2.2). What's up with $\ln Y_i$ on the left-hand side? Why use logs and not the variable Y_i itself? The answer is easiest to see in a bivariate regression, say,

$$\ln Y_i = \alpha + \beta P_i + e_i, \qquad (2.13)$$

where P_i is a dummy for private school attendance. Because this is a case of regression for dummies, we have

$$E[\ln Y_i | P_i] = \alpha + \beta P_i.$$

In other words, regression in this case fits the CEF perfectly.

Suppose we engineer a *ceteris paribus* change in P_i for student i. This reveals potential outcome Y_{0i} when $P_i = 0$ and Y_{1i} when $P_i = 1$. Thinking now of equation (2.13) as a model for the log of these potential outcomes, we have

$$\ln Y_{0i} = \alpha + e_i$$
$$\ln Y_{1i} = \alpha + \beta + e_i.$$

The difference in potential outcomes is therefore

$$\ln Y_{1i} - \ln Y_{0i} = \beta. \qquad (2.14)$$

Rearranging further gives

$$\beta = \ln\frac{Y_{1i}}{Y_{0i}} = \ln\left\{1 + \frac{Y_{1i} - Y_{0i}}{Y_{0i}}\right\}$$
$$= \ln\{1 + \Delta\%Y_p\}$$
$$\approx \Delta\%Y_p,$$

where $\Delta\%Y_p$ is shorthand for the percentage change in potential outcomes induced by P_i. Calculus tells us that $\ln\{1 + \Delta\%Y_p\}$ is close to $\Delta\%Y_p$, when the latter is small. From this, we conclude that the regression slope in a model with $\ln Y_i$ on the left-hand side gives the approximate percentage change in Y_i generated by changing the corresponding regressor.

To calculate the exact percentage change generated by changing P_i, exponentiate both sides of equation (2.14)

$$\frac{Y_{1i}}{Y_{0i}} = \exp(\beta),$$

so

$$\frac{Y_{1i} - Y_{0i}}{Y_{0i}} = \exp(\beta) - 1.$$

When β is less than about .2, $\exp(\beta) - 1$ and β are close enough to justify reference to the latter as percentage change.[19]

You might hear masters describe regression coefficients from a log-linear model as measuring "log points." This terminology reminds listeners that the percentage change interpretation is approximate. In general, log points underestimate percentage change, that is,

$$\beta < \exp(\beta) - 1,$$

with the gap between the two growing as β increases. For example, when $\beta = .05$, $\exp(\beta) - 1 = .051$, but when $\beta = .3$, $\exp(\beta) - 1 = .35$.

---

[19] The percentage change interpretation of regression models built with logs does not require a link with potential outcomes, but it's easier to explain in the context of models with such a link.

Regression Standard Errors and Confidence Intervals

Our regression discussion has largely ignored the fact that our data come from samples. As we noted in the appendix to the first chapter, sample regression estimates, like sample means, are subject to sampling variance. Although we imagine the underlying relationship quantified by a regression to be fixed and nonrandom, we expect estimates of this relationship to change when computed in a new sample drawn from the same population. Suppose we're after the relationship between the earnings of college graduates and the types of colleges they've attended. We're unlikely to have data on the entire population of graduates. In practice, therefore, we work with samples drawn from the population of interest. (Even if we had a complete enumeration of the student population in one year, different students will have gone to school in other years.) The data set analyzed to produce the estimates in Tables 2.2–2.5 is one such sample. We would like to quantify the sampling variance associated with these estimates.

Just as with a sample mean, the sampling variance of a regression coefficient is measured by its standard error. In the appendix to Chapter 1, we explained that the standard error of a sample average is

$$SE(\bar{Y}_n) = \frac{\sigma_Y}{\sqrt{n}}.$$

The standard error of the slope estimate in a bivariate regression $(\hat{\beta})$ looks similar and can be written as

$$SE(\hat{\beta}) = \frac{\sigma_e}{\sqrt{n}} \times \frac{1}{\sigma_X},$$

where σ_e is the standard deviation of the regression residuals, and σ_X is the standard deviation of the regressor, X_i.

Like the standard error of a sample average, regression standard errors decrease with sample size. Standard errors increase (that is, regression estimates are less precise) when the residual variance is large. This isn't surprising, since a large residual variance means the regression line doesn't fit very well. On the other hand, variability in regressors is good: as σ_X increases, the slope estimate becomes more precise. This is

FIGURE 2.2
Variance in X is good

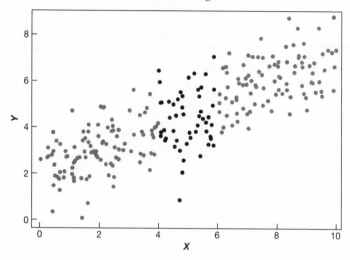

illustrated in Figure 2.2, which shows how adding variability in X_i (specifically, adding the observations plotted in gray) helps pin down the slope linking Y_i and X_i.

The regression anatomy formula for multiple regression carries over to standard errors. In a multivariate model like this,

$$Y_i = \alpha + \sum_{k=1}^{K} \beta_k X_{ki} + e_i,$$

the standard error for the kth sample slope, $\hat{\beta}_k$, is

$$SE(\hat{\beta}_k) = \frac{\sigma_e}{\sqrt{n}} \times \frac{1}{\sigma_{\tilde{X}_k}}, \qquad (2.15)$$

where $\sigma_{\tilde{X}_k}$ is the standard deviation of $\tilde{X}_{ki}$, the residual from a regression of X_{ki} on all other regressors. The addition of controls has two opposing effects on $SE(\hat{\beta}_k)$. The residual variance (σ_e in the numerator of the standard error formula) falls when covariates that predict Y_i are added to the regression. On the other hand, the standard deviation of $\tilde{X}_{ki}$ in the denominator of the standard error formula is less than the standard deviation of X_{ki}, increasing the standard error. Additional covariates explain some of the variation in other regressors, and this variation is removed by virtue of regression anatomy. The upshot of these changes to top and bottom can be either an increase or decrease in precision.

Standard errors computed using equation (2.15) are nowadays considered old-fashioned and are not often seen in public. The old-fashioned formula is derived assuming the variance of residuals is unrelated to regressors—a scenario that masters call *homoskedasticity*. Homoskedastic residuals can make regression estimates a statistically efficient matchmaker. However, because the homoskedasticity assumption may not be satisfied, kids today rock a more complicated calculation known as *robust standard errors*.

The robust standard error formula can be written as

$$RSE(\hat{\beta}) = \sqrt{\frac{V(\tilde{X}_{ki}e_i)}{n(\sigma^2_{\tilde{X}_k})^2}}. \tag{2.16}$$

Robust standard errors allow for the possibility that the regression line fits more or less well for different values of X_i, a scenario known as *heteroskedasticity*. If the residuals turn out to be homoskedastic after all, the robust numerator simplifies:

$$V(\tilde{X}_{ki}e_i) = V(\tilde{X}_{ki})V(e_i) = \sigma^2_{\tilde{X}_k}\sigma^2_e.$$

In this case, estimates of $RSE(\hat{\beta})$ should be close to estimates of $SE(\hat{\beta})$, since the theoretical standard errors are then identical. But if residuals are indeed heteroskedastic, estimates of $RSE(\hat{\beta})$ usually provide a more accurate (and typically somewhat larger) measure of sampling variance.[20]

---

[20] The distinction between robust and old-fashioned standard errors for regression estimates parallels the distinction (noted in the appendix to Chapter 1) between standard error estimators for the difference in two means that use separate or common estimates of σ^2_Y for the variance of data from treatment and control groups.

Chapter 3

Instrumental Variables

||||||||||||||||||||||||||||||||||||||||||||||||||||||||||||❦||||||||||||||||||||||||||||||||||||||||||||||||||||||||

KWAI CHANG CAINE: From a single action, you draw an entire universe.

Kung Fu, Season 1, Episode 1

Our Path

S tatistical control through regression may fail to produce convincing estimates of causal effects. Luckily, other paths lead to *other things equal*. Just as in randomized trials, the forces of nature, including human nature, sometimes manipulate treatment in a manner that obviates the need for controls. Such forces are rarely the only source of variation in treatment, but this is an obstacle easily surmounted. The *instrumental variables* (IV) method harnesses partial or incomplete random assignment, whether naturally occuring or generated by researchers. We illustrate this important idea three ways. The first evaluates an American education innovation—charter schools—with an elementary IV analysis that exploits randomized school admissions lotteries. A second IV application, examining the question of how best to respond to domestic violence, shows how IV can be used to analyze field experiments in which the subjects randomly assigned to treatment are free to opt out. The third application explores the long-run effects of growing up in a larger or smaller family. This application illustrates *two-stage least squares* (2SLS), an elaboration on the IV method and one of our most powerful tools.

3.1   The Charter Conundrum

INTERVIEWER: Have your mom and dad told you about the lottery?

DAISY: The lottery . . . isn't that when people play and they win money?

Waiting for Superman, 2010

The release of *Waiting for Superman*, a documentary film that tells the story of applicants to charter schools in New York and California, intensified an already feverish debate over American education policy. *Superman* argues that charter schools offer the best hope for poor minority students who would otherwise remain at inner city public schools, where few excel and many drop out.

Charter schools are public schools that operate with considerably more autonomy than traditional American public schools. A charter—the right to operate a public school—is typically awarded to an independent operator (mostly private, nonprofit management organizations) for a limited period, subject to renewal conditional on good performance. Charter schools are free to structure their curricula and school environments. Many charter schools expand instruction time by running long school days and continuing school on weekends and during the summer. Perhaps the most important and surely the most controversial difference between charters and traditional public schools is that the teachers and staff who work at the former rarely belong to labor unions. By contrast, most big-city public school teachers work under teachers' union contracts that regulate pay and working conditions, often in a very detailed manner. These contracts may improve working conditions for teachers, but they can make it hard to reward good teachers or dismiss bad ones.

Among the schools featured in *Waiting for Superman* is KIPP LA College Prep, one of more than 140 schools affiliated with the Knowledge Is Power Program. KIPP schools are emblematic of the No Excuses approach to public education, a widely replicated charter model that emphasizes discipline and comportment and features a long school day, an extended school year, selective teacher hiring, and a focus on traditional reading and math skills. KIPP was started in Houston and New York City in 1995 by veterans of Teach for America, a program that recruits thousands of recent graduates of America's most selective colleges and universities to teach in low-performing school districts. Today, the KIPP network serves a student body that is 95% black and Hispanic, with more than 80% of KIPP students poor enough to qualify for the federal government's subsidized lunch program.[1]

The American debate over education reform often focuses on the achievement gap, shorthand for uncomfortably large test score differences by race and ethnicity. Black and Hispanic children generally score well below white and Asian children on standardized tests. The question of how policymakers should react to large and persistent racial achievement gaps generates two sorts of responses. The first looks to schools to produce better outcomes; the second calls for broader social change, arguing that schools alone are unlikely to close achievement gaps. Because of its focus on minority students, KIPP is often central in this debate, with supporters pointing out that nonwhite KIPP students have markedly higher average test scores than nonwhite students from nearby schools. KIPP skeptics have argued that KIPP's apparent success reflects the fact that KIPP attracts families whose children are more likely to succeed anyway:

> KIPP students, as a group, enter KIPP with substantially higher achievement than the typical achievement of schools from which they came. . . . [T]eachers told us either that they referred students who were more able than their peers, or that the most motivated and educationally sophisticated parents were those likely to take the initiative . . . and enroll in KIPP.[2]

---

[1] Jay Mathews' book, *Work Hard. Be Nice,* Algonquin Books, 2009, details the history of KIPP. In 2012, Teach for America was the largest single employer of graduating seniors on 55 American college campuses, ranging from Arizona State to Yale.

[2] Martin Carnoy, Rebecca Jacobsen, Lawrence Mishel, and Richard Rothstein, *The Charter School Dust-Up: Examining Evidence on Student Achievement*, Economic Policy Institute Press, 2005, p. 58.

This claim raises the important question of whether *ceteris* is *paribus* when KIPP students are compared to other public school children.

Playing the Lottery

The first KIPP school in New England was a middle school in the town of Lynn, Massachusetts, just north of Boston. An old ditty warns: "Lynn, Lynn, city of sin, you never come out the way you came in." Alas, there's not much coming out of Lynn today, sinful or otherwise. Once a shoe manufacturing hub, Lynn has more recently been distinguished by high rates of unemployment, crime, and poverty. In 2009, more than three-quarters of Lynn's mostly nonwhite public school students were poor enough to qualify for a subsidized lunch. Poverty rates are even higher among KIPP Lynn's entering cohorts of fifth graders. Although urban charter schools typically enroll many poor, black students, KIPP Lynn is unusual among charters in enrolling a high proportion of Hispanic children with limited English proficiency.

KIPP Lynn got off to a slow start when it opened in fall 2004, with fewer applicants than seats. A year later the school was oversubscribed, but not by much. After 2005, however, demand accelerated, with more than 200 students applying for about 90 seats in fifth grade each year. As required by Massachusetts law, scarce charter seats are allocated by lottery. More than a colorful institutional detail, these lotteries allow us to untangle the charter school causality conundrum. Our IV tool uses these admissions lotteries to frame a naturally occurring randomized trial.

The decision to attend a charter school is never entirely random: even among applicants, some of those offered a seat nevertheless choose to go elsewhere, while a few lottery losers find their way in by other means. However, comparisons of applicants who are and are not *offered* a seat as a result of random admissions lotteries should be satisfyingly apples to apples in nature. Assuming the only difference created by winning the lottery is in the likelihood of charter enrollment (an assumption called an *exclusion restriction*), IV turns randomized offer effects into causal estimates of the effect of charter attendance. Specifically, IV estimates capture causal effects on the sort of child who enrolls in KIPP when offered a seat in a lottery but wouldn't manage to get in otherwise. As we explain below, this group is known as the set of KIPP lottery *compliers*.

Master Joshway and his collaborators collected data on applicants to KIPP Lynn from fall 2005 through fall 2008.[3] Some applicants bypass the lottery: those with previously enrolled siblings are (for the most part) guaranteed admission. A few applicants are categorically excluded (those too old for middle school, for example). Among the 446 applicants for fifth-grade entry who were subject to random assignment in the four KIPP lotteries held from 2005 to 2008, 303 (68%) were offered a seat. Perhaps surprisingly, however, a fair number of these students failed to enroll come September. Some had moved away, while others ultimately preferred a nearby neighborhood school. Among those offered a seat, 221 (73%) appeared at KIPP the following school year. At the same time, a handful of those not offered a place (about 3.5%) nevertheless found their way into KIPP (a few losing applicants were offered charter seats at a later date or in a later lottery). Figure 3.1 summarizes this important information.

KIPP lotteries randomize the offer of a charter seat. Random assignment of offers should balance the demographic characteristics of applicants who were and were not offered seats. Balance by offer status indeed looks good, as can be seen in panel A of Table 3.1. As a benchmark, the first column reports demographic characteristics and elementary school test scores for all Lynn public school fifth graders. The second and third columns, which report averages for KIPP lottery winners and the difference in means between winners and losers, show

[3] Joshua D. Angrist et al., "Inputs and Impacts in Charter Schools: KIPP Lynn," *American Economic Review Papers and Proceedings*, vol. 100, no. 2, May 2010, pages 239–243, and Joshua D. Angrist et al., "Who Benefits from KIPP?" *Journal of Policy Analysis and Management*, vol. 31, no. 4, Fall 2012, pages 837–860.

FIGURE 3.1
Application and enrollment data from KIPP Lynn lotteries

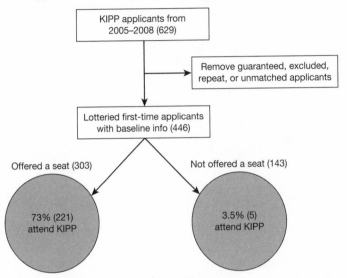

Note: Numbers of Knowledge Is Power Program (KIPP) applicants are shown in parentheses.

that winners and losers are about equally likely to be black or Hispanic or poor enough to qualify for a free lunch.

An especially important feature of Table 3.1 is the check for balance in pretreatment outcomes, namely, the test scores of lottery applicants in fourth grade, prior to KIPP enrollment (these are labeled "baseline scores" in the table). As is common in research on student achievement, these scores have been *standardized* by subtracting the mean and dividing by the standard deviation of scores in a reference population, in this case, the population of Massachusetts fourth graders. After standardization, scores are measured in units defined by the standard deviation of the reference population. As in many poorer cities and towns in Massachusetts, average math scores in Lynn fall about three-tenths of a standard deviation below the state mean. This level of scores is written $-.3\sigma$ (as in

TABLE 3.1
Analysis of KIPP lotteries

	Lynn public fifth graders (1)	KIPP Lynn lottery winners (2)	KIPP applicants		
			Winners vs. losers (3)	Attended KIPP (4)	Attended KIPP vs. others (5)
Panel A. Baseline characteristics					
Hispanic	.418	.510	−.058 (.058)	.539	.012 (.054)
Black	.173	.257	.026 (.047)	.240	−.001 (.043)
Female	.480	.494	−.008 (.059)	.495	−.009 (.055)
Free/Reduced price lunch	.770	.814	−.032 (.046)	.828	.011 (.042)
Baseline (4th grade) math score	−.307	−.290	.102 (.120)	−.289	.069 (.109)
Baseline (4th grade) verbal score	−.356	−.386	.063 (.125)	−.368	.088 (.114)
Panel B. Outcomes					
Attended KIPP	.000	.787	.741 (.037)	1.000	1.000 —
Math score	−.363	−.003	.355 (.115)	.095	.467 (.103)
Verbal score	−.417	−.262	.113 (.122)	−.211	.211 (.109)
Sample size	3,964	253	371	204	371

Notes: This table describes baseline characteristics of Lynn fifth graders and reports estimated offer effects for Knowledge Is Power Program (KIPP) Lynn applicants. Means appear in columns (1), (2), and (4). Column (3) shows differences between lottery winners and losers. These are coefficients from regressions that control for risk sets, namely, dummies for year and grade of application and the presence of a sibling applicant. Column (5) shows differences between KIPP students and applicants who did not attend KIPP. Standard errors are reported in parentheses.

the appendix to Chapters 1 and 2, standard deviation is represented by the Greek letter "sigma"). The small and statistically insignificant baseline differences between KIPP lottery winners and losers reported in column (3) of Table 3.1 are most likely due to chance.

The final two columns in Table 3.1 show averages for fifth graders who enrolled at KIPP Lynn, along with differences between KIPP applicants who did and did not enroll at KIPP. Since enrollment is not randomly assigned, differences between enrolled and nonenrolled students potentially reflect selection bias: Lottery winners who chose to go elsewhere may care less about school than those who accepted a KIPP enrollment opportunity. This is the selection bias scenario described by KIPP skeptics. As it turns out, however, the gaps in column (5) are small, and none approach statistical significance, suggesting that selection bias may not be important in this context after all.

Most KIPP applicants apply to enter KIPP in fifth grade, one year before regular middle school starts, but some apply to enter in sixth. We look here at effects of KIPP attendance on test scores for tests taken at the end of the grade following the application grade. These scores are from the end of fifth grade for those who applied to KIPP when they were in fourth grade and the end of sixth grade for those who applied to KIPP while in fifth. The resulting sample, which includes 371 applicants, omits young applicants who applied for entry after finishing third grade and a few applicants with missing baseline or outcome scores.[4]

Panel B of Table 3.1 shows that KIPP applicants who were offered a seat had standardized math scores close to 0, that is, near the state mean. Because KIPP applicants start with fourth-grade scores that average roughly $.3\sigma$ below the state mean, achievement at the level of the state mean should be seen as

---

[4] As noted in Chapter 1, attrition (missing data) is a concern even in randomized trials. The key to the integrity of a randomized design with missing data is an equal probability that data are missing in treatment and control groups. In the KIPP sample used to construct Table 3.1, winners and losers are indeed about equally likely to have complete data.

impressive. By contrast, the average outcome (fifth or sixth grade) score among those not offered a seat is about $-.36\sigma$, a little below the fourth-grade starting point.

Since lottery offers are randomly assigned, the difference between 0 and $-.36$, reported in column (3), is an average causal effect: the offer of a seat at KIPP Lynn boosts math scores by $.36\sigma$, a large gain (the effect of KIPP offers on reading scores, though also positive, is smaller and not statistically significant). As a technical note, the analysis here is slightly more complicated than a simple comparison of means, though the idea is the same. The results in column (3) come from regressions of scores on a dummy variable indicating KIPP offers, along with dummies for year and grade of application and the presence of a sibling applicant. These control variables are necessary because the probability of winning the lottery varies from year to year and from grade to grade, and is much higher for siblings. The control variables used here describe groups of students (sometimes called *risk sets*) for whom the odds of a lottery offer are constant.[5]

What does an offer effect of $.36\sigma$ tell us about the effects of KIPP Lynn attendance? The IV estimator converts KIPP offer effects into KIPP attendance effects. In this case, the *instrumental variable* (or "instrument" for short) is a dummy variable indicating KIPP applicants who receive offers. In general, an instrument meets three requirements:

(i) The instrument has a causal effect on the variable whose effects we're trying to capture, in this case KIPP enrollment. For reasons that will soon become clear, this causal effect is called the *first stage*.

(ii) The instrument is randomly assigned or "as good as randomly assigned," in the sense of being unrelated to the omitted variables we might like to control for (in this case variables like family background or motivation). This is known as the *independence assumption*.

(iii) Finally, IV logic requires an *exclusion restriction*. The exclusion restriction describes a single channel through which the instrument affects outcomes. Here, the exclusion restriction amounts to the claim that the

[5] Section 3.3 details the role of covariates in IV estimation.

.36σ score differential between winners and losers is attributable solely to the .74 win-loss difference in attendance rates shown in column (3) of Table 3.1 (at the top of panel B).

The IV method uses these three assumptions to characterize a chain reaction leading from the instrument to student achievement. The first link in this causal chain—the first stage—connects randomly assigned offers with KIPP attendance, while the second link—the one we're after—connects KIPP attendance with achievement. By virtue of the independence assumption and the exclusion restriction, the product of these two links generates the effect of offers on test scores:

$$\text{Effect of offers on scores}$$
$$= (\{Effect\ of\ offers\ on\ attendance\}$$
$$\times \{Effect\ of\ attendance\ on\ scores\}).$$

Rearranging, the causal effect of KIPP attendance is

$$\text{Effect of attendance on scores}$$
$$= \frac{\{Effect\ of\ offers\ on\ scores\}}{\{Effect\ of\ offers\ on\ attendance\}}. \qquad (3.1)$$

This works out to be .48σ, as shown at the left in Figure 3.2.

The logic generating equation (3.1) is easily summarized: KIPP offers are assumed to affect test scores via KIPP attendance alone. Offers increase attendance rates by about 75 percentage points (.74 to be precise), so multiplying effects of offers on scores by about 4/3 ($\approx 1/.74$) generates the attendance effect. This adjustment corrects for the facts that roughly a quarter of those who were offered a seat at KIPP chose to go elsewhere, while a few of those not offered nevertheless wound up at KIPP.[6]

---

[6] We can make a similar adjustment for the OHP health insurance lottery discussed in Chapter 1: The effect of OHP offers on the proportion with health insurance is about .25. Dividing the health effects of an insurance *offer* by .25 therefore reveals the effect of insurance *coverage* on health. Since the health consequences of an insurance offer were about zero in OHP, this correction leaves our bottom line for insurance effects unchanged.

An alternative estimate of the KIPP attendance effect appears in columns (4) and (5) in Table 3.1. Column (4) reports means for KIPP students, while column (5) shows the contrast between KIPP students and everyone else in the applicant pool. The differences in column (5) ignore randomized lottery offers and come from a regression of post-enrollment math scores on a dummy variable for KIPP attendance, along with the same controls used to construct the win/loss differences in column (3). The variation in KIPP attendance in this regression comes mostly, but not entirely, from the lottery. Because KIPP enrollment involves random assignment as well as individual choices (made, for example, when winners opt out), comparisons between those who do and don't enroll may be compromised by selection bias. However, the estimate for math

FIGURE 3.2
IV in school: the effect of KIPP attendance on math scores

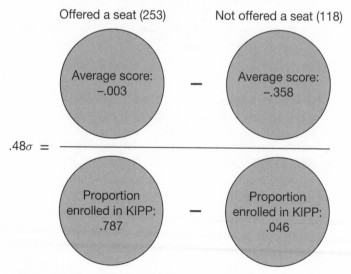

Note: The effect of Knowledge Is Power Program (KIPP) enrollment described by this figure is $.48\sigma = .355\sigma/.741$.

in column (5) (about .47σ) is close to the IV estimate in Figure 3.2, confirming our earlier conjecture that selection bias is unimportant in this case.

A gain of half a standard deviation in math scores after one school year is a remarkable effect. Lynn residents lucky enough to have attended KIPP really don't come out the way they came in.

LATE for Charter School

The KIPP lottery exemplifies an IV chain reaction. The components of such reactions have been named, so masters can discuss them efficiently. We've noted that the original randomizer (in this case, a KIPP offer) is called an instrumental variable or just an instrument for short. As we've seen, the link from the instrument to the causal variable of interest (in this case, the effect of lottery offers on KIPP attendance) is called the first-stage, because this is the first link in the chain. The direct effect of the instrument on outcomes, which runs the full length of the chain (in this case, the effect of offers on scores), is called the *reduced form*. Finally, the causal effect of interest—the second link in the chain—is determined by the ratio of reduced form to first-stage estimates. This causal effect is called a *local average treatment effect* (*LATE* for short).

The links in the IV chain are made of differences between conditional expectations, that is, comparisons of population averages for different groups. In practice, population averages are estimated using sample means, usually with data from random samples. The necessary data are

- the *instrument, Z_i*: in this case, a dummy variable that equals 1 for applicants randomly offered a seat at KIPP (defined only for those participating in the lottery);
- the *treatment variable, D_i*: in this case, a dummy variable that equals 1 for those who attended KIPP (for historical reasons, this is sometimes called the endogenous variable); and
- the *outcome variable, Y_i*: in this case, fifth-grade math scores.

Key relationships between these variables, that is, the links in the IV chain, are parameters. We therefore christen them, you guessed it, in Greek.

THE FIRST STAGE $E[D_i|Z_i = 1] - E[D_i|Z_i = 0]$; call this ϕ.

In the KIPP study, ϕ ("phi") is the difference in KIPP attendance rates between those who were and were not offered a seat in the lottery (equal to .74 in Figure 3.2).

THE REDUCED FORM $E[Y_i|Z_i = 1] - E[Y_i|Z_i = 0]$; call this ρ.

In the KIPP study, ρ ("rho") is the difference in average test scores between applicants who were and were not offered a seat in the lottery (equal to .36 in Figure 3.2).

THE LOCAL AVERAGE TREATMENT EFFECT (LATE)

$$\lambda = \frac{\rho}{\phi} = \frac{E[Y_i|Z_i = 1] - E[Y_i|Z_i = 0]}{E[D_i|Z_i = 1] - E[D_i|Z_i = 0]}; \quad (3.2)$$

LATE, denoted here by λ ("lambda"), is the ratio of the reduced form to the first stage.

In the KIPP study, LATE is the difference in scores between winners and losers divided by the difference in KIPP attendance rates between winners and losers (equal to .48 in Figure 3.2).

We can estimate λ by replacing the four population expectations on the right-hand side of equation (3.2) with the corresponding sample averages, an estimator masters call IV. In practice, however, we usually opt for a method known as two-stage least squares (2SLS), detailed in Section 3.3 below. 2SLS implements the same idea, with added flexibility. Either way, the fact that parameters are estimated using samples requires us to quantify their sampling variance with the appropriate standard errors. It won't surprise you to learn that there's a formula for IV standard errors and that your econometric software knows it. Problem solved!

A more interesting question concerns the interpretation of λ: just who is LATE for charter school, you might ask. Children probably differ in the extent to which they benefit from KIPP. For some, perhaps those with a supportive family environment, the choice of KIPP Lynn or a Lynn public school matters little; the causal effect of KIPP attendance on such applicants is 0. For others, KIPP attendance may matter greatly. LATE is an average of these different individual causal effects. Specifically, LATE is the average causal effect for children whose KIPP enrollment status is determined solely by the KIPP lottery.

The biblical story of Passover explains that there are four types of children, and so it is with children today. We'll start with the first three types: Applicants like Alvaro are dying to go to KIPP; if they lose the lottery, their mothers get them into KIPP anyway. Applicants like Camila are happy to go to KIPP if they win, but stoically accept the verdict if they lose. Finally, applicants like Normando worry about long days and lots of homework. Normando doesn't really want to go to KIPP and refuses to do so when hearing that he has won a seat. Normando is called a *never-taker*, because his choice of school is unaffected by the lottery (it's the social worker who put his name in the hat). At the other end of KIPP kommitment, Alvaro is called an *always-taker*. He'll happily take a seat when offered, while his mother finds a way to make it happen for him even when he loses, perhaps by falsely claiming a sibling among the winners. For Alvaro, too, choice of school is unaffected by the lottery.

Camila attends KIPP when she wins the lottery but will regretfully take a seat in her neighborhood school if she loses (Camila's foster mother has her hands full; she wants the best for her daughter, but plays the hand she's dealt). Camila is the type of applicant who gives IV its power, because the instrument changes her treatment status. When her $Z_i = 0$, Camila's $D_i = 0$; and when her $Z_i = 1$, Camila's $D_i = 1$. IV strategies depend on applicants like Camila, who are called *compliers*, a group we indicate with the dummy variable, C_i. The term "compliers" comes from the world of randomized trials. In many randomized trials, such as those used to evaluate new drugs, the decision to comply with a randomized treatment

TABLE 3.2
The four types of children

		Lottery losers $Z_i = 0$	
		Doesn't attend KIPP $D_i = 0$	Attends KIPP $D_i = 1$
Lottery winners $Z_i = 1$	Doesn't attend KIPP $D_i = 0$	Never-takers (*Normando*)	Defiers
	Attends KIPP $D_i = 1$	Compliers (*Camila*)	Always-takers (*Alvaro*)

Note: KIPP = Knowledge Is Power Program.

assignment remains voluntary and nonrandom (experimental subjects who are randomly offered treatment may decline it, for example). Compliers in such trials are those who take treatment when randomly offered treatment but not otherwise. With lottery instruments, LATE is the average causal effect of KIPP attendance on Camila and other compliers who enroll at KIPP if and only if they win the lottery. IV methods are uninformative for always-takers like Alvaro and never-takers like Normando, because the instrument is unrelated to their treatment status.

Table 3.2 classifies children like Alvaro, Normando, and Camila, as well as a fourth type, called *defiers*. The columns indicate attendance choices made when $Z_i = 0$; rows indicate choices made when $Z_i = 1$. The table covers all possible scenarios for every applicant, not only those we observe (for example, for applicants who won an offer, the table describes what they would have done had they lost). Never-takers like Normando and always-takers like Alvaro appear on the main diagonal. Win or lose, their choice of school is unchanged. At the bottom left, Camila complies with her lottery offer, attending KIPP if and only if she wins. The first stage, $E[D_i|Z_i = 1] - E[D_i|Z_i = 0]$, is driven by such applicants, and LATE reflects average treatment effects in this group.

The defiers in Table 3.2 are those who enroll in KIPP only when *not* offered a seat in the lottery. The Bible refers to such rebels as "wicked," but we make no moral judgments. We note, however, that such perverse behavior makes IV estimates hard to interpret. With defiers as well as compliers in the data, the average effect of a KIPP offer might be 0 even if everyone benefits from KIPP attendance. Luckily, defiant behavior is unlikely in charter lotteries and many other IV settings. We therefore assume defiant behavior is rare to nonexistent. This no-defiers assumption is called *monotonicity,* meaning that the instrument pushes affected applicants in one direction only.

We've argued that instrumental variables can be understood as initiating a causal chain in which an instrument, Z_i, changes the variable of interest, D_i, in turn affecting outcomes, Y_i. The notion of a complier population tied to each instrument plays a key role in our interpretation of this chain reaction. The LATE theorem says that for any randomly assigned instrument with a nonzero first stage, satisfying both monotonicity and an exclusion restriction, the ratio of reduced form to first stage is LATE, the average causal effect of treatment on compliers.[7] Recall (from Section 1.1) that Y_{1i} denotes the outcome for i with the treatment switched on, while Y_{0i} is the outcome for the same person with treatment switched off. Using this notation and the parameters defined above, LATE can be written:

$$\lambda = \frac{\rho}{\phi} = E[Y_{1i} - Y_{0i} | C_i = 1].$$

Without stronger assumptions, such as a constant causal effect for everybody (this is the model described by equation (1.3) in Chapter 1), LATE needn't describe causal effects on never-takers and always-takers.

It shouldn't surprise you that an instrumental variable is not necessarily helpful for learning about effects on people whose treatment status cannot be changed by manipulating

---

[7] This theorem comes from Guido W. Imbens and Joshua D. Angrist, "Identification and Estimation of Local Average Treatment Effects," *Econometrica,* vol. 62, no. 2, March 1994, pages 467–475. The distinction between compliers, always-takers, and never-takers is detailed in Joshua D. Angrist, Guido W. Imbens, and Donald B. Rubin, "Identification of Causal Effects Using Instrumental Variables," *Journal of the American Statistical Association,* vol. 91, no. 434, June 1996, pages 444–455.

the instrument. The good news here is that the population of compliers is a group we'd like to learn about. In the KIPP example, compliers are children likely to attend KIPP were the network to expand and offer additional seats in a lottery, perhaps as a consequence of opening a new school in the same area. In Massachusetts, where the number of charter seats is capped by law, the consequences of charter expansion is the education policy question of the day.

Researchers and policymakers are sometimes interested in average causal effects for the entire treated population, as well as in LATE. This average causal effect is called the *treatment effect on the treated* (TOT for short). TOT is written $E[Y_{1i} - Y_{0i} | D_i = 1]$. As a rule, there are two ways to be treated, that is, to have D_i switched on. One is to be treated regardless of whether the instrument is switched off or on. As we've discussed, this is the story of Alvaro, an always-taker. The remainder of the treated population consists of compliers who were randomly assigned $Z_i = 1$. In the KIPP study, the treated sample includes compliers who were offered a seat (like Camila) and always-takers (like Alvaro) who attend KIPP no matter what. The population of compliers who were randomly offered a seat is representative of the population of all compliers (including compliers who lose the lottery and go to public schools), but effects on always-takers need not be the same as effects on compliers. We might imagine, for example, that Alvaro is an always-taker because his mother senses that KIPP will change his life. The causal effect he experiences is therefore larger than that experienced by less-committed treated applicants, that is, by treated compliers.

Because the treated population includes always-takers, LATE and TOT are usually not the same. Moreover, neither of these average causal effects need be the same over time or in different settings (such as at charter schools with fewer minority applicants). The question of whether a particular causal estimate has predictive value for times, places, and people beyond those represented in the study that produced it is called *external validity*. When assessing external validity, masters must ask themselves why a particular LATE estimate is big or small.

It seems likely, for example, that KIPP boosts achievement because the KIPP recipe provides a structured educational environment in which many children—but perhaps not all—find it easy to learn. Children who are especially bright and independent might not thrive at KIPP. To explore the external validity of a particular LATE, we can use a single instrument to look at estimates for different types of students—say, those with higher or lower baseline scores. We can also look for additional instruments that affect different sorts of compliers, a theme taken up in Section 3.3. As with estimates from randomized trials, the best evidence for the external validity of IV estimates comes from comparisons of LATEs for the same or similar treatments across different populations.

3.2   Abuse Busters

The police were called to O. J. Simpson's Los Angeles mansion at least nine times over the course of his marriage to Nicole Brown Simpson. But the former National Football League superstar, nicknamed "The Juice," was arrested only once, in 1989, when he pleaded no contest to a charge of spousal abuse in an episode that put Nicole in the hospital. Simpson paid a small fine, did token community service, and was ordered to seek counseling from the psychiatrist of his choice. The prosecutor in the 1989 case, Robert Pingle, noted that Nicole had not been very cooperative with authorities in the aftermath of her severe beating. Five years later, Nicole Brown Simpson and her companion Ronald Goldman were murdered by an unknown intruder whom many believe was Nicole's ex-husband, O.J.[8]

---

[8] Simpson was acquitted of murder in a criminal trial but was held responsible for the deaths in a civil trial. He later authored a book titled *If I Did It: Confessions of the Killer,* Beaufort Books, 2007. Our account of repeated police visits to Simpson's home is based on Sara Rimer, "The Simpson Case: The Marriage; Handling of 1989 Wife-Beating Case Was a 'Terrible Joke,' Prosecutor Says," *The New York Times,* June 18, 1994.

How should police respond to domestic violence? Like Nicole Brown Simpson, abuse victims are often reluctant to press charges. Arresting batterers without victim cooperation may be pointless and could serve to aggravate an already bad situation. To many observers and not a few police officers, social service agencies seem best equipped to respond to domestic violence. At the same time, victim advocates worry that the failure to arrest batterers signals social tolerance for violent acts that, if observed between strangers, would likely provoke a vigorous law enforcement response.

In the wake of a heated policy debate, the mayor and police chief of Minneapolis embarked on a pathbreaking experiment in the early 1980s. The Minneapolis Domestic Violence Experiment (MDVE) was designed to assess the value of arresting batterers.[9] The MDVE research design incorporated three treatments: arrest, ordering the suspected offender off the premises for 8 hours (separation), and a counseling intervention that might include mediation by the officers called to the scene (advice). The design called for one of these three treatments to be randomly selected whenever participating Minneapolis police officers encountered a situation meeting experimental criteria (specifically, probable cause to believe that a cohabitant or spouse had committed misdemeanor assault against a partner in the past 4 hours). Cases of life-threatening or severe injury (that is, felony assault) were excluded. Both suspect and victim had to be present at the time officers arrived. The primary outcome examined by the MDVE was the reoccurrence of a domestic assault at the same address within 6 months of the original random assignment.

The MDVE randomization device was a pad of report forms randomly color-coded for three possible responses: arrest, separation, and advice. Officers who encountered a situation that met experimental criteria were to act according to the color of the form on top of the pad. The police officers who participated

---

[9] The original analysis of the MDVE appears in Lawrence W. Sherman and Richard A. Berk, "The Specific Deterrent Effects of Arrest for Domestic Assault," *American Sociological Review,* vol. 49, no. 2, April 1984, pages 261–272.

TABLE 3.3
Assigned and delivered treatments in the MDVE

Assigned treatment	Delivered treatment			
		Coddled		
	Arrest	Advise	Separate	Total
Arrest	98.9 (91)	0.0 (0)	1.1 (1)	29.3 (92)
Advise	17.6 (19)	77.8 (84)	4.6 (5)	34.4 (108)
Separate	22.8 (26)	4.4 (5)	72.8 (83)	36.3 (114)
Total	43.4 (136)	28.3 (89)	28.3 (89)	100.0 (314)

Notes: This table shows percentages and counts for the distribution of as-signed and delivered treatments in the Minneapolis Domestic Violence Experi-ment (MDVE). The first three columns show row percentages. The last column reports column percentages. The number of cases appears in parentheses.

in the experiment had volunteered to take part and were there-fore expected to implement the research design. At the same time, everyone involved with the study understood that strict adherence to the randomization protocol was unrealistic and inappropriate.

In practice, officers often deviated from the responses called for by the color of the report form drawn at the time of an in-cident. In some cases, suspects were arrested even though ran-dom assignment called for separation or advice. Most arrests in these cases occurred when a suspect attempted to assault an officer, a victim persistently demanded an arrest, or when both parties were injured. A few deviations arose when offi-cers forgot their report forms. As a result of these deviations from the experimental protocol, *treatment delivered* was not random. This can be seen in Table 3.3, which tabulates treat-ments assigned and delivered. Almost every case assigned to arrest resulted in arrest (91 of 92 cases assigned), but many cases assigned to the separation or advice treatments also re-sulted in arrest.

The contrast between arrest, which usually resulted in a night in jail, and gentler alternatives generates the most in-teresting and controversial findings in the MDVE. Table 3.3

therefore combines the two nonarrest treatments under the heading "coddled." Random assignment had a large but not deterministic effect on the likelihood a suspected batterer was coddled: A case assigned to be coddled was coddled with probability .797 ($\frac{(84+5)+(5+83)}{108+114} = \frac{177}{222}$); while a case not assigned to coddling (that is, assigned to arrest) was coddled with probability .011 (1/92). Because coddling was not delivered randomly, the MDVE looks like a broken experiment. IV methods, however, readily fix it.

When LATE Is the Effect on the Treated

The LATE framework is motivated by an analogy between IV and randomized trials. But some instrumental variables really come from randomized trials. IV methods allow us to capture the causal effect of treatment on the treated in spite of the nonrandom compliance decisions made by participants in experiments like the MDVE. In fact, the use of IV is usually necessary in such experiments. A naive analysis of the MDVE data based on treatment delivered is misleading.

Analysis of the MDVE based on treatment delivered is misleading because the cases in which police officers were supposed to coddle suspected batterers and actually did so are a nonrandom subset of all cases assigned to coddling. Comparisons of those who were and were not coddled are therefore contaminated by selection bias. Batterers who were arrested when assigned to coddling were often especially aggressive or agitated. Use of randomly assigned intention to treat as an instrumental variable for treatment delivered eliminates this source of selection bias.

As always, an IV chain reaction begins with the first stage.[10] The MDVE first stage is the difference between the probability of being coddled when assigned to be coddled and the probability of being coddled when assigned to be arrested. Let Z_i

[10] Our IV analysis of the MDVE is based on Joshua D. Angrist, "Instrumental Variables Methods in Experimental Criminological Research: What, Why and How," *Journal of Experimental Criminology*, vol. 2, no. 1, April 2006, pages 23–44.

indicate assignment to coddling, and let D_i indicate incidents where coddling was delivered. The first stage for this setup is

$$E[D_i|Z_i = 1] - E[D_i|Z_i = 0] = .797 - .011 = .786,$$

a large gap, but still far from the difference of 1 we'd get if compliance had been perfect.

Unfortunately, domestic abuse is often a repeat offense, as can be seen in the fact the police were called for a second domestic violence intervention at 18% of the addresses in the MDVE sample. Most importantly from the point of view of MDVE researchers, recidivism was greater among suspects assigned to be coddled than among those assigned to be arrested. We learn this by calculating the effect of random assignment to coddling on an outcome variable, Y_i, that indicates at least one post-treatment episode of suspected abuse:

$$E[Y_i|Z_i = 1] - E[Y_i|Z_i = 0] = .211 - .097 = .114. \quad (3.3)$$

Given that the overall recidivism rate is 18%, this estimated difference of 11 percentage points is substantial.

In randomized trials with imperfect compliance, where treatment assigned differs from treatment delivered, effects of random assignment such as that calculated in equation (3.3) are called *intention-to-treat* (ITT) effects. An ITT analysis captures the causal effect of being assigned to treatment. But an ITT analysis ignores the fact that some of those assigned to be coddled were nevertheless arrested. Because the ITT effect does not take this noncompliance into account, it's too small relative to the average causal effect of coddling on those who were indeed coddled. This problem, however, is easily addressed: ITT effects divided by the difference in compliance rates between treatment and control groups capture the causal effect of coddling on compliers who were coddled as a result of the experiment.

Dividing ITT estimates from a randomized trial by the corresponding difference in compliance rates is another case of IV in action: We recognize ITT as the reduced form for a randomly assigned instrument, specifically, random assignment to coddling. As we've seen, many suspected batterers assigned to be coddled were nevertheless arrested. The regression of a dummy for having been coddled on a dummy for random assignment to coddling is the first stage that goes with this reduced form. The IV causal chain begins with random assignment to treatment, runs through treatment delivered, and ultimately affects outcomes.

The LATE estimate that emerges from the MDVE data is impressive: $.114/.786 = .145$, a large coddling effect, even in comparison with the corresponding ITT estimates. Remarkably, even though officers on the scene were highly selective in choosing whether to follow the experimental protocol, this estimate of LATE is likely to be a good measure of the causal effect of treatment delivered.

As always, the causal interpretation of LATE turns in part on the relevant exclusion restriction, which requires that the treatment variable of interest be the only channel through which the instrument affects outcomes. In the MDVE, the IV chain reaction begins with the color of police officers' incident report forms. The exclusion restriction here requires that randomly assigned form color affect recidivism solely through the decision to arrest or to coddle suspected batterers. This seems like a reasonable assumption, all the more so as batterers and victims were unaware of their participation in an experimental study.

Are the modest complications of an IV analysis really necessary? Suppose we analyze the MDVE using information on treatment delivered, ignoring the nonrandom nature of decisions to comply with random assignment. The resulting analysis compares recidivism among those who were and were not coddled, with no further complications or adjustments:

$$E[Y_i|D_i = 1] - E[Y_i|D_i = 0] = .216 - .129 = .087.$$

The estimated effect here is quite a bit smaller than the IV estimate of almost 15 percentage points.

Chapter 1 shows that without random assignment, comparisons of treated and untreated subjects equal the causal effect of interest plus selection bias. The selection bias that contaminates a naive analysis of the MDVE is the difference in potential recidivism (that is, in Y_{0i}) between batterers who were and were not coddled. Although much of the variation in coddling was produced by random assignment, officers on the scene also used discretion. Batterers who were arrested even though they'd been randomly assigned to be coddled were often especially violent or agitated, while suspects in cases where officers complied with a coddling assignment were typically more subdued. In other words, batterers who were coddled were less likely to abuse again in any case. The resulting selection bias leads the calculation based on treatment delivered to underestimate the impact of coddling. In contrast with the KIPP study (discussed in Section 3.1), selection bias matters here.

IV analysis of the MDVE eliminates selection bias, capturing average causal effects on compliers (in this case, the effect of coddling batterers in incidents in which officers were willing to comply with random assignment to coddling). An interesting and important feature of the MDVE is the virtually one-sided nature of noncompliance in treatment delivered. When randomized to arrest, the police faithfully arrested (with only one exception in 92 cases). By contrast, more than 20% of those assigned to be coddled were nevertheless arrested.

The asymmetry in coddling compliance means there were almost no always-takers in the MDVE. In our IV analysis of the MDVE, always-takers are suspected batterers who were coddled without regard to treatment assigned. The size of this group is given by the probability of coddling when assigned to arrest, in this case, only 1/92. As we noted in Section 3.1, any treated population is the union of two groups, the set of compliers randomly assigned to be treated and the set of always-takers. With no always-takers, all of the treated are compliers, in which case, LATE is TOT:

$$\lambda = E[Y_{1i} - Y_{0i}|C_i = 1] = E[Y_{1i} - Y_{0i}|D_i = 1].$$

Applying the no-always-takers property to the MDVE, we see that LATE is the average causal effect of coddling on the coddled. Specifically, the TOT estimate emerging from the MDVE contrasts recidivism among the coddled $(E[Y_{1i}|D_i = 1])$ with the rates we would observe in a counterfactual world in which coddled batterers were arrested instead $(E[Y_{0i}|D_i = 1])$. This important simplification of the usual LATE story emerges in any IV analysis with no always-takers, including many other randomized trials with one-sided noncompliance. When some of those randomly assigned to treatment go untreated, but no one randomly assigned to the control group gets treated, IV methods using random intention to treat as an instrument for treatment delivered capture TOT.[11]

A final note on how much good 'metrics matters: It's hard to overstate the impact of the MDVE on U.S. law enforcement. Batterers in misdemeanor domestic assault cases are now routinely arrested. In many states, arrest in cases of suspected domestic abuse has become mandatory.

GRASSHOPPER: Master, the O.J. case came a decade after the MDVE. The pathbreaking MDVE research design did not save Nicole Brown and Ron Goldman.

MASTER JOSHWAY: Social change happens slowly, Grass-hopper. And the original MDVE analysts reported naive estimates based on treatment delivered, along with intention-to-treat effects. The IV estimates in my 2006 study are much larger.

---

[11] This theoretical result originates with Howard S. Bloom, "Accounting for No-Shows in Experimental Evaluation Designs," *Evaluation Review*, vol. 8, no. 2, April 1984, pages 225–246. The LATE interpretation of the Bloom result appears in Imbens and Angrist, "Identification and Estimation," *Econometrica*, 1994. See also Section 4.4.3 in Joshua D. Angrist and Jörn-Steffen Pischke, *Mostly Harmless Econometrics: An Empiricist's Companion*, Princeton University Press, 2009. An example from our field of labor economics is the Job Training Partnership Act (JTPA). The JTPA experiment randomly assigned the opportunity to participate in a federally funded job-training program. About 60% of those offered training received JTPA services, but no controls got JTPA training. An IV analysis of the JTPA using treatment assigned as an instrument for treatment delivered captures the effect of training on trainees. For details, see Larry L. Orr et al., *Does Training for the Disadvantaged Work? Evidence from the National JTPA Study*, Urban Institute Press, 1996.

GRASSHOPPER: Would Nicole and Ron have been saved if earlier analysts had used instrumental variables?

MASTER JOSHWAY: There are some things we can never know.

3.3   The Population Bomb

Population control or race to oblivion?
    Paul Ehrlich, 1968

World population increased from 3 billion to 6 billion be-tween 1960 and 1999, a doubling time of 39 years, and about half as long as the time it took to go from 1.5 billion to 3 billion. Only a dozen years passed before the seventh bil-lion came along. But contemporary demographers agree that population growth has slowed dramatically. Projections using current fertility rates point to a doubling time of 100 years or more, perhaps even forever. One widely quoted estimate has population peaking at 9 billion in 2070.[12] Contemporary hand-wringing about sustainable growth notwithstanding, the population bomb has been defused—what a relief!

The question of how population growth affects living stan-dards has both a macro side and a micro side. Macro demog-raphy traces its roots to the eighteenth-century English scholar Thomas Malthus, who argued that population size increases when food output increases, so much so that productivity gains fail to boost living standards. The unhappy Malthusian outcome is characterized by a permanent subsistence-level ex-istence for most people. This pessimistic view of economic growth has repeatedly been falsified by history, but that hasn't

[12] See David Lam, "How the World Survived the Population Bomb: Lessons from 50 Years of Extraordinary Demographic History," *Demography*, vol. 48, no. 4, November 2011, pages 1231–1262, and Wolfgang Lutz, Warren San-derson, and Sergei Scherbov, "The End of World Population Growth," *Nature*, vol. 412, no. 6846, August 2, 2001, pages 543–545.

prevented it from gaining traction among latter-day doom-sayers. Biologist Paul Ehrlich's 1968 blockbuster *The Population Bomb* famously argued for a Malthusian scenario featuring imminent mass starvation in India. Since then, India's population has tripled, while Indian living standards have increased markedly.[13]

Economists have turned a micro lens on the relationship between family size and living standards. Here, attention focuses on the ability of households of different sizes to support a comfortable standard of living. We might indeed expect increases in family size to be associated with increased poverty and reduced education—more mouths to feed means less for each—and that's what simple correlations show. A more elaborate theoretical rationalization for this powerful relation comes from the work of the late Gary Becker and his collaborators. These studies introduced the notion of a "quantity-quality trade-off," the idea that reductions in family size increase parental investment in children. For example, parents with fewer children might guard their children's health more closely and invest more in their schooling.[14]

On the policy side, the view that smaller families are essential for increasing living standards has motivated international agencies and many governments to promote, and occasionally even to require, smaller families. China led the way with the controversial One Child Policy, implemented in 1979. Other aggressive government-sponsored family planning efforts include a forced-sterilization program in India and the public promotion of family planning in Mexico and Indonesia. By

[13] Just how much Indian living standards have risen is debated. Still, scholars generally agree that conditions have improved dramatically since 1970 (see, for example, Angus Deaton, *The Great Escape: Health, Wealth, and the Origins of Inequality,* Princeton University Press, 2013).

[14] Gary S. Becker and H. Gregg Lewis, "On the Interaction between the Quantity and Quality of Children," *Journal of Political Economy,* vol. 81, no. 2, part 2, March/April 1973, pages S279–288, and Gary S. Becker and Nigel Tomes, "Child Endowments and the Quantity and Quality of Children," *Journal of Political Economy,* vol. 84, no. 4, part 2, August 1976, pages S143–S162.

1990, 85% of people in the developing world lived in countries where the government considered high fertility to be a major force perpetuating poverty.[15]

The negative correlation between average family size and development indicators like schooling is hard to argue with. Is there a causal connection between family size and children's education? The challenge in answering this question, as always, is the *paribus*-ness of the *ceteris*. For the most part, fertility is determined by the choices parents make.[16] Not surprisingly, therefore, women with large families differ in many ways from those with smaller families; they tend to be less educated, for example. And the children of less-educated mothers tend to be less educated themselves. Marked differences in observable characteristics across families of different sizes raise the red flag of selection bias. Since women with different numbers of children are so observably different, we must acknowledge the possibility of important unobserved differences associated with family size as well.

As always, the ideal solution to an omitted variables problem is random assignment. In this case, the experiment might go like this. (i) Draw a sample of families with one child. (ii) In some of these households, randomly distribute an additional child. (iii) Wait 20 years and collect data on the educational attainment of firstborns who did and did not get an extra sibling. Of course, we aren't likely to see such an experiment any time soon. Clever masters might, however, find sources of

---

[15] John Bongaarts, "The Impact of Population Policies: Comment," *Population and Development Review*, vol. 20, no. 3, September 1994, pages 616–620.

[16] You might think this is true only of societies with access to modern contraceptive methods, such as the pill or the penny (held between the knees as needed). But demographers have shown that even without access to modern contraceptives, potential parents exert a remarkable degree of fertility control. For example, in an extensive body of work, Ansley Coale documented the dramatic decline in marital fertility in nineteenth- and twentieth-century Europe (see http://opr.princeton.edu/archive/pefp/). This pattern, since repeated in most of the world, is called the *demographic transition*.

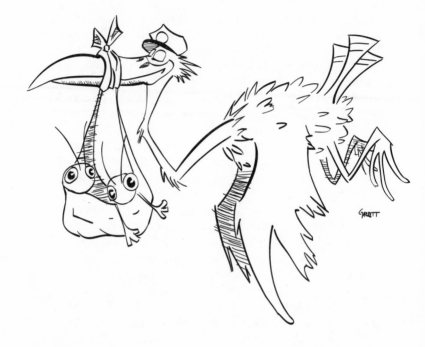

variation that reveal the causal connection between family size and schooling without the benefit of a real experiment.

Which brings us to the question of where babies come from. As most of our readers will know, human infants are delivered to households by a long-legged, long-necked bird called a stork (though it's a myth that the infant is dropped down the chimney—chimneys have a damper that prevents delivery of a live infant). Delivery occurs 9 months after a woman, whom we will refer to as the "mother," declares her intention to have a child. Storks are unresponsive to the wishes of men (except when these wishes are passed on by women), so we focus here on the notional experiment from the point of view of the mother and her oldest child.

The experiment we have in mind is the addition of children to households that have one already. The first-born child is our experimental subject. The 'metrics challenge is how to generate "as good as randomly assigned" variation in family size for these subjects. Unfortunately, the Association of Stork Midwives rejects random assignment as unnatural. But storks nevertheless generate circumstantially random variation in family size by sometimes delivering more than one child in the form of twins (a consequence of the fact that storks are large and infants are small, so storks sometimes scoop multiples when picking babies in the infant storage warehouse). The fact that twins induce a family size experiment was first recognized in a pioneering study by Mark Rosenzweig and Kenneth Wolpin, who used a small sample of twins to investigate the quantity-quality trade-off in India.[17]

To exploit the twins experiment, we turn to a large sample from Israel, analyzed in a study of the quantity-quality trade-off by Master Joshway, with colleagues Victor Lavy and Analia Schlosser (the "ALS study" for short).[18] Israel makes for an interesting case study because it has a very diverse population, including many people who were born in developing countries and into large families. About half of the Israeli Jewish population is of European ancestry, while the other half has roots in Asia or Africa. Quite a few Arabs live in Israel as well, but the data for Israeli non-Jews are less complete than for Jews. An attractive feature of the Israeli Jewish sample, besides ethnic diversity and larger families than are found in most developed countries, is the availability of information on respondents' families of origin, including the age and sex of their siblings. This unusual data structure is the foundation of the ALS empirical strategy.

We focus here on a group of first-born adults in a random sample of men and women born to mothers with at least two children. These firstborns have at least one younger sibling, but many have two or more. Consider a family in which the

[17] Mark R. Rosenzweig and Kenneth I. Wolpin, "Testing the Quantity-Quality Fertility Model: The Use of Twins as a Natural Experiment," *Econometrica*, vol. 48, no. 1, January 1980, pages 227–240.

[18] Joshua D. Angrist, Victor Lavy, and Analia Schlosser, "Multiple Experiments for the Causal Link between the Quantity and Quality of Children," *Journal of Labor Economics*, vol. 28, no. 4, October 2010, pages 773–824.

second birth is a singleton. On average, such families include 3.6 children. A second twin birth, however, increases average family size by .32, that is, by about one-third of a child. Why do twin births increase family size by a Solomonic fractional child? Many Israeli parents would like three or four children; their family size is largely unaffected by the occurrence of a multiple twin birth, since they were going to have more than two children either way. On the other hand, some families are happy with only two children. The latter group is forced to increase family size from two to three when the stork delivers twins. The one-third-of-a-child twins differential in family size reflects a difference in probabilities: the likelihood of having a third child increases from about .7 with a singleton second birth to a certainty when the second birth is multiple. The .3 figure comes from the fact that the difference between a probability of 1 and probability of .7 is .3.

A simple regression of adult firstborns' highest grade completed on family size shows that each extra sibling is associated with a reduction of about one-quarter of a year of schooling (these results come from a model with age and sex controls). On the other hand, as the ALS study shows, even though first-born adults with second-born twin siblings were raised in larger families, they are no less educated than first-born adults in families where the second-born child was a singleton. The comparison of schooling between firstborns with twin and singleton siblings constitutes the reduced form for an IV estimate that uses twin births as an instrument for family size.

IV estimates are constructed from the ratio of reduced-form to first-stage estimates, so a reduced form of zero immediately suggests the causal effect of sibship size is also zero. The fact that the twins reduced-form and associated IV estimates are close to zero weighs against the view that a larger family of origin reduces children's schooling. In other words, the twins experiment generates no evidence of a quantity-quality trade-off.

Multiple births have a marked effect on family size, but the twins experiment isn't perfect. Because the Association of Stork Midwives refuses to use random assignment, there's some imbalance in the incidence of twinning. Multiple births are more frequent among mothers who are older and for women in some racial and ethnic groups. This potentially leads to omitted variables bias in our analysis of the twins experiment, especially if some of the characteristics that boost twinning are hard to observe and control for.[19] Luckily, a second fertility experiment provides evidence on the quantity-quality trade-off.

In many countries, fertility is affected by sibling sex composition. For one thing, parents often hope for a son; son preference is particularly strong in parts of Asia. In Europe, the Americas, and Israel, parents seem to care little about whether children are male or female. Rather, many parents hope for a diversified sibling-sex portfolio: Families whose first two children are both boys or both girls are more likely to have a third child. Because the sex of a newborn is essentially randomly assigned (male births occur about half the time and, in the absence of sex-selective abortion, little can be done to change this), parental preferences for mixed sibling-sex composition generate sex-mix instruments.

First-born Israeli adults who have a second-born sibling of the opposite sex grew up in households with about 3.60 children. But firstborns whose second-born sibling is of the same sex were raised in families with 3.68 children. In other words, the same-sex first stage for Israeli firstborns is about .08. As with the twins first stage, this differential reflects changes in the probability of childbearing induced by an instrument. In this case, the instrumental variable is a dummy variable that equals 1 for families whose first two children are both male or both female and equals 0 for families with one boy and one girl. While the sex-mix first stage is smaller than that arising from twinning, the number of families affected by same-sex sibships is much larger than the number of families affected by twinning. About half of all families with at least two children have either two boys or two girls at births number one

---

[19] In more recent samples, twins instruments are also compromised by the proliferation of in vitro fertilization, a treatment for infertility. Mothers who turn to in vitro fertilization, which increases twin birth rates sharply, tend to be older and more educated than other mothers.

and number two. By contrast, only about 1% of mothers have twins. Sibling sex composition also has a leg up on twinning in being unrelated to maternal characteristics, such as age at birth and race (as shown by ALS and in an earlier study by Master Joshway and William Evans).[20]

As it turns out, the educational attainment of first-born Israeli adults is unaffected by their siblings' sex composition. For example, the average highest grade completed by first-borns from families with mixed- and same-sex sibships is about equal at 12.6. Thus, the same-sex reduced form, and therefore the corresponding IV estimates, are both zero. Like the twins experiment, fertility changes generated by differences in sibling sex composition show no evidence of a quantity-quality trade-off.

The exclusion restriction required for a causal interpretation of sex-mix IV estimates asserts that sibling sex composition matters for adult outcomes only insofar as it changes family size. Might the sex-mix of the first two children affect children's educational outcomes for other reasons? Two boys and two girls are likely to share a bedroom longer than mixed-sex siblings, for example, and same-sex siblings may make better use of hand-me-down clothing. Such household efficiencies might make families with a same-sex sibship feel a little richer, a feeling that may ultimately increase parental investment in their children's schooling.

Can we test the exclusion restriction? Not directly, but, as is often the case, evidence can be brought to bear on the question. For some mothers, sex composition is unlikely to affect fertility. For example, in an Israeli sample, religious women who plan to have three or more children are always-takers for sex-mix instruments. On the other hand, highly educated women, most of whom plan small families, are never-takers if their fertility behavior is unchanged by sex mix. Because the fertility of always-takers and never-takers is unchanged by

[20] Joshua D. Angrist and William Evans, "Children and Their Parents' Labor Supply: Evidence from Exogenous Variation in Family Size," *American Economic Review*, vol. 88, no. 3, June 1998, pages 450–477.

sibling sex composition, any relationship between sex-mix instruments and outcomes in samples with few compliers may signal violations of the underlying exclusion restriction.

We can express this idea more formally using the representation of LATE in equation (3.2). This expression defines LATE as the ratio of reduced-form to first-stage parameters, that is:

$$\lambda = \frac{\rho}{\phi},$$

which implies in turn that the reduced form, ρ, is the product of the first stage and LATE:

$$\rho = \phi\lambda.$$

From this we conclude that in samples where the first stage, ϕ, is zero, the reduced form should be zero as well. On the other hand, a statistically significant reduced-form estimate with no evidence of a corresponding first stage is cause for worry, because this suggests some channel other than the treatment variable (in this case, family size) links instruments with outcomes. In this spirit, ALS identified demographic groups for which the effect of twins and sex-composition instruments on family size is small and not significantly different from zero. These "no-first-stage samples" generate no evidence of significant reduced-form effects that might signal violations of the exclusion restriction.

One-Stop Shopping with Two-Stage Least Squares

IV estimates of causal effects boil down to reduced-form comparisons across groups defined by the instrument, scaled by the appropriate first stage. This is a universal IV principle, but the details vary across applications. The quantity-quality scenario differs from the KIPP story in that we have more than one instrument for the same underlying causal relation. Assuming that twins and sex-mix instruments both satisfy the required assumptions and capture similar average causal effects, we'd like to combine the two IV estimates they generate to increase statistical precision. At the same time, twinning might be correlated with maternal characteristics like age at birth and ethnicity, leading to bias in twins IV estimates. We'd therefore like a simple IV procedure that controls for maternal age and any other confounding factors. This suggests a payoff to integrating the IV idea with the regression methods discussed in Chapter 2.

Two-stage least squares (2SLS) generalizes IV in two ways. First, 2SLS estimates use multiple instruments efficiently. Second, 2SLS estimates control for covariates, thereby mitigating OVB from imperfect instruments. To see how 2SLS works, it helps to rewrite the first stage (ϕ) and reduced form (ρ) parameters as regression coefficients instead of differences in means. Starting with a single instrument, say, a dummy variable for multiple second births denoted by Z_i, the reduced-form effect can be written as the coefficient ρ in the regression equation:

$$Y_i = \alpha_0 + \rho Z_i + e_{0i}. \qquad (3.4)$$

As we noted in the appendix to Chapter 2, regression on a constant term and a single dummy variable produces the difference in the conditional means of the dependent variable with the dummy switched off and on. The coefficient on Z_i in equation (3.4) is therefore

$$\rho = E[Y_i|Z_i = 1] - E[Y_i|Z_i = 0].$$

Likewise, the first-stage effect of Z_i is the coefficient ϕ in the first-stage equation:

$$D_i = \alpha_1 + \phi Z_i + e_{1i}, \qquad (3.5)$$

where $\phi = E[D_i|Z_i = 1] - E[D_i|Z_i = 0]$. Since $\lambda = \rho/\phi$, we conclude that LATE is the ratio of the slope coefficients in regressions (3.4) and (3.5).

The 2SLS procedure offers an alternative way of computing ρ/ϕ. The 2SLS name comes from the fact that LATE can be obtained from a sequence of two regressions. In the 2SLS first stage, we estimate equation (3.5) and save the fitted values, $\hat{D}_i$. These "first-stage fits" are defined as

$$\hat{D}_i = \alpha_1 + \phi Z_i. \qquad (3.6)$$

The 2SLS second stage regresses Y_i on $\hat{D}_i$, as in

$$Y_i = \alpha_2 + \lambda_{2SLS}\hat{D}_i + e_{2i}.$$

The value of λ_{2SLS} generated by this second step is identical to the ratio of reduced form to first-stage regression coefficients, ρ/ϕ, a theoretical relationship derived in the chapter appendix.

Control variables like maternal age fit neatly into this two-step regression framework.[21] Adding maternal age, denoted A_i, the reduced form and first stage look like

$$\text{Reduced form:} \quad Y_i = \alpha_0 + \rho Z_i + \gamma_0 A_i + e_{0i} \qquad (3.7)$$

$$\text{First stage:} \quad D_i = \alpha_1 + \phi Z_i + \gamma_1 A_i + e_{1i}. \qquad (3.8)$$

Here, the first-stage fitted values come from models that include the control variable, A_i:

$$\hat{D}_i = \alpha_1 + \phi Z_i + \gamma_1 A_i.$$

2SLS estimates are again constructed by regressing Y_i on both $\hat{D}_i$ and A_i. Hence, the 2SLS second-stage equation is

$$Y_i = \alpha_2 + \lambda_{2SLS}\hat{D}_i + \gamma_2 A_i + e_{2i}, \qquad (3.9)$$

which also includes A_i.

The 2SLS setup allows as many control variables as you like, provided they appear in both the first and second stages. As discussed in the chapter appendix, the corresponding covariate-adjusted LATE can still be constructed from the ratio of reduced-form to first-stage coefficients, ρ/ϕ. Indeed, we should separately inspect the upstairs and downstairs in this ratio to make sure all on both floors is kosher. But when it comes time to report results to the public, 2SLS is the way to go even in relatively simple scenarios like this one. Econometrics software packages compute 2SLS estimates directly,

---

[21] We've seen a version of IV with covariates already. The KIPP offer effects reported in column (3) of Table 3.1 come from regression models for the first stage and reduced form that include covariates in the form of dummies for application risk sets.

reducing the scope for mistakes and generating appropriate standard errors at no extra charge.[22]

What about our second family-size instrument, a dummy for same-sex sibships? Call this W_i (where $W_i = 1$ indicates two girls or two boys, and $W_i = 0$ otherwise). Here, too, control variables are called for, in particular, the sex of the first-born, which we code as a dummy, B_i, indicating first-born boys (as a rule, boys are born slightly more often than girls, so the probability of a same-sex pair is slightly higher when the first-born is male). With two instruments, W_i and Z_i, and the extra control variable, B_i, the 2SLS first stage becomes

$$D_i = \alpha_1 + \phi_t Z_i + \phi_s W_i + \gamma_1 A_i + \delta_1 B_i + e_{1i}. \quad (3.10)$$

The first-stage effects of the twins and sex-mix instruments are distinguished by subscripts t for twins and s for sex-mix: we write these as ϕ_t and ϕ_s. Both instruments appear with similarly subscripted coefficients in the corresponding reduced form as well:

$$Y_i = \alpha_0 + \rho_t Z_i + \rho_s W_i + \gamma_0 A_i + \delta_0 B_i + e_{0i}.$$

With these ingredients at hand, it's time to cook!

Second-stage estimates with two instruments and two co-variates are generated by the regression equation

$$Y_i = \alpha_2 + \lambda_{2SLS} \hat{D}_i + \gamma_2 A_i + \delta_2 B_i + e_{2i}, \quad (3.11)$$

where the fitted values, $\hat{D}_i$, come from first-stage equation (3.10). Note that the covariates appear at every turn: in the first

---

[22] Alert readers will have noticed that the treatment variable here, family size, is not a dummy variable like KIPP enrollment, but rather an ordered treatment that counts children. You might wonder whether it's OK to describe 2SLS estimates of the effects of variables like family size as LATE. Although the details differ, 2SLS estimates can still be said to capture average causal effects on compliers in this context. The extension of LATE to ordered treatments is developed in Joshua D. Angrist and Guido W. Imbens, "Two Stage Least Squares Estimation of Average Causal Effects in Models with Variable Treatment Intensity," *Journal of the American Statistical Association*, vol. 90, no. 430, June 1995, pages 431–442. Along the same lines, 2SLS easily accommodates instruments that aren't dummies. We'll see an example of this in Chapter 6.

TABLE 3.4
Quantity-quality first stages

	Twins instruments		Same-sex instruments		Twins and same-sex instruments
	(1)	(2)	(3)	(4)	(5)
Second-born twins	.320 (.052)	.437 (.050)			.449 (.050)
Same-sex sibships			.079 (.012)	.073 (.010)	.076 (.010)
Male		−.018 (.010)		−.020 (.010)	−.020 (.010)
Controls	No	Yes	No	Yes	Yes

Notes: This table reports coefficients from a regression of the number of children on instruments and covariates. The sample size is 89,445. Standard errors are reported in parentheses.

and second stages, and in the reduced form. Equation (3.11) produces a weighted average of the estimates we'd get using the instruments Z_i and W_i one at a time, while controlling for covariates A_i and B_i. When the instruments generate similar results when used one at a time, the 2SLS weighted average is typically a more precise estimate of this common causal effect.

2SLS offers a wonderfully flexible framework for IV estimation. In addition to incorporating control variables and using multiple instruments efficiently, the framework accommodates instruments of all shapes and sizes, not just dummy variables. In practice, however, masters use special-purpose statistical software to calculate 2SLS estimates instead of estimating regressions on fitted values like (3.11). Estimation of this equation, known as "manual 2SLS," doesn't produce the correct standard errors needed to measure sampling variance. The chapter appendix explains why.

Estimates of twins and sex-mix first stages with and without covariates appear in Table 3.4. The estimate from a first-stage model with controls, reported in column (2) of the table, shows that first-born Israeli adults whose second-born siblings were twin were raised in families with about .44 more children than those raised in families where the second birth was a singleton. This first-stage estimate is larger than the estimate of .32 computed without controls (reported in column (1)). The OVB formula therefore tells us that twin births are associated with factors that reduce family size, like older maternal age. Adjusting for maternal age and other possible confounding factors boosts the twins first stage. On the other hand, the same-sex first stage of .073 generated by a model with covariates is close to the uncontrolled estimate of .079, since sex mix is essentially unrelated to the included controls (these estimates can be seen in columns (3) and (4)). The fact that the first-born is male also has little effect on the size of his family. This can be seen in the small, marginally significant male coefficients reported in the last row (this is the only covariate coefficient reported in the table, though the presence of other controls is indicated in the bottom row).[23]

Second-stage estimates of the quantity-quality trade-off are reported in Table 3.5, along with the corresponding estimates from a conventional (that is, uninstrumented) OLS regression of the form

$$Y_i = \alpha_3 + \beta D_i + \gamma_3 A_i + \delta_3 B_i + e_{3i}.$$

The conventional regression estimates in column (1) show a strong negative relation between family size and education outcomes, even after adjusting for family background variables related to ethnicity and mother's age at birth. By contrast, the 2SLS estimates generated by twins instruments, reported in column (2) of the table, mostly go the other way, though the 2SLS estimates in this case are not significantly different from zero. Estimation using sex-composition instruments reinforces the twins findings. The 2SLS estimates in column (3) show uni-

---

[23] In addition to the male dummy, other covariates include indicators for census year, parents' ethnicity, age, missing month of birth, mother's age, mother's age at first birth, and mother's age at immigration (where relevant). See the Empirical Notes section for details.

TABLE 3.5

OLS and 2SLS estimates of the quantity-quality trade-off

| | | 2SLS estimates | | |
Dependent variable	OLS estimates (1)	Twins instruments (2)	Same-sex instruments (3)	Twins and same-sex instruments (4)
Years of schooling	−.145 (.005)	.174 (.166)	.318 (.210)	.237 (.128)
High school graduate	−.029 (.001)	.030 (.028)	.001 (.033)	.017 (.021)
Some college (for age ≥ 24)	−.023 (.001)	.017 (.052)	.078 (.054)	.048 (.037)
College graduate (for age ≥ 24)	−.015 (.001)	−.021 (.045)	.125 (.053)	.052 (.032)

Notes: This table reports OLS and 2SLS estimates of the effect of family size on schooling. OLS estimates appear in column (1). Columns (2), (3), and (4) show 2SLS estimates constructed using the instruments indicated in column headings. Sample sizes are 89,445 for rows (1) and (2); 50,561 for row (3); and 50,535 for row (4). Standard errors are reported in parentheses.

formly positive effects of family size on education (though only one of these is significantly different from zero).

An important feature of both the twins and sex-composition second stages is their precision, or lack thereof. IV methods discard all variation in fertility except that generated by the instrument. This can leave too little variation for statistically conclusive findings. We can increase precision, however, by pooling multiple instruments, especially if, when taken one at a time, the instruments generate similar findings (in this case, both twins and sex-composition instruments show little evidence of a quantity-quality trade-off). The resulting pooled first-stage estimates appear in column (5) of Table 3.4, while the corresponding second-stage results are reported in column (4) of Table 3.5.

The pooled second-stage estimates are not very different from those generated using the instruments one at a time, but the standard errors are appreciably smaller. For example, the estimated effect of family size on highest grade completed using both instruments is .24, with a standard error of .13, a marked drop from the standard errors of about .17 and .21 using twins and same-sex instruments one at a time. Importantly, the regression estimate in column (1), a very precise $-.15$ for highest grade completed, lies well outside the confidence interval associated with the 2SLS estimate in column (4).[24] This suggests that the strong negative association between family size and schooling is driven in large part and perhaps entirely by selection bias.

❦

MASTER JOSHWAY: Build the house of IV, Grasshopper.

GRASSHOPPER: The foundation has three layers: (i) the *first-stage* requires instruments that affect the causal channel of interest; (ii) the *independence assumption* requires instruments to be as good as randomly assigned; (iii) the *exclusion restriction* asserts that a single causal channel connects instruments with outcomes.

MASTER JOSHWAY: Can these assumptions be checked?

GRASSHOPPER: Check the first stage by looking for a strong relationship between instruments and the proposed causal channel; check independence by checking covariate balance with the instrument switched off and on, as in a randomized trial.

MASTER JOSHWAY: And exclusion?

GRASSHOPPER: The exclusion restriction is not easily verified. Sometimes, however, we may find a sample where the first stage is very small. Exclusion implies such samples should generate small reduced-form estimates, since the hypothesized causal channel is absent.

MASTER JOSHWAY: How are IV estimates computed?

---

[24] Specifically, the regression estimate of $-.145$ lies outside the multi-instrument 2SLS confidence interval of $.237 \pm (2 \times .128) = [-.02, .49]$. You can, in some cases, have too many instruments, especially if they have little explanatory power in the first stage. The chapter appendix elaborates on this point.

GRASSHOPPER: Statistical software computes two-stage least squares estimates for us. This allows us to add covariates and use more than one instrument at a time. But we look at the first-stage and reduced-form estimates as well.

Masters of 'Metrics: The Remarkable Wrights

The IV method was invented by economist Philip G. Wright, assisted by his son, Sewall, a geneticist. Philip wrote frequently about agricultural markets. In 1928, he published *The Tariff on Animal and Vegetable Oils*.[25] Most of this book is concerned with the question of whether the steep tariffs on farm products imposed in the early 1920s benefited domestic producers. A 1929 reviewer noted that "Whatever the practical value of the intricate computation of elasticity of demand and supply as applied particularly to butter in this chapter, the discussion has high theoretical value."[26]

In competitive markets, shifting supply and demand curves simultaneously generate equilibrium prices and quantities. The path from these observed equilibrium prices and quantities to the underlying supply and demand curves that generate them is unclear. The challenge of how to derive supply and demand elasticities from the observed relationship between prices and quantities is called an *identification problem*. At the time Philip was writing, econometric identification was poorly understood. Economists knew for sure only that the observed relationship between price and quantity fails to capture either supply or demand, and is somehow determined by both.

Appendix B of *The Tariff on Animal and Vegetable Oils* begins with an elegant statement of the identification problem in simultaneous equations models. The appendix then goes on

[25] Philip G. Wright, *The Tariff on Animal and Vegetable Oils,* Macmillan Company, 1928.

[26] G. O. Virtue, "*The Tariff on Animal and Vegetable Oils* by Philip G. Wright," *American Economic Review,* vol. 19, no. 1, March 1929, pages 152–156. The quote is from page 155.

to explain how variables present in one equation but excluded from another solve the identification problem. Philip referred to such excluded variables as "external factors," because, by shifting the equation in which they appear, they trace out the equation from which they're omitted (that is, to which they are external). Today we call such shifters instruments. Philip derived and then used IV to estimate supply and demand curves in markets for butter and flaxseed (flaxseed is used to make linseed oil, an ingredient in paint). Philip's analysis of the flaxseed market uses prices of substitutes as demand shifters, while farm yields per acre, mostly driven by weather conditions, shift supply.

Appendix B was a major breakthrough in 'metrics thought, remarkable and unexpected, so much so that some have wondered whether Philip really wrote it. Perhaps Appendix B was written by Sewall, a distinguished scholar in his own right. Like 'metrics masters Galton and Fisher, profiled at the end of Chapters 1 and 2, Sewall was a geneticist and statistician. Well before the appearance of Appendix B, Sewall had developed a statistical method called "path analysis" that was meant to solve problems related to omitted variables bias. Today we recognize path analysis as an application of the multivariate regression methods discussed in Chapter 2; it doesn't solve the identification problem raised by simultaneous equations models. Some of Appendix B references Sewall's idea of "path coefficients," but Philip's method of external factors was entirely new.

Masters James Stock and Francesco Trebbi investigated the case for Sewall's authorship using Stylometrics.[27] Stylometrics identifies authors by the statistical regularities in their word usage and sentence structure. Stylometrics confirms Philip's authorship of Appendix B. Recently, however, Stock and his student Kerry Clark uncovered letters between father and son that show the ideas in Appendix B developing jointly in a self-effacing give and take. In this exchange, Philip describes the

---

[27] James H. Stock and Francesco Trebbi, "Who Invented Instrumental Variables Regression?" *Journal of Economic Perspectives*, vol. 17, no. 3, Summer 2003, pages 177–194.

In February 1926, Philip Wright wrote his son, Sewall: "I expect I am stupid but I don't seem to be able to pick up a new branch of mathematics as quickly as I could once..."

power and simplicity of IV. But he wasn't naive about the ease with which the method could be applied. In a March 1926 letter to Sewall, writing on the prospect of finding external factors, Philip commented: "Such factors, I fear, especially in the case of demand conditions, are not easy to find."[28] The search for identification has not gotten easier in the intervening decades.

Philip's journey was personal as well as intellectual. He worked for many years as a teacher at obscure Lombard College in Galesburg, Illinois. Lombard College failed to survive the Great Depression, but Philip's time there bore impressive fruit. At Lombard, he mentored young Carl Sandburg, whose loosely structured and evocative poetry later made him

[28] This quote and the one in the sketch are from from unpublished letters, uncovered by James H. Stock and Kerry Clark. See "Philip Wright, the Identification Problem in Econometrics, and Its Solution," presented at the Tufts University Department of Economics Special Event in honor of Philip Green Wright, October 2011 (http://ase.tufts.edu/econ/news/documents/wright PhilipAndSewall.pdf), and Kerry Clark's 2012 Harvard senior thesis, "The Invention and Reinvention of Instrumental Variables Regression."

an American icon. Here's Sandburg's description of the path blazed by experience:[29]

> THIS morning I looked at the map of the day
> And said to myself, "This is the way! This is the way I will go;
> Thus shall I range on the roads of achievement,
> The way is so clear—it shall all be a joy on the lines
>   marked out."
> And then as I went came a place that was strange,—
> 'Twas a place not down on the map!
> And I stumbled and fell and lay in the weeds,
> And looked on the day with rue.
>
> I am learning a little—never to be sure—
> To be positive only with what is past,
> And to peer sometimes at the things to come
> As a wanderer treading the night
> When the mazy stars neither point nor beckon,
> And of all the roads, no road is sure.
>
> I see those men with maps and talk
> Who tell how to go and where and why;
> I hear with my ears the words of their mouths,
> As they finger with ease the marks on the maps;
> And only as one looks robust, lonely, and querulous,
> As if he had gone to a country far
> And made for himself a map,
> Do I cry to him, "I would see your map!
> I would heed that map you have!"

Appendix: IV Theory

IV, LATE, and 2SLS

We first refresh notation for an IV setup with one instrument and no covariates. The first stage links instrument and treatment:

---

[29] "Experience." From *In Reckless Ecstasy*, Asgard Press, 1904, edited and with a foreword by Philip Green Wright.

$$D_i = \alpha_1 + \phi Z_i + e_{1i}.$$

The reduced form links instrument and outcomes:

$$Y_i = \alpha_0 + \rho Z_i + e_{0i}.$$

The 2SLS second stage is the regression of outcomes on first-stage fitted values:

$$Y_i = \alpha_2 + \lambda \hat{D}_i + e_{2i}.$$

Note that the LATE formula (3.2) can be written in terms of first-stage and reduced-form regression coefficients as

$$\lambda = \frac{\rho}{\phi} = \frac{C(Y_i, Z_i)/V(Z_i)}{C(D_i, Z_i)/V(Z_i)} = \frac{C(Y_i, Z_i)}{C(D_i, Z_i)}. \qquad (3.12)$$

Here, we've used the fact that the differences in means on the top and bottom of equation (3.2) are the same as the regression coefficients, ϕ and ρ. Written this way, that is, as a ratio of covariances, λ is called the *IV formula*. It's sample analogue is the IV estimator.

In this simple setup, the regression of Y_i on $\hat{D}_i$ (the 2SLS second step) is the same as equation (3.12). This is apparent once we write out the 2SLS second stage:

$$\lambda_{2SLS} = \frac{C(Y_i, \hat{D}_i)}{V(\hat{D}_i)} = \frac{C(Y_i, \alpha_1 + \phi Z_i)}{V(\alpha_1 + \phi Z_i)}$$

$$= \frac{\phi C(Y_i, Z_i)}{\phi^2 V(Z_i)} = \frac{\rho}{\phi} = \lambda.$$

In deriving this, we've used the rules for variances and covariances detailed in the appendix to Chapter 2.

With covariates included in the first and second stage— say, the variable A_i, as in our investigation of the population bomb—the 2SLS second stage is equation (3.9). Here, too, 2SLS and the IV formula are equivalent, with the latter again given by the ratio of reduced-form to first-stage coefficients. In this case, these coefficients are estimated with A_i included, as in equations (3.7) and (3.8):

$$\frac{\rho}{\phi} = \frac{C(Y_i, \tilde{Z}_i)/V(\tilde{Z}_i)}{C(D_i, \tilde{Z}_i)/V(\tilde{Z}_i)} = \lambda_{2SLS},$$

where $\tilde{Z}_i$ is the residual from a regression of Z_i on A_i (this we know from regression anatomy). The details behind the second equals sign are left for you to fill in.

2SLS Standard Errors

Just as with sample means and regression estimates, we expect IV and 2SLS estimates to vary from one sample to another. We must gauge the extent of sampling variability in any particular set of estimates as we decide whether they're meaningful. The sampling variance of 2SLS estimates is quantified by the appropriate standard errors.

2SLS standard errors for a model that uses Z_i to instrument D_i, while controlling for A_i, are computed as follows. First the 2SLS residual is constructed using

$$\eta_i = Y_i - \alpha_2 - \lambda_{2SLS}D_i - \gamma_2 A_i.$$

The standard error for $\hat{\lambda}_{2SLS}$ is then given by

$$SE(\hat{\lambda}_{2SLS}) = \frac{\sigma_\eta}{\sqrt{n}} \times \frac{1}{\sigma_{\hat{D}}}, \qquad (3.13)$$

where σ_η is the standard deviation of η_i, and $\sigma_{\hat{D}}$ is the standard deviation of the first-stage fitted values, $\hat{D}_i = \alpha_1 + \phi Z_i + \gamma_1 A_i$.

It's important to note that η_i is not the residual generated by manual estimation of the 2SLS second stage, equation (3.9). This incorrect residual is

$$e_{2i} = Y_i - \alpha_2 - \lambda_{2SLS}\hat{D}_i - \gamma_2 A_i.$$

The variance of e_{2i} plays no role in equation (3.13), so a manual 2SLS second stage generates incorrect standard errors. The moral is clear: explore freely in the privacy of your own computer, but when it comes to the estimates and standard errors you plan to report in public, let professional software do the work.

2SLS Bias

IV is a powerful and flexible tool, but masters use their most powerful tools wisely. As we've seen, 2SLS combines multiple instruments in an effort to generate precise estimates of a single causal effect. Typically, a researcher blessed with many instruments knows that some produce a stronger first stage than others. The temptation is to use them all anyway (econometrics software doesn't charge more for this). The risk here is that 2SLS estimates with many weak instruments can be misleading. A weak instrument is one that isn't highly correlated with the regressor being instrumented, so the first-stage coefficient associated with this instrument is small or imprecisely estimated. 2SLS estimates with many such instruments tend to be similar to OLS estimates of the same model. When 2SLS is close to OLS, it's natural to conclude you needn't worry about selection bias in the latter, but this conclusion may be unwarranted. Because of *finite sample bias*, 2SLS estimates in a many-weak IV scenario tell you little about the causal relationship of interest.

When is finite sample bias worth worrying about? Masters often focus on the first-stage F-statistic testing the joint hypothesis that all first-stage coefficients in a many-instrument setup are zero (an F-statistic extends the t-statistic to tests of multiple hypotheses at once). A popular rule of thumb requires an F value of at least 10 to put many-weak fears to rest. An alternative to 2SLS, called the limited information maximum likelihood estimator (LIML for short) is less affected by finite sample bias. You'd like LIML estimates and 2SLS estimates to be close to one another, since the former are unlikely to be biased even with many weak instruments (though LIML estimates typically have larger standard errors than do the corresponding 2SLS estimates).

The many-weak instruments problem loses its sting when you use a single instrument to estimate a single causal effect. Estimates of the quantity-quality trade-off using either a single dummy for multiple births or a single dummy for same-sex sibships as an instrument for family size are therefore unlikely to be plagued by finite sample bias. Such estimates appear in columns (2) and (3) of Table 3.5. Finally, reduced-form estimates are always worth a careful look, since these are OLS estimates, unaffected by finite sample bias. Reduced-form estimates that are small and not significantly different from zero provide a strong and unbiased hint that the causal relationship of interest is weak or nonexistent as well, at least in the data at hand (multiple reduced-form coefficients are also tested together using an F-test). We always tell our students: *If you can't see it in the reduced form, it ain't there.*

Chapter 4

Regression Discontinuity Designs

YOUNG CAINE: Master, may we speak further on the forces of destiny?

MASTER PO: Speak.

CAINE: As we stand with two roads before us, how shall we know whether the left road or the right road will lead us to our destiny?

MASTER PO: You spoke of chance, Grasshopper. As if such a thing were certain to exist. In the matter you speak of, destiny, there is no such thing as chance.

Kung Fu, Season 3, Episode 62

Our Path

Human behavior is constrained by rules. The State of California limits elementary school class size to 32 students; 33 is one too many. The Social Security Administration won't pay you a penny in retirement benefits until you've reached age 62. Potential armed forces recruits with test scores in the lower deciles are ineligible for American military service. Although many of these rules seem arbitrary, with little grounding in science or experience, we say: bring 'em on! For rules that constrain the role of chance in human affairs often generate interesting experiments. Masters of 'metrics exploit these experiments with a tool called the *regression discontinuity* (RD) design. RD doesn't work for all causal questions, but it works for many. And when it does, the results have almost the same causal force as those from a randomized trial.

4.1   Birthdays and Funerals

KATY: Is this really what you're gonna do for the rest of your life?

BOON: What do you mean?

KATY: I mean hanging around with a bunch of animals getting drunk every weekend.

BOON: No! After I graduate, I'm gonna get drunk every night.
    Animal House, 1978 . . . of course

Your twenty-first birthday is an important milestone. American over-21s can drink legally, "at last," some would say. Of course, those under age drink as well. As we learn from the exploits of Boon and his fraternity brothers, not all underage drinking is in moderation. In an effort to address the social and public health problems associated with underage drinking, a group of American college presidents have lobbied states to return the minimum legal drinking age (MLDA) to the Vietnam-era threshold of 18. The theory behind this effort (known as the Amethyst Initiative) is that legal drinking at age 18 discourages binge drinking and promotes a culture of mature alcohol consumption. This contrasts with the traditional view that the age-21 MLDA, while a blunt and imperfect tool, reduces youth access to alcohol, thereby preventing some harm.

Fortunately, the history of the MLDA generates two natural experiments that can be used for a sober assessment of alcohol policy. We discuss the first experiment in this chapter and the second in the next.[1] The first MLDA experiment emerges from the fact that a small change in age (measured in months or even days) generates a big change in legal access. The difference a day makes can be seen in Figure 4.1, which plots the relationship between birthdays and funerals. This figure shows the number of deaths among Americans aged 20–22 between

[1] Our MLDA discussion draws on Christopher Carpenter and Carlos Dobkin, "The Effect of Alcohol Consumption on Mortality: Regression Discontinuity Evidence from the Minimum Drinking Age," *American Economic Journal—Applied Economics,* vol. 1, no. 1, January 2009, pages 164–182, and "The Minimum Legal Drinking Age and Public Health," *Journal of Economic Perspectives,* vol. 25, no. 2, Spring 2011, pages 133–156.

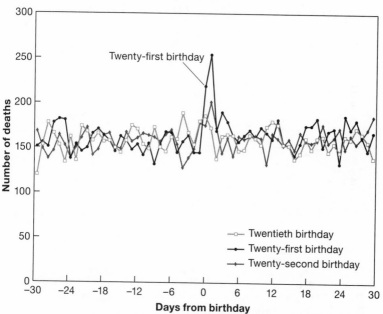

FIGURE 4.1
Birthdays and funerals

1997 and 2003. Deaths here are plotted by day, relative to birthdays, which are labeled as day 0. For example, someone who was born on September 18, 1990, and died on September 19, 2012, is counted among deaths of 22-year-olds occurring on day 1.

Mortality risk shoots up on and immediately following a twenty-first birthday, a fact visible in the pronounced spike in daily deaths on these days. This spike adds about 100 deaths to a baseline level of about 150 per day. The age-21 spike doesn't seem to be a generic party-hardy birthday effect. If this spike reflects birthday partying alone, we should expect to see deaths shoot up after the twentieth and twenty-second birthdays as well, but that doesn't happen. There's something special about the twenty-first birthday. It remains to be seen, however, whether the age-21 effect can be attributed to the MLDA, and whether the elevated mortality risk seen in Figure 4.1 lasts long enough to be worth worrying about.

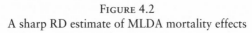

FIGURE 4.2
A sharp RD estimate of MLDA mortality effects

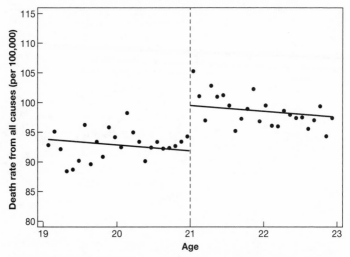

Notes: This figure plots death rates from all causes against age in months. The lines in the figure show fitted values from a regression of death rates on an over-21 dummy and age in months (the vertical dashed line indicates the minimum legal drinking age (MLDA) cutoff).

Sharp RD

The story linking the MLDA with a sharp and sustained rise in death rates is told in Figure 4.2. This figure plots death rates (measured as deaths per 100,000 persons per year) by month of age (defined as 30-day intervals), centered around the twenty-first birthday. The *X*-axis extends 2 years in either direction, and each dot in the figure is the death rate in one monthly interval. Death rates fluctuate from month to month, but few rates to the left of the age-21 cutoff are above 95. At ages over 21, however, death rates shift up, and few of those to the right of the age-21 cutoff are below 95.

Happily, the odds a young person dies decrease with age, a fact that can be seen in the downward-sloping lines fit to the death rates plotted in Figure 4.2. But extrapolating the trend line drawn to the left of the cutoff, we might have expected an age-21 death rate of about 92; in the language of Chapter 1, this is the average of the unseen counterfactual outcomes, Y_{0i}. In the real world, however, the trend line to the right of 21 starts markedly higher, at around 100. The jump in trend lines at age 21 illustrates the subject of this chapter, regression discontinuity designs (RD designs for short). RD is based on the seemingly paradoxical idea that rigid rules—which at first appear to reduce or even eliminate the scope for randomness—create valuable experiments.

The causal question addressed by Figure 4.2 is the effect of legal access to alcohol on death rates. The treatment variable in this case can be written D_a, where $D_a = 1$ indicates legal drinking and is 0 otherwise. D_a is a function of age, a: the MLDA transforms 21-year-olds from underage minors to legal alcohol consumers. We capture this transformation in mathematical notation by writing

$$D_a = \begin{cases} 1 & \text{if } a \geq 21 \\ 0 & \text{if } a < 21. \end{cases} \quad (4.1)$$

This representation highlights two signal features of RD designs:

- Treatment status is a deterministic function of a, so that once we know a, we know D_a.
- Treatment status is a discontinuous function of a, because no matter how close a gets to the cutoff, D_a remains unchanged until the cutoff is reached.

The variable that determines treatment, age in this case, is called the *running variable*. Running variables play a central role in the RD story. In *sharp* RD designs, treatment switches cleanly off or on as the running variable passes a cutoff. The MLDA is a sharp function of age, so an investigation of MLDA effects on mortality is a sharp RD study. The second half of the chapter discusses a second RD scenario, known as *fuzzy RD*, in which the probability or intensity of treatment jumps at a cutoff.

Mortality clearly changes with the running variable, a, for reasons unrelated to the MLDA. Death rates from disease-related causes like cancer (known to epidemiologists as internal causes) are low but increasing for those in their late teens and early 20s, while deaths from external causes, primarily car accidents, homicides, and suicides, fall. To separate this trend variation from any possible MLDA effects, an RD analysis controls for smooth variation in death rates generated by a. RD gets its name from the practice of using regression models to implement this control.

A simple RD analysis of the MLDA estimates causal effects using a regression like

$$\bar{M}_a = \alpha + \rho D_a + \gamma a + e_a, \qquad (4.2)$$

where $\bar{M}_a$ is the death rate in month a (again, month is defined as a 30-day interval counting from the twenty-first birthday). Equation (4.2) includes the treatment dummy, D_a, as well as a linear control for age in months. Fitted values from equation (4.2) produce the lines drawn in Figure 4.2. The negative slope, captured by γ, reflects smoothly declining death rates among young people as they mature. The parameter ρ captures the jump in deaths at age 21. Regression (4.2) generates an estimate of ρ equal to 7.7. When cast against average death rates of around 95, this estimate indicates a substantial increase in risk at the MLDA cutoff.

Is this a credible estimate of the causal effect of the MLDA? Should we not control for other things? The OVB formula tells us that the difference between the estimate of ρ in this short regression and the results any longer regression might produce depend on the correlation between variables added to the long regression and D_a. But equation (4.1) tells us that D_a is determined solely by a. Assuming that the effect of a on death rates is captured by a linear function, we can be sure that no OVB afflicts this short regression.

The lack of OVB in equation (4.2) is the payoff to inside information: although treatment isn't randomly assigned, we know where it comes from. Specifically, treatment is determined by the running variable—an implication of the deterministic link noted above. The question of causality therefore turns on whether the relationship between the running variable and outcomes has indeed been nailed by a regression with a linear control for age.

Although RD uses regression methods to estimate causal effects, RD designs are best seen as a distinct tool that differs importantly from the regression methods discussed in Chapter 2. In Chapter 2, we compared treatment and control outcomes at particular values of the control variables, in the hope that treatment is as good as randomly assigned after conditioning on controls. Here, there is no value of the running variable at which we get to observe both treatment and control observations. Whoa, Grasshopper! Unlike the matching and regression strategies discussed in Chapter 2, which are based on treatment-control comparisons conditional on covariate values, the validity of RD turns on our willingness to extrapolate across values of the running variable, at least for values in the neighborhood of the cutoff at which treatment switches on.

The local nature of such neighborly comparisons is apparent in Figure 4.2. The jump in trend lines at the MLDA cutoff implicitly compares death rates for people on either side of—but close to—a twenty-first birthday. In other words, the notional experiment here involves changes in access to alcohol for young people, in a world where alcohol is freely available to adults. The results from this experiment, though relevant for contemporary discussions of alcohol policy, need not tell us much about the consequences of more dramatic policy changes, such as Prohibition.

RD Specifics

RD tools aren't guaranteed to produce reliable causal estimates. Figure 4.3 shows why not. In panel A, the relationship between the running variable (X) and the outcome (Y) is linear, with a clear jump in $E[Y|X]$ at the cutoff value of one-half. Panel B looks similar, except that the relationship between average Y and X is nonlinear. Still, the jump at $X = .5$ is plain to see. Panel C of Figure 4.3 highlights the challenge RD designers face. Here, the figure exhibits a baroque nonlinear trend, with sharp turns to the left and right of the cutoff, but no discontinuity. Estimates constructed using a linear model like equation (4.2) mistake this nonlinearity for a discontinuity.

FIGURE 4.3
RD in action, three ways

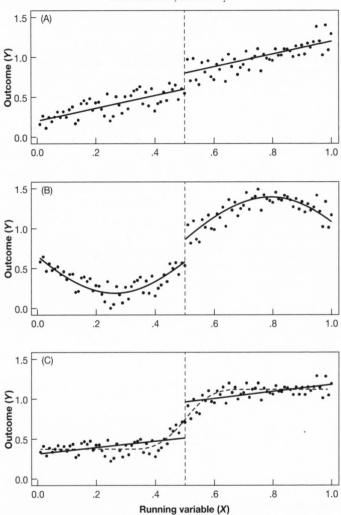

Notes: Panel A shows RD with a linear model for $E[Y_i|X_i]$; panel B adds some curvature. Panel C shows nonlinearity mistaken for a discontinuity. The vertical dashed line indicates a hypothetical RD cutoff.

Two strategies reduce the likelihood of RD mistakes, though neither provides perfect insurance. The first models nonlinearities directly, while the second focuses solely on observations near the cutoff. We start with the nonlinear modeling strategy, briefly taking up the second approach at the end of this section.

Nonlinearities in an RD framework are typically modeled using polynomial functions of the running variable. Ideally, the results that emerge from this approach are insensitive to the degree of nonlinearity the model allows. Sometimes, however, as in the case of panel C of Figure 4.3, they are not. The question of how much nonlinearity is enough requires a judgment call. A risk here is that you'll pick the model that produces the results that seem most appealing, perhaps favoring those that conform most closely to your prejudices. RD practitioners therefore owe their readers a report on how their RD estimates change as the details of the regression model used to construct them change.

Figure 4.2 suggests the possibility of mild curvature in the relationship between $\bar{M}_a$ and a, at least for the points to the right of the cutoff. A simple extension that captures this curvature uses quadratic instead of linear control for the running variable. The RD model with quadratic running variable control becomes

$$\bar{M}_a = \alpha + \rho D_a + \gamma_1 a + \gamma_2 a^2 + e_a,$$

where $\gamma_1 a + \gamma_2 a^2$ is a quadratic function of age, and the γs are parameters to be estimated.

A related modification allows for different running variable coefficients to the left and right of the cutoff. This modification generates models that interact a with D_a. To make the model with interactions easier to interpret, we center the running variable by subtracting the cutoff, a_0. Replacing a by $a - a_0$ (here, $a_0 = 21$), and adding an *interaction term*, $(a - a_0)D_a$, the RD model becomes

$$\bar{M}_a = \alpha + \rho D_a + \gamma (a - a_0) + \delta [(a - a_0)D_a] + e_a. \quad (4.3)$$

Centering the running variable ensures that ρ in equation (4.3) is still the jump in average outcomes at the cutoff (as can be seen by setting $a = a_0$ in the equation).

Why should the trend relationship between age and death rates change at the cutoff? Data to the left of the cutoff reflect the relationship between age and death rates for a sample whose drinking behavior is restricted by the MLDA. In this sample, we might expect steadily declining death rates as young people mature and take fewer risks. After age 21, however, unrestricted access to alcohol might change this process, perhaps slowing a declining trend. On the other hand, if the college presidents who back the Amethyst Initiative are right, responsible legal drinking accelerates the development of mature behavior. The direction of such a change in slopes is merely a hypothesis—the main point is that equation (4.3) allows for slope changes either way.

A subtle implication of the model with interaction terms is that away from the a_0 cutoff, the MLDA treatment effect is given by $\rho + \delta(a - a_0)$. This can be seen by subtracting the regression line fit to observations where D_a is switched off from the line fit to observations where D_a is switched on:

$$[\alpha + \rho + (\gamma + \delta)(a - a_0)] - [\alpha + \gamma(a - a_0)]$$
$$= \rho + \delta(a - a_0).$$

Estimates away from the cutoff constitute a bold extrapolation, however, and should be consumed with a slice of lime and a shaker of salt. There is no data on counterfactual death rates in a world where drinking at ages substantially older than 21 is forbidden. Likewise, far to the left of the cutoff, it's hard to say what death rates would be in a world where drinking at very young ages is allowed. By contrast, it seems reasonable to say that those just under 21 provide a good counterfactual comparison for those just over 21. This leads us to see estimates of the parameter ρ (the causal effect right at the cutoff) as most reliable, even when the model used for estimation implicitly tells us more than that.

Nonlinear trends and changes in slope at the cutoff can also be combined in a model that looks like

$$\bar{M}_a = \alpha + \rho D_a + \gamma_1(a - a_0) + \gamma_2(a - a_0)^2 \qquad (4.4)$$
$$+ \delta_1\big[(a - a_0)D_a\big] + \delta_2\big[(a - a_0)^2 D_a\big] + e_a.$$

In this setup, both the linear and quadratic terms change as we cross the cutoff. As before, the jump in death rates at the MLDA cutoff is captured by the MLDA treatment effect, ρ. The treatment effect away from the cutoff is now $\rho + \delta_1(a - a_0) + \delta_2 (a - a_0)^2$, though again the causal interpretation of this quantity is more speculative than the causal interpretation of ρ itself.

Figure 4.4 shows that the estimated trend function generated by equation (4.4) has some curvature, mildly concave to the left of age 21 and markedly convex thereafter. This model generates a larger estimate of the MLDA effect at the cutoff than does a linear model, equal to about 9.5 deaths per 100,000. Figure 4.4 also shows the linear trend line generated by equation (4.2). The more elaborate model seems to give a better fit than the simple model: Death rates jump sharply at age 21, but then recover somewhat in the first few months after a twenty-first birthday. This echoes the spike in daily death rates on or around the twenty-first birthday seen in Figure 4.1. Unlike Boon and his fraternity brothers, many newly legalized drinkers seem eventually to tire of getting trashed every night. Specification (4.4) captures this jump—and decline—nicely, though at the cost of some technical fanciness.

Which model is better, fancy or simple? There are no general rules here, and no substitute for a thoughtful look at the data. We're especially fortunate when the results are not highly sensitive to the details of our modeling choices, as appears true in Figure 4.4. The simple RD model seems flexible enough to capture effects right at the cutoff, in this case around a twenty-first birthday. The fancier version fits the spike in death rates near twenty-first birthdays, while also capturing the subsequent partial recovery in death rates.

Effects at the cutoff need not be the most important. Suppose we raise the drinking age to 22. In a world where excess alcohol deaths are due entirely to MLDA birthday parties, such a change might extend some lives by a year but otherwise have little effect. The sustained increase in death rates apparent in Figure 4.4 is therefore important, since this suggests restricted alcohol access has lasting benefits. We commented above that evidence for effects away from the cutoff is more speculative than the evidence found in a jump near the cutoff. On the other

FIGURE 4.4
Quadratic control in an RD design

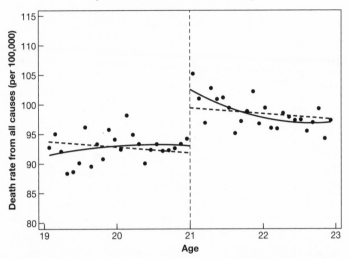

Notes: This figure plots death rates from all causes against age in months. Dashed lines in the figure show fitted values from a regression of death rates on an over-21 dummy and age in months. The solid lines plot fitted values from a regression of mortality on an over-21 dummy and a quadratic in age, interacted with the over-21 dummy (the vertical dashed line indicates the minimum legal drinking age [MLDA] cutoff).

hand, when the trend relationship between running variable and outcomes is approximately linear, limited extrapolation seems justified. The jump in death rates at the cutoff shows that drinking behavior responds to alcohol access in a manner that is reflected in death rates, an important point of principle, while the MLDA treatment effect extrapolated as far out as age 23 still looks substantial and seems believable, on the order of 5 extra deaths per 100,000. This pattern highlights the value of "visual RD," that is, careful assessment of plots like Figure 4.4.

How convincing is the argument that the jump in Figure 4.4 is indeed due to drinking? Data on death rates by cause of death help us make the case. Although alcohol is poisonous, few people die from alcohol poisoning alone, and deaths from alcohol-related diseases occur only at older ages. But alcohol is closely tied to motor vehicle accidents (MVA), the number-one killer of young people. If drunk driving is the primary alcohol-related cause of deaths, we should see a large jump in motor vehicle fatalities alongside little change in death rates due to internal causes. Like the balancing tests reported for the RAND HIE experiment in Table 1.3 and for the KIPP offer instrument in panel A of Table 3.1, zero effects on outcomes that should be unchanged by treatment raise our confidence in the causal effects we are after.

As a benchmark for results related to specific causes of death, the first row of Table 4.1 shows estimates for all deaths, constructed using both simple RD equation (4.2) and fancy RD equation (4.4). These are displayed in columns (1) and (2). The second row of Table 4.1 reveals strong effects of legal drinking on MVA fatalities, effects large enough to account for most of the excess deaths related to the MLDA. The estimates here are largely insensitive to whether the fancy or simple model is used to construct them. Other causes of death we might expect to see affected by drinking are suicide and other external causes, which include accidents other than car crashes. Indeed, estimated effects on suicide and deaths from other external causes (excluding homicide) also show small but statistically significant increases at the MLDA cutoff.

Importantly, the estimates reported in columns (1) and (2) for deaths from all internal causes (these include deaths from cancer and other diseases) are small and and not significantly different from zero. As the last row in the table shows, effects from direct alcohol poisoning also appear to be modest and of roughly the same magnitude as those from internal causes, though the estimated jump in deaths from alcohol poisoning is significantly different from zero. On balance, therefore, Table 4.1 supports the MLDA story, showing clear effects for causes most likely attributable to alcohol but little evidence of an increase due to internal causes.

Also in support of this conclusion, Figure 4.5 plots fitted values for MVA fatalities, constructed using the model that generates the estimates in column (2) of Table 4.1. The figure shows a clear break at the MLDA cutoff, with no evidence

TABLE 4.1
Sharp RD estimates of MLDA effects on mortality

Dependent variable	Ages 19–22		Ages 20–21	
	(1)	(2)	(3)	(4)
All deaths	7.66	9.55	9.75	9.61
	(1.51)	(1.83)	(2.06)	(2.29)
Motor vehicle accidents	4.53	4.66	4.76	5.89
	(.72)	(1.09)	(1.08)	(1.33)
Suicide	1.79	1.81	1.72	1.30
	(.50)	(.78)	(.73)	(1.14)
Homicide	.10	.20	.16	−.45
	(.45)	(.50)	(.59)	(.93)
Other external causes	.84	1.80	1.41	1.63
	(.42)	(.56)	(.59)	(.75)
All internal causes	.39	1.07	1.69	1.25
	(.54)	(.80)	(.74)	(1.01)
Alcohol-related causes	.44	.80	.74	1.03
	(.21)	(.32)	(.33)	(.41)
Controls	age	age, age^2, interacted with over-21	age	age, age^2, interacted with over-21
Sample size	48	48	24	24

Notes: This table reports coefficients on an over-21 dummy from regressions of month-of-age-specific death rates by cause on an over-21 dummy and linear or interacted quadratic age controls. Standard errors are reported in parentheses.

of potentially misleading nonlinear trends. At the same time, there isn't much of a jump in deaths due to internal causes, while the standard errors in Table 4.1 suggest that the small jump in internal deaths seen in the figure is likely due to chance.

In addition to straightforward regression estimation, an approach that masters refer to as *parametric RD,* a second RD strategy exploits the fact that the problem of distinguishing jumps from nonlinear trends grows less vexing as we zero in

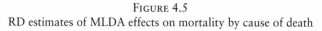

FIGURE 4.5
RD estimates of MLDA effects on mortality by cause of death

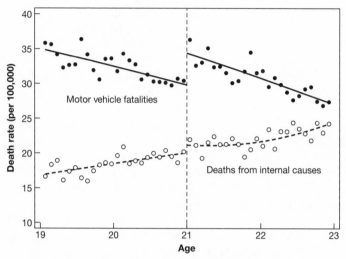

Notes: This figure plots death rates from motor vehicle accidents and internal causes against age in months. Lines in the figure plot fitted values from regressions of mortality by cause on an over-21 dummy and a quadratic function of age in months, interacted with the dummy (the vertical dashed line indicates the minimum legal drinking age [MLDA] cutoff).

on points close to the cutoff. For the small set of points close to the boundary, nonlinear trends need not concern us at all. This suggests an approach that compares averages in a narrow window just to the left and just to the right of the cutoff. A drawback here is that if the window is very narrow, there are few observations left, meaning the resulting estimates are likely to be too imprecise to be useful. Still, we should be able to trade the reduction in bias near the boundary against the increased variance suffered by throwing data away, generating some kind of optimal window size.

The econometric procedure that makes this trade-off is *nonparametric RD*. Nonparametric RD amounts to estimating equation (4.2) in a narrow window around the cutoff. That is, we estimate

$$\bar{M}_a = \alpha + \rho D_a + \gamma a + e_a;$$

$$\text{in a sample such that } a_0 - b \leq a \leq a_0 + b. \quad (4.5)$$

The parameter b describes the width of the window and is called a *bandwidth*. The results in Table 4.1 can be seen as nonparametric RD with a bandwidth equal to 2 years of age for the estimates reported in columns (1) and (2) and a bandwidth half as large (that is, including only ages 20–21 instead of 19–22) for the estimates shown in columns (3) and (4). The choice of the simple model in equation (4.5) vs. the fancier equation (4.4) should matter little when both are estimated in narrower age windows around the cutoff. The results in Table 4.1 support this conjecture, though there is some wobbliness in the estimates across columns that we might reasonably attribute to sampling variance.[2]

Simple enough! But how shall we pick the bandwidth? On one hand, to obviate concerns about polynomial choice, we'd like to work with data close to the cutoff. On the other hand, less data means less precision. For starters, therefore, the bandwidth should vary as a function of the sample size. The more information available about outcomes in the neighborhood of an RD cutoff, the narrower we can set the bandwidth while still hoping to generate estimates precise enough to be useful. Theoretical econometricians have proposed sophisticated strategies for making such bias-variance trade-offs efficiently, though here too, the bandwidth selection algorithm is not completely data-dependent and requires researchers to choose certain parameters.[3] In practice, bandwidth choice—like the choice of polynomial in parametric models—requires a judgment call. The goal here is not so much to find the one perfect

---

[2] Nonparametric RD mavens typically estimate models like equation (4.2) using weighted least squares. This is a procedure that puts the most weight on observations right at the cutoff and less weight on observations farther away. The weighting function used for this purpose is called a *kernel*. The estimates in Table 4.1 implicitly use a *uniform kernel*; that is, they weight observations inside the bandwidth equally.

[3] See Guido W. Imbens and Karthik Kalyanaraman, "Optimal Bandwidth Choice for the Regression Discontinuity Estimator," *Review of Economic Studies*, vol. 79, no. 3, July 2012, pages 933–959.

bandwidth as to show that the findings generated by any particular choice of bandwidth are not a fluke.

In this spirit, the studies upon which our investigation of the MLDA is based appear to have been written in RD heaven (perhaps a reward for their authors' temperance). The RD estimates generated by parametric models with alternative polynomial controls come out similar to one another and close to a corresponding set of nonparametric estimates. These nonparametric estimates are largely insensitive to the choice of bandwidth over a wide range.[4] This alignment of results suggests the findings generated by an RD analysis of the MLDA capture real causal effects. Some young people appear to pay the ultimate price for the privilege of downing a legal drink.

4.2   The Elite Illusion

KWAI CHANG CAINE: I seek not to know the answers, but to understand the questions.
Kung Fu, Season 1, Episode 14

The Boston and New York City public school systems include a handful of selective exam schools. Unlike most other American public schools, exam schools screen applicants on the basis of a competitive admissions test. Just as many American high school seniors compete to enroll in the country's most selective colleges and universities, younger students and their parents in a few cities aspire to coveted seats at top exam schools. Fewer than half of Boston's exam school applicants win a seat at the John D. O'Bryant School, Boston Latin Academy, or the Boston Latin School (BLS); only one-sixth of New York applicants are offered a seat at one of the three original exam schools in the Big Apple (Stuyvesant, Bronx Science, and Brooklyn Tech).

---

[4] A comparison of parametric and nonparametric estimates appears in Tables 4 and 5 of Carpenter and Dobkin, "The Effect of Alcohol Comsumption," *American Economic Journal: Applied Economics*, 2009. Sensitivity to choice of bandwidth is explored in their online appendix (DOI: 10.1257/app.1.1 .164). The 2009 study analyzes mortality by exact day of birth, while here we work with monthly data.

At first blush, the intense competition for exam school seats is understandable. Many exam school students go on to distinguished careers in science, the arts, and politics. By any measure, exam school students are well ahead of other public school students. It's easy to see why some parents would give a kidney (perhaps a liver!) to place their children in such schools. Economists and other social scientists are also interested in the consequences of the exam school treatment. For one thing, exam schools bring high-ability students together. Surely that's a good thing: bright students learn as much from their peers as from their teachers, or so we say at highly selective institutions like MIT and the London School of Economics.

The case for an exam school advantage is easy to make, but it's also clear that at least some of the achievement difference associated with exam school attendance reflects these schools' selective admissions policies. When schools admit only high achievers, then the students who go there are necessarily high achievers, regardless of whether the school itself adds value. This sounds like a case of selection bias, and it is. Taking a cue from the far-sighted Oregon Health Authority and its health insurance lottery, we might hope to convince Stuyvesant and Boston Latin to admit students at random, instead of on the basis of a test. We could then use the resulting experimental data to learn whether exam schools add value. Or could we? For if exam schools were to admit students randomly, then they wouldn't be *exam* schools after all.

If selective admissions are a necessary part of what it means to be an exam school, how can we hope to design an experiment that reveals exam school effectiveness? Necessity is the mother of invention, as revered philosophers Plato and Frank Zappa remind us. The discrete nature of exam school admissions policies creates a natural experiment. Among applicants with scores close to admissions cutoffs, whether an applicant falls to the right or left of the cutoff might be as good as randomly assigned. In this case, however, the experiment is subtle: rather than a simple on-off switch, it's the nature of the exam school experience that changes discontinuously at the cutoff, since some admitted students choose to go elsewhere while many of those rejected at one exam school end up at another. When discontinuities change treatment probabilities or average characteristics (treatment intensity, for short), instead of flicking a simple on-off switch, the resulting RD design is said to be *fuzzy*.

Fuzzy RD

Just what is the exam school treatment? Figures 4.6–4.8, which focus on applicants to BLS, help us craft an answer. BLS applicants, like all who aspire to an exam school seat in Boston, take the Independent Schools Entrance Exam (ISEE for short). The sample used to construct these figures consists of applicants with ISEE scores near the BLS entrance cutoff. The dots in the figures are averages of the variable on the Y-axis calculated for applicants with ISEE scores in bins one point wide, while the line through the dots shows a fit obtained by smoothing these

FIGURE 4.6
Enrollment at BLS

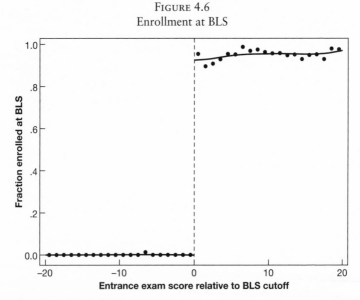

Notes: This figure plots enrollment rates at Boston Latin School (BLS), conditional on admissions test scores, for BLS applicants scoring near the BLS admissions cutoff. Solid lines show fitted values from a local linear regression estimated separately on either side of the cutoff (indicated by the vertical dashed line).

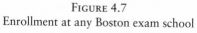

FIGURE 4.7
Enrollment at any Boston exam school

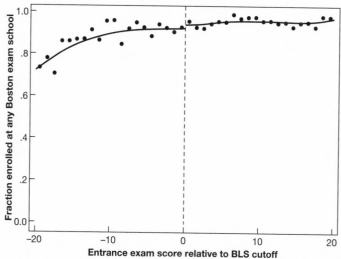

Notes: This figure plots enrollment rates at any Boston exam school, conditional on admissions test scores, for Boston Latin School (BLS) applicants scoring near the BLS admissions cutoff. Solid lines show fitted values from a local linear regression, estimated separately on either side of the cutoff (indicated by the vertical dashed line).

data in a manner explained in a footnote.[5] Figure 4.6 shows that most but not all qualifying applicants enroll at BLS.

BLS is the most prestigious exam school in Boston. Where do applicants who miss the BLS cutoff go? Most go to Boston

[5] The variable that determines admissions in these figures is a weighted average of each applicant's ISEE score and GPA, but we refer to this running variable as the ISEE score for short. The dots here come from a smoothing method known as local linear regression, which works by fitting regressions to small samples defined by a bandwidth around each point. Smoothed values are the fitted values generated by this procedure. For details, see the study on which our discussion here is based: Atila Abdulkadiroglu, Joshua D. Angrist, and Parag Pathak, "The Elite Illusion: Achievement Effects at Boston and New York Exam Schools," *Econometrica,* vol. 81, no. 1, January 2014, pages 137–196.

FIGURE 4.8
Peer quality around the BLS cutoff

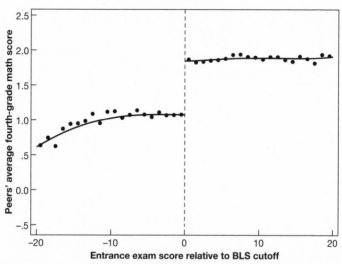

Notes: This figure plots average seventh-grade peer quality for applicants to Boston Latin School (BLS), conditional on admissions test scores, for BLS applicants scoring near the admissions cutoff. Peer quality is measured by seventh-grade schoolmates' fourth-grade math scores. Solid lines show fitted values from a local linear regression, estimated separately on either side of the cutoff (indicated by the vertical dashed line).

Latin Academy, a venerable institution that's one school down in the Boston exam school hierarchy. This enrollment shift is documented in Figure 4.7, which plots enrollment rates at any Boston exam school around the BLS cutoff. Figure 4.7 shows that most students who miss the BLS cutoff indeed end up at another exam school, so that the odds of enrolling at *some* exam school are virtually unchanged at the BLS cutoff. It would seem, therefore, that we have to settle for a parochial-sounding experiment comparing highly selective BLS to the somewhat less selective Boston Latin Academy, instead of a more interesting evaluation of the whole exam school idea.

Or do we? One of the most controversial questions in education research is the nature of peer effects; that is, whether the ability of your classmates has a causal effect on your learning. If you're lucky enough to attend high school with other good students, this may contribute to your success. On the other hand, if you're relegated to a school where most students do poorly, this may hold you back. Peer effects are important for policies related to school assignment, that is, the rules and regulations that determine where children attend school. In many American cities, for example, students attend schools near their homes. Because poor, nonwhite, and low-achieving students tend to live far from well-to-do, high-achieving students in mostly white neighborhoods, school assignment by neighborhood may reduce poor minority children's chances to excel. Many school districts therefore bus children to schools far from where they live in an effort to increase the mixing of children from different backgrounds and races.

Exam schools induce a dramatic experiment in peer quality. Specifically, applicants who qualify for admission at one of Boston's exam schools attend school with much higher-achieving peers than do applicants who just miss the cut, even when the alternative is another exam school. Figure 4.8 documents this for BLS applicants. Here, peer achievement is measured by the math score of applicants' schoolmates on a test they took in fourth grade (2 years before they applied to exam schools). As in the charter school investigation discussed in Chapter 3, test scores in this figure are measured in standard deviation units, where one standard deviation is written in Greek as 1σ. Successful applicants to BLS study with much higher-scoring schoolmates, enjoying a jump in peer math achievement of $.8\sigma$, equivalent to the difference in average peer quality between inner city Boston and its wealthy suburbs. Such dramatic variation in treatment intensity lies at the heart of any fuzzy RD research design. The difference between fuzzy and sharp designs is that, with fuzzy, applicants who cross a threshold are exposed to a more intense treatment, while in a sharp design treatment switches cleanly on or off at the cutoff.

Fuzzy RD Is IV

In a regression rite of passage, social scientists around the world link student achievement to the average ability of their

schoolmates. Such regressions reliably reveal a strong association between the performance of students and the achievement
of their peers. Among all Boston exam school applicants, a regression of students' seventh-grade math scores on the average
fourth-grade scores of their seventh-grade classmates generates a coefficient of about one-quarter. This putative peer effect
comes from the regression model

$$Y_i = \theta_0 + \theta_1 \bar{X}_{(i)} + \theta_2 X_i + u_i, \qquad (4.6)$$

where Y_i is student i's seventh-grade math score, X_i is i's
fourth-grade math score, and $\bar{X}_{(i)}$ is the average fourth-grade
math score of i's seventh-grade classmates (the subscript "(i)"
reminds us that student i is not included when calculating the
average achievement of his or her peers). The estimated coefficient on peer quality (θ_1) is around .25, meaning that a
one standard deviation increase in the ability of middle school
peers, as measured by their elementary school scores and controlling for a student's own elementary school performance,
is associated with a $.25\sigma$ gain in middle school achievement.

Parents and teachers have a powerful intuition that "peers
matter," so the strong positive association between the achievement of students and their classmates rings true. But this naive
peer regression is unlikely to have a causal interpretation for
the simple reason that students educated together tend to be
similar for many reasons. Your authors' four children, for example, precocious high-achievers like their parents, have been
fortunate to attend schools attended by many children from
similar families. Because family background is not held fixed
in regressions like equation (4.6), the observed association
between students and their classmates undoubtedly reflects
some of these shared influences. To break the resulting causal
deadlock, we'd like to randomly assign students to a range of
different peer groups.

Exam schools to the rescue! Figure 4.8 documents the remarkable difference in peer ability that BLS admission produces, with a jump of four-fifths of a standard deviation in
peer quality at the BLS cutoff. The jump in peer quality at
exam school admissions cutoffs arises—by design—from the

mix of students enrolled in selective schools. This is just what the econometrician ordered by way of an ideal peer experiment (this improvement in peer quality also makes many parents hope and dream of an exam school seat for their children). Moreover, while peer quality jumps at the cutoff, cross-cutoff comparisons of variables related to applicants' own abilities, motivation, and family background—the sources of selection bias we usually worry about—show no similar jumps. For example, there's no jump in applicants' own elementary school scores. Peers change discontinuously at admissions cutoffs, but exam school applicants' own characteristics do not.[6]

Hopes, dreams, and the results from our naive peer regression (equation (4.6)) notwithstanding, the exam school experiment casts doubt on the notion of a causal peer effect on the achievement of Boston exam school applicants. The seeds of doubt are planted by Figure 4.9, which plots seventh- and eighth-grade math scores (on tests taken after 1 or 2 years of middle school) against ISEE scores (the exam school running variable) for applicants scoring near the BLS cutoff. Admitted applicants are exposed to a much stronger peer group, but this exposure generates no parallel jump in applicants' middle school achievement.

As in equation (4.2), the size of the jump in Figure 4.9 can be estimated by fitting an equation like

$$Y_i = \alpha_0 + \rho D_i + \beta_0 R_i + e_{0i}. \tag{4.7}$$

Here, D_i is a dummy variable indicating applicants who qualify, while R_i is the running variable that determines qualification. In a sample of seventh-grade applicants to BLS, where Y_i is a middle school math score as in the figures, this regression produces an estimate of $-.02$ with a standard error of $.10$, a statistical zero in our book.

How should we interpret this estimate of ρ? Through the lens of the corresponding first stage, of course! Equation (4.7) is the reduced form for a 2SLS setup where the endogenous

[6] This is documented in Abdulkadiroglu et al., "The Elite Illusion," *Econometrica*, 2014.

FIGURE 4.9
Math scores around the BLS cutoff

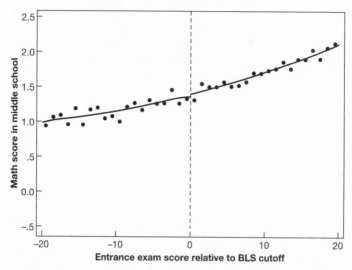

Notes: This figure plots seventh- and eighth-grade math scores for applicants to the Boston Latin School (BLS), conditional on admissions test scores, for BLS applicants scoring near the admissions cutoff. Solid lines show fitted values from a local linear regression, estimated separately on either side of the cutoff (indicated by the vertical dashed line).

variable is average peer quality, $\bar{X}_{(i)}$. The first-stage equation that goes with this reduced form is

$$\bar{X}_{(i)} = \alpha_1 + \phi D_i + \beta_1 R_i + e_{1i}, \qquad (4.8)$$

where the parameter ϕ captures the jump in mean peer quality induced by an exam school offer. This is the jump shown in Figure 4.8, a precisely estimated $.80\sigma$.

The last piece of our 2SLS setup is the causal relationship of interest, the 2SLS second stage. In this case, the second stage captures the effect of peer quality on seventh- and eighth-grade math scores. As always, the second stage includes the same control variables as appear in the first stage. This leads to a second-stage equation that can be written

$$Y_i = \alpha_2 + \lambda \hat{X}_{(i)} + \beta_2 R_i + e_{2i}, \qquad (4.9)$$

where λ is the causal effect of peer quality, and the variable $\hat{X}_{(i)}$ is the first-stage fitted value produced by estimating equation (4.8).

Note that equation (4.9) inherits a covariate from the first stage and reduced form, the running variable, R_i. On the other hand, the jump dummy, D_i, is excluded from the second stage, since this is the instrument that makes the 2SLS engine run. Substantively, we've assumed that in the neighborhood of admissions cutoffs, after adjusting for running variable effects with a linear control, exam school qualification has no direct effect on test scores, but rather influences achievement, if at all, solely through peer quality. This assumption is the all-important IV exclusion restriction in this context.

The 2SLS estimate of λ in equation (4.9) is $-.023$ with a standard error of $.132$.[7] Since the reduced-form estimate is close to and not significantly different from zero, so is the corresponding 2SLS estimate. This estimate is also far from the estimate of $.25\sigma$ generated by OLS estimation of the naive peer effects regression, equation (4.6). On the other hand, who's to say that the only thing that matters about an exam school education is peer quality? The exclusion restriction requires us to commit to a specific causal channel. But the assumed channel need not be the only one that matters in practice.

A distinctive feature of the exam school environment besides peer achievement is racial composition. In Boston's mostly minority public schools, exam schools offer the opportunity to go to school with a more diverse population, where diversity means more white classmates. The court-mandated

---

[7] This standard error is clustered by applicant. As explained in the appendix to Chapter 5, we use clustered standard errors to adjust for the fact that the data contain correlated observations (in this case, the seventh- and eighth-grade test scores for each BLS applicant are correlated).

dismantling of segregated American school systems was motivated by an effort to improve educational outcomes. In 1954, the U.S. Supreme Court famously declared: "Separate educational facilities are inherently unequal," laying the framework for court-ordered busing to increase racial balance in public schools. Does increasing racial balance indeed boost achievement? Exam schools are relevant to the debate over racial integration because exam school admission sharply increases exposure to white peers. At the same time, we know that if we replace peer quality, $\bar{X}_{(i)}$, with peer proportion white, this too will produce a zero second-stage coefficient, a consequence of the fact that the underlying reduced form is unchanged by the choice of causal channel.

Exam schools might differ in other ways as well, perhaps attracting better teachers or offering more Advanced Placement (college-level) courses than nonselective public schools. Importantly, however, school resources and other features of the school environment that might change at exam school admissions cutoffs seem likely to be beneficial. This in turn suggests that any omitted variables bias associated with 2SLS estimates of exam school peer effects is positive. This claim echoes that made in Chapter 2 regarding the likely direction of OVB in our evaluation of selective colleges. Because omitted variables with positive effects are probably positively correlated with exam school offers, the 2SLS estimate using exam school qualification as an instrument for peer quality is, if anything, too big relative to the pure peer effect we're after. All the more surprising, then, that this estimate turns out to be zero.

As with any IV story, fuzzy RD requires tough judgments about the causal channels through which instruments affect outcomes. In practice, multiple channels might mediate causal effects, in which case we explore alternatives. Likewise, the channels we measure readily need not be the only ones that matter. The causal journey never ends; new questions emerge continuously. But the fuzzy framework that uses RD to generate instruments is no less useful for all that.

MASTER STEVEFU: Summarize RD for me, Grasshopper.

GRASSHOPPER: The RD design exploits abrupt changes in treatment status that arise when treatment is determined by a cutoff.

MASTER STEVEFU: Is RD as good as a randomized trial?

GRASSHOPPER: RD requires us to know the relationship between the running variable and potential outcomes in the absence of treatment. We must control for this relationship when using discontinuities to identify causal effects. Randomized trials require no such control.

MASTER STEVEFU: How can you know that your control strategy is adequate?

GRASSHOPPER: One can't be sure, Master. But our confidence in causal conclusions increases when RD estimates remain similar as we change details of the RD model.

MASTER STEVEFU: And sharp versus fuzzy?

GRASSHOPPER: Sharp is when treatment itself switches on or off at a cutoff. Fuzzy is when the probability or intensity of treatment jumps. In fuzzy designs, a dummy for clearing the cutoff becomes an instrument; the fuzzy design is analyzed by 2SLS.

MASTER STEVEFU: You approach the threshold for mastery, Grasshopper.

Masters of 'Metrics: Donald Campbell

The RD story was first told by psychologists Donald L. Thistlethwaite and Donald T. Campbell, who used RD in 1960 to evaluate the impact of National Merit Scholarship awards on awardees' careers and attitudes.[8] As many of our readers will know, the American National Merit Scholarship program is a multi-round process, at the end of which a few thousand high-achieving high school seniors are awarded a college scholarship. Selection is based on applicants' scores on the PSAT and SAT tests, the college entrance exams taken by most U.S. college applicants.

Successful candidates in the National Merit competition have PSAT scores above a cutoff (and have their PSAT scores validated by doing well on the SAT, taken later). Among these, a few are awarded scholarships by the National Merit screening committee, while the rest get a Certificate of Merit. Students receiving this certificate, known as National Merit finalists, are justifiably pleased: in recognition of this accomplishment, their names are distributed to colleges, universities, and to other scholarship sponsors. Colleges with many National Merit finalists in their incoming classes also like to advertise this fact. Thistlethwaite and Campbell asked whether recognition as a National Merit finalist has any lasting consequences for those so recognized.

In earlier work relying on matching methods (of the sort described in Chapter 2), Thistlethwaite estimated that applicants who were awarded a Certificate of Merit were 4 percentage points more likely to plan to become college teachers or researchers than they otherwise would have been.[9] But an RD design exploiting discontinuities at the PSAT cutoff for a Certificate of Merit generated a statistically insignificant estimate of only about 2 points for this outcome. The plot that goes with this finding is reproduced here as Figure 4.10. Public recognition by itself seems to have little effect on career choice or plans for graduate study.

---

[8] Donald L. Thistlethwaite and Donald T. Campbell, "Regression-Discontinuity Analysis: An Alternative to the Ex Post Facto Experiment," *Journal of Educational Psychology,* vol. 51, no. 6, December 1960, pages 309–317.

[9] Donald L. Thistlethwaite, "Effects of Social Recognition upon the Educational Motivation of Talented Youths," *Journal of Educational Psychology,* vol. 50, no. 3, 1959, pages 111–116.

FIGURE 4.10
Thistlethwaite and Campbell's Visual RD

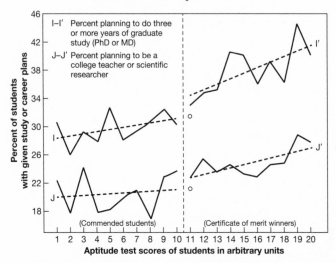

Notes: This figure plots PSAT test takers' plans for graduate study (line I–I') and a measure of test takers' career plans (line J–J') against the running variable that determines National Merit recognition.

Donald Campbell is remembered not just for inventing RD but also for his 1963 essay, "Experimental and Quasi-Experimental Designs for Research on Teaching," written with Julian C. Stanley and later released in book form. The Campbell and Stanley essay was a pioneering exploration of the 'metrics methods discussed in this and the following chapter of our book. A subsequent update written with Thomas D. Cook remains an important reference to this day.[10]

[10] Donald T. Campbell and Julian C. Stanley, "Experimental and Quasi-Experimental Designs for Research on Teaching," Chapter 5 in Nathaniel L. Gage (ed.), *Handbook of Research on Teaching,* Rand McNally, 1963; and Donald T. Campbell and Thomas D. Cook, *Quasi-Experimentation: Design and Analysis Issues for Field Settings,* Houghton Mifflin, 1979.

Chapter 5

Differences-in-Differences

|||||||||||||||||||||||||||||||||||||||||||||||||||||||❧|||||||||||||||||||||||||||||||||||||||||||||||||||||||

MASTER KAN: If while building a house, a carpenter strikes a nail and it proves faulty by bending, does the carpenter lose faith in all nails and stop building? So it is with empirical work.

Kung Fu, Season 1, Episode 7

Our Path

C redible instrumental variables and dramatic policy discontinuities can be hard to find; you'll need other 'metrics tools in your kit too. The *differences-in-differences* (DD) method recognizes that in the absence of random assignment, treatment and control groups are likely to differ for many reasons. Sometimes, however, treatment and control outcomes move in parallel in the absence of treatment. When they do, the divergence of a post-treatment path from the trend established by a comparison group may signal a treatment effect. We demonstrate DD with a study of the effects of monetary policy on bank failures during the Great Depression. We also revisit the MLDA.

5.1 A Mississippi Experiment

On the eve of the largest economic downturn in American history—the Great Depression—economic spirits ran high in the halls of high finance. Caldwell and Company's slogan "We Bank on the South" reflected the confidence of a regional financial empire. Based in Nashville, Caldwell ran the largest Southern banking chain in the 1920s, and owned many non-banking businesses as well. Rogers Caldwell, known as the

J. P. Morgan of the South, lived large on an estate that housed his stable of prize-winning thoroughbreds. Alas, in November of 1930, mismanagement and fallout from the stock market crash of October 1929 brought the Caldwell empire down. Within days, Caldwell's collapse felled closely tied banking networks in Tennessee, Arkansas, Illinois, and North Carolina. The Caldwell crisis was a harbinger of a surge in bank failures across the country.

Banking is a business built on confidence and trust. Banks lend to businesses and property owners in the expectation that most loans will be paid off when they come due. Depositors trust they'll be able to withdraw their funds on demand. This confidence notwithstanding, banks hold less cash than needed to pay all depositors, because most deposits are out on loan. The resulting maturity mismatch poses no problem in normal times, when few depositors make withdrawals on any given day.

If confidence falters, the banking system breaks down. In the 1930s, when your bank went out of business, your savings very likely disappeared with it. Even if your bank's mortgage and loan portfolios looked safe, you wouldn't have wanted to be the last depositor to try to get your money out. Once other depositors are seen to withdraw in panic, you'd do well to panic too. That's how a bank run starts.

Caldwell's demise shook depositor confidence throughout the American South and precipitated a run on Mississippi banks in December 1930. Deposits in Mississippi fell slowly at first, but on December 19, the floodgates opened when savers panicked. On that day, the Mississippi state Banking Department closed three banks. Two more banks ceased operations the day after, and another 29 folded in the next six months. The regional panic of 1930 was one of many more to come. In 1933, the year Depression-era bank failures peaked, more than 4,000 banks failed nationwide.

Economists have long sought to understand whether and how monetary policy contributed to the Great Depression, and whether more aggressive monetary intervention might have stemmed the financial collapse and economic free fall seen in

those dark days. Depression-era lessons may help us understand the present. Although financial markets today are more
sophisticated, the pillars of finance remain much as they were:
banks borrow and lend, typically at different maturities, and
bet on being able to raise the cash (known in banking jargon
as "liquidity") needed to cover liabilities as they come due.

We're unlucky enough to live in economically interesting
times. The year 2008 saw the U.S. financial system shaken
by a collapse in the market for mortgage-backed securities,
followed by a European sovereign debt crisis beginning in late
2009. Carmen Reinhart and Kenneth Rogoff have recently
chronicled financial crises since the fourteenth century, arguing
they share a common anatomy. The apparent similarity of such
episodes makes you wonder whether they can be avoided, or at
least whether their effects can be mitigated. In their masterful
1963 monetary history of the United States, Milton Friedman
and Anna Schwartz convinced many economists that a proper
understanding of the effects of monetary policy is the key to
answering this question.[1]

One Mississippi, Two Mississippi

Policymakers facing a bank run can open the flow of credit
or turn off the tap. Friedman and Schwartz argued that the
Federal Reserve (America's central bank) foolishly restricted
credit as the Great Depression unfolded. Easy money might
have allowed banks to meet increasingly urgent withdrawal
demands, staving off depositor panic. By lending to troubled
banks freely, the central bank has the power to stem a liquidity
crisis and obviate the need for a bailout in the first place.

But who's to say when a crisis is merely a crisis of confidence?
Some crises are real. Bank balance sheets may be so sickened
by bad debts that no amount of temporary liquidity support
will cure 'em. After all, banks don't lose their liquidity by

---

[1] Carmen Reinhart and Kenneth Rogoff, *This Time Is Different: Eight
Centuries of Financial Folly*, Princeton University Press, 2009; and Milton
Friedman and Anna Schwartz, *A Monetary History of the United States,
1867–1960*, Princeton University Press, 1963.

random assignment. Rather, bank managers make loans that either fail or are fruitful. Injecting central bank funds into bad banks may throw good money after bad. Better in such cases to declare bankruptcy and hope for an orderly distribution of any remaining assets.

Support for bad banks also raises the specter of what economists call *moral hazard*. If bankers know that the central bank will lend cheaply when liquidity runs dry, they needn't take care to avoid crises in the first place. In 1873, *The Economist*'s editor-in-chief Walter Bagehot described the danger this way:

> If the banks are bad, they will certainly continue bad and will probably become worse if the Government sustains and encourages them. The cardinal maxim is, that any aid to a present bad Bank is the surest mode of preventing the establishment of a future good Bank.[2]

Bagehot was a professed Social Darwinist, believing that evolutionary principles applied in social affairs just as in biology. Which policy stance is more likely to speed a happy ending to an economic downturn, liquidity backstopping or survival of banking's fittest? As always, masters of 'metrics would like to settle this question with a randomized trial. We have a grant proposal to fund such a bank liquidity experiment under review; we'll surely blog the results if it comes through. In the meantime, we must learn about the effects of monetary policy from the history of banking crises and policy responses to them.

Fortunately for this research agenda, the U.S. Federal Reserve System is organized into 12 districts, each run by a regional Federal Reserve Bank. Depression-era heads of the regional Feds had considerable policy independence. The Atlanta Fed, running the Sixth District, favored lending to troubled banks. By contrast, the St. Louis Fed ran the Eighth District according to a philosophy known as the Real Bills Doctrine,

---

[2] From Chapter IV.4 in Walter Bagehot, *Lombard Street: A Description of the Money Market*, Henry S. King and Co., 1873.

which holds that the central bank should restrict credit in a recession. Especially happily for research on monetary policy, the border between the Sixth and Eighth Districts runs east-west smack through the middle of the state of Mississippi (District borders were determined by population size in 1913, at the birth of the Federal Reserve System). This border defines a within-state natural experiment from which we can profit.

Masters Gary Richardson and William Troost analyzed Mississippi's monetary two-step.[3] As we might expect from their differing approaches to monetary policy, the Atlanta and St. Louis Feds reacted very differently to the Caldwell crisis. Within 4 weeks of Caldwell's collapse, the Atlanta Fed had increased bank lending by about 40% in the Sixth District. In the same period, bank lending by the St. Louis Fed in the Eighth District fell almost 10%.

The Richardson and Troost policy experiment imagines the Eighth District as a control group, where policy was to do little or even restrict lending, while the Sixth District is a treatment group, where policy was to increase lending. A first-line outcome is the number of banks still operating in each District on July 1, 1931, about 8 months after the beginning of the crisis. On that day, 132 banks were open in the Eighth District and 121 were open in the Sixth District, a deficit of 11 banks in the Sixth District. This suggests easy money was counterproductive. But look again: the Sixth and Eighth Districts were similar but not identical. We see this in the fact that the number of banks operating in the two districts differed markedly across districts on July 1, 1930, well before the Caldwell crisis, with 135 banks open in the Sixth District and 165 banks open in the Eighth. To adjust for this difference across districts in the pre-treatment period, we analyze the Mississippi experiment using a tool called differences-in-differences, or DD for short.

---

[3] Gary Richardson and William Troost, "Monetary Intervention Mitigated Banking Panics during the Great Depression: Quasi-Experimental Evidence from a Federal Reserve District Border, 1929–1933," *Journal of Political Economy*, vol. 117, no. 6, December 2009, pages 1031–1073. Numbers in this section are our tabulations from the Richardson and Troost data.

Parallel Worlds

Let Y_{dt} denote the number of banks open in District d in year t, where the subscript d tells us whether we're looking at data from the Sixth or Eighth District and the subscript t tells us whether we're looking at data from 1930 (before the Caldwell crisis) or 1931 (after). The DD estimate (δ_{DD}) of the effect of easy money in the Sixth District is

$$\delta_{DD} = (Y_{6,1931} - Y_{6,1930}) - (Y_{8,1931} - Y_{8,1930})$$
$$= (121 - 135) - (132 - 165)$$
$$= -14 - (-33) = 19. \qquad (5.1)$$

Instead of comparing the number of banks open in the Sixth and Eighth Districts after Caldwell, DD contrasts the change in the number of banks operating in the two districts.

Comparing changes instead of levels adjusts for the fact that in the pre-treatment period, the Eighth District had more banks open than the Sixth. To see this, note that we can also construct the DD bottom line this way:

$$\delta_{DD} = (Y_{6,1931} - Y_{8,1931}) - (Y_{6,1930} - Y_{8,1930})$$
$$= (121 - 132) - (135 - 165)$$
$$= -11 - (-30) = 19. \qquad (5.2)$$

This version of the DD calculation subtracts the pre-treatment difference between the Sixth and Eighth Districts from the post-treatment difference, thereby adjusting for the fact that the two districts weren't the same initially. DD estimates suggest that lending to troubled banks kept many of them open. Specifically, the Atlanta Fed appears to have saved 19 banks—more than 10% of those operating in Mississippi's Sixth District in 1930.

DD logic is depicted in Figure 5.1, which plots the number of banks in the Sixth and Eighth Districts in 1930 and 1931, with data from the two periods connected by solid lines. Figure 5.1 highlights the fact that while banks failed in both Federal Reserve Districts, they did so much more sharply in the Eighth.

FIGURE 5.1

Bank failures in the Sixth and Eighth Federal Reserve Districts

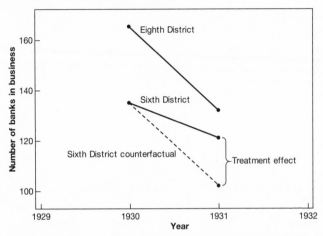

Notes: This figure shows the number of banks in operation in Mississippi in the Sixth and Eighth Federal Reserve Districts in 1930 and 1931. The dashed line depicts the counterfactual evolution of the number of banks in the Sixth District if the same number of banks had failed in that district in this period as did in the Eighth.

The DD tool amounts to a comparison of changes or trends across districts. The dotted line in Figure 5.1 is the counterfactual outcome—our imagined Y_{0i} in the notation of Chapter 1—that lies at the heart of the DD research design: this line tells us what would have happened in the Sixth District had everything evolved as it did in the Eighth. The fact that the solid line for the Sixth District declines much more gradually than this counterfactual line is evidence for the effectiveness of easy money. The 19 bank failures uncovered by our DD calculation is the difference between what really happened and what would have happened had bank activity in the two districts unfolded in parallel.

The DD counterfactual comes from a strong but easily stated assumption: *common trends*. In the Mississippi experiment, DD presumes that, absent any policy differences, the Eighth District trend is what we should have expected to see in the

FIGURE 5.2
Trends in bank failures in the Sixth and Eighth Federal
Reserve Districts

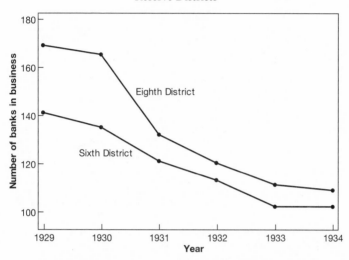

Note: This figure shows the number of banks in operation in Mississippi in the Sixth and Eighth Federal Reserve Districts between 1929 and 1934.

Sixth. Although strong, the common trends assumption seems like a reasonable starting point, one that takes account of pre-treatment differences in levels. With more data, the assumption can also be probed, tested, and relaxed.

Figure 5.2 provides evidence on the common trends assumption for Mississippi's Federal Reserve Districts. The evidence comes in the form of a longer time series on bank activity. Before 1931, the Great Depression had not yet hit Mississippi hard. Regional Fed policies in the two districts were also similar in this more relaxed period. The fact that bank failures moved almost in parallel in the two districts between 1929 and 1930, with the number of banks declining slightly in both districts, is therefore consistent with the common trends hypothesis for untreated periods. Figure 5.3 adds the Sixth District counterfactual implied by extrapolating Eighth District trends to the Sixth District for years after 1930. The gap

FIGURE 5.3

Trends in bank failures in the Sixth and Eighth Federal Reserve
Districts, and the Sixth District's DD counterfactual

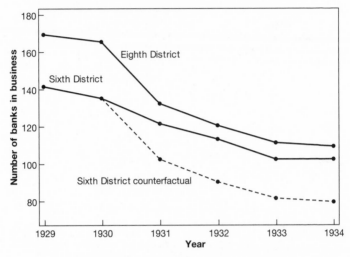

Notes: This figure adds DD counterfactual outcomes to the banking data
plotted in Figure 5.2. The dashed line depicts the counterfactual evolution of
the number of banks in the Sixth District if the same number of banks had
failed in that district after 1930 as did in the Eighth.

between actual and counterfactual Sixth District banking activity changed little through 1934.

As in Figure 5.1, the relatively steep fall-off in bank activity in the Eighth District after the Caldwell collapse emerges
clearly in Figures 5.2 and 5.3. But these figures document
something further. Beginning in July 1931, the St. Louis Fed
abandoned tight money and started lending to troubled banks
freely. In other words, after 1931, Federal Reserve policy in
the two districts was again similar, with both regional Feds
willing to provide liquidity with a free hand. Moreover, while
the Depression was far from over in 1932, the Caldwell crisis had petered out and withdrawals had returned to pre-crisis
levels. Given the two regional Feds' common readiness to lend
as the need arose, trends in bank activity should again have

been common after 1931. The 1931–1934 data line up well with this hypothesis.

Just DDo It: A Depression Regression

The simplest DD calculation involves only four numbers, as in equations (5.1) and (5.2). In practice, however, the DD recipe is best cooked with regression models fit to samples of more than four data points, such as the 12 points plotted in Figure 5.2. In addition to allowing for more than two periods, regression DD neatly incorporates data on more than two cross-sectional units, as we'll see in a multistate analysis of the MLDA in Section 5.2. Equally important, regression DD facilitates statistical inference, often a tricky matter in a DD setup (for details, see the appendix to this chapter).

The regression DD recipe associated with Figure 5.2 has three ingredients:

(i) A dummy for the treatment district, written $TREAT_d$, where the subscript d reminds us that this varies across districts; $TREAT_d$ controls for fixed differences between the units being compared.

(ii) A dummy for post-treatment periods, written $POST_t$, where the subscript t reminds us that this varies over time; $POST_t$ controls for the fact that conditions change over time for everyone, whether treated or not.

(iii) The interaction term, $TREAT_d \times POST_t$, generated by multiplying these two dummies; the coefficient on this term is the DD causal effect.

We think of the Caldwell-era experimental treatment as provision of easy credit in the face of a liquidity crisis, so $TREAT_d$ equals one for data points from the Sixth District and zero otherwise. The bank failure rate slowed after 1931 as the Caldwell crisis subsided. In the 1930s, however, there were no zombie banks: dead banks were gone for good. The Caldwell-era failures resulted in fewer banks open in the years 1932–1934 as well, even though the St. Louis Fed had by then begun to lend freely. We therefore code $POST_t$ to indicate

all the observations from 1931 onward. Finally, the interaction term, $TREAT_d \times POST_t$, indicates observations in the
Sixth District in the post-treatment period. More precisely,
$TREAT_d \times POST_t$ indicates observations from the Sixth District in periods when the Atlanta Fed's response to Caldwell
mattered for the number of active banks.

Regression DD for the Mississippi experiment puts these
pieces together by estimating

$$Y_{dt} = \alpha + \beta \, TREAT_d + \gamma \, POST_t$$
$$+ \, \delta_{rDD}(TREAT_d \times POST_t) + e_{dt} \quad (5.3)$$

in a sample of size 12. This sample is constructed by stacking
observations from both districts and all available years (6 years
for each district). The coefficient on the interaction term, δ_{rDD},
is the causal effect of interest. With only two periods, as in
Figure 5.1, estimates of δ_{DD} and δ_{rDD} coincide (a consequence
of the properties of dummy variable regression outlined in the
appendix to Chapter 2). With more than two periods, as in
Figure 5.2, estimates based on equation (5.3) should be more
precise and provide a more reliable picture of policy effects
than the simple four-number DD recipe.[4]

Fitting equation (5.3) to the 12 observations plotted in Figure 5.2 generates the following estimates (with standard errors
shown in parentheses):

$$Y_{dt} = 167 - \underset{(8.8)}{29} \, TREAT_d - \underset{(7.6)}{49} \, POST_t$$
$$+ \underset{(10.7)}{20.5} \, (TREAT_d \times POST_t) + e_{dt}.$$

These results suggest that roughly 21 banks were kept alive by
Sixth District lending. This estimate is close to the estimate
of 19 banks saved using the four-number DD recipe. The
standard error for the estimated δ_{rDD} is about 11, so 21 is

---

[4] In fact, as we explain in the chapter appendix, it's hard to gauge the
precision of a DD estimate constructed from only two cross-sectional units
and two periods.

a marginally significant result, the best we can hope for with such a small sample.

Let's Get Real

The Atlanta Fed very likely saved many Sixth District banks from failure. But banks are not valued for their own sakes. Did the Atlanta Fed's policy of easy money support real economic activity, that is, non-bank businesses and jobs? Statistics on business activity within states are scarce for this period. Still, the few numbers available suggest the Atlanta Fed's bank liquidity backstopping generated real economic benefits. This is documented in Table 5.1, which lists the ingredients for a

TABLE 5.1
Wholesale firm failures and sales in 1929 and 1933

	1929	1933	Difference (1933–1929)
Panel A. Number of wholesale firms			
Sixth Federal Reserve District (Atlanta)	783	641	−142
Eighth Federal Reserve District (St. Louis)	930	607	−323
Difference (Sixth–Eighth)	−147	34	181
Panel B. Net wholesale sales ($ million)			
Sixth District Federal Reserve (Atlanta)	141	60	−81
Eighth District Federal Reserve (St. Louis)	245	83	−162
Difference (Sixth–Eighth)	−104	−23	81

Notes: This table presents a DD analysis of Federal Reserve liquidity effects on the number of wholesale firms and the dollar value of their sales, paralleling the DD analysis of liquidity effects on bank activity in Figure 5.1.

simple DD analysis of Federal Reserve liquidity effects on the number of active wholesalers and their sales.

DD estimates for Mississippi wholesalers parallel those for Mississippi banks. Between 1929 and 1933, the number of wholesale firms and their sales fell in both the Sixth and Eighth Districts, with a much sharper drop in the Eighth District, where more banks failed. In the 1920s and 1930s, wholesalers relied heavily on bank credit to finance inventories. The estimates in Table 5.1 suggest that the reduction in bank credit in the Eighth District in the wake of Caldwell brought wholesale business activity down as well, with a likely ripple effect throughout the local economy. Sixth District wholesalers were more likely to have been spared this fate. Cooked with only a four-number DD recipe, however, the evidence for a liquidity treatment effect in Table 5.1 is weaker than that produced by the larger sample for bank activity.

The Caldwell experiment offers a hard-won lesson in how to nip a banking crisis in the bud. Perhaps the governor of the St. Louis Fed, seeing a more modest collapse in the Sixth

District than in the Eighth, had absorbed the Caldwell lesson by the time he reversed course in 1931. But the palliative power of monetary policy in a financial crisis was understood by national authorities only much later. In their memoirs, Milton Friedman and his wife Rose famously recounted:

> Instead of using its powers to offset the Depression, [the Federal Reserve Board in Washington, D.C.] presided over a decline in the quantity of money by one-third from 1929 to 1933. If it had operated as its founders intended, it would have prevented that decline and, indeed, converted it into the rise that was called for to accommodate the normal growth in the economy.[5]

Which isn't to say that the problem of financial crisis management has since been nailed. Today's complex financial markets run off the rails for many reasons, not all of which can be contained by the Fed and its printing presses. That hard lesson is being learned by the monetary authorities of our day.

5.2 Drink, Drank, . . .

SHEN: Are you willing to die to find the truth?

PO: You bet I am! . . . Although, I'd prefer not to.
  Kung Fu Panda 2

With the repeal of federal alcohol Prohibition in 1933, U.S. states were free to regulate alcohol. Most instituted an MLDA of 21, but Kansas, New York, and North Carolina, among others, allowed drinking at 18. Following the twenty-sixth amendment to the constitution in 1971, which lowered the voting age to 18 in response to agitation sparked by the Vietnam War, many states reduced the MLDA. But not all: Arkansas, California, and Pennsylvania are among the states that held the line at 21. In 1984, the National Minimum Drinking Age Act punished youthful intemperance by withholding

---

[5] Milton Friedman and Rose D. Friedman, *Two Lucky People: Memoirs*, University of Chicago Press, 1998, page 233.

federal aid for highway construction from states with an age-18 MLDA. By 1988, all 50 states and the District of Columbia had opted for an MLDA of 21, though some had taken the federal highway hint more quickly than others.

As with much American policymaking, the interaction of federal and state law produces a colorful and oft-changing quilt of legal standards. This policy variation is a boon to masters of 'metrics: variation in state MLDA laws is easily exploited in a DD framework. In efforts to uncover effects of alcohol policy, this framework provides an alternative to the RD approach detailed in Chapter 4.[6]

Patterns from Patchwork

Alabama lowered its MLDA to 19 in 1975, but alphabetically and geographically proximate Arkansas has had an MLDA of 21 since Prohibition's repeal. Did Alabama's indulgence of its youthful drinkers cost some of them their lives? We tackle this question by fitting a regression DD model to data on the death rates of 18–20-year-olds from 1970 to 1983. The dependent variable is denoted Y_{st}, for death rates in state s and year t. With a sample including only Alabama and Arkansas, the regression DD model for Y_{st} takes the form

$$Y_{st} = \alpha + \beta \ TREAT_s + \gamma \ POST_t$$
$$+ \ \delta_{rDD}(TREAT_s \times POST_t) + e_{st}, \quad (5.4)$$

where $TREAT_s$ is a dummy variable indicating Alabama, $POST_t$ is a dummy indicating years from 1975 onward, and the interaction term $TREAT_s \times POST_t$ indicates Alabama observations from low-drinking-age years. The coefficient δ_{rDD} captures the effect of an age-19 MLDA on death rates.

Equation (5.4) parallels the regression DD model for Mississippi's two Federal Reserve Districts. But why look only at Alabama and Arkansas? There's more than one MLDA experi-

---

[6] Carpenter and Dobkin, "The Minimum Legal Drinking Age," *Journal of Economic Perspectives*, 2011, analyzed the MLDA in a DD framework.

ment in the legislative record. For example, Tennessee's MLDA fell to 18 in 1971, then rose to 19 in 1979. A complicating but manageable consequence of differences in the timing of MLDA reductions in Alabama and Tennessee is the absence of a common post-treatment period. When combining multiple MLDA experiments in a DD framework, we swap the single $POST_t$ dummy for a set of dummies indicating each year in the sample, with one omitted as a reference group. The coefficients on these dummies, known as *time effects,* capture temporal changes in death rates that are common to all states.[7]

Our multi-MLDA regression DD procedure should also reflect the fact that there are many states driving causal comparisons. Instead of controlling only for the difference between, say, the Sixth and Eighth Federal Reserve Districts as in the Mississippi experiment of Section 5.1, or the difference between Alabama and Arkansas in the example above, the multistate setup controls for the differing death rates in each of many states. This is accomplished by introducing *state effects,* a set of dummies for every state in the sample, except for one, which is omitted as a reference group. A regression DD analysis of data from Alabama, Arkansas, and Tennessee, for example, includes two state effects. State effects replace the single $TREAT_s$ dummy included in a two-state (or two-group) analysis.

A final complication in this scenario is the absence of a common treatment variable that discretely switches off and on. The MLDA runs from age 18 to age 21, generating treatment effects for legal drinking at ages 18, 19, or 20. Masters of 'metrics simplify such things by reducing them to a single measure of exposure to the policy of interest, in this case, access to alcohol. Our simplification strategy replaces $TREAT_d \times POST_t$ with a variable we'll call $LEGAL_{st}$. This variable measures the proportion of 18–20-year-olds allowed to drink in state s and year t. In some states, no one under 21 is allowed to drink, while in states

---

[7] We include one less time effect than there are years in our data. Time effects measure temporal changes relative to a starting point, usually the first year in the sample.

with an age-19 MLDA, roughly two-thirds of 18–20-year-olds can drink, and in states with an age-18 MLDA, all 18–20-year-olds can drink. Our definition of $LEGAL_{st}$ also captures variation due to within-year timing. For example, Alabama's age-19 MLDA came into effect in July 1975. $LEGAL_{AL,1975}$ is therefore scaled to reflect the fact that Alabama's 19–20-year-olds were free to drink for only half that year.

The multistate regression DD model looks like

$$Y_{st} = \alpha + \delta_{rDD} LEGAL_{st}$$

$$+ \sum_{k=\text{Alaska}}^{\text{Wyoming}} \beta_k STATE_{ks} + \sum_{j=1971}^{1983} \gamma_j YEAR_{jt} + e_{st}. \quad (5.5)$$

Don't let the big sums in this equation scare you. This notation describes models with many dummy variables compactly, just as in the models with college selectivity group dummies in Chapter 2. Here every state but one (the reference state) gets its own dummy variable, indexed by the subscript k for state k. The index s keeps track of the state supplying the observations. The kth state dummy, $STATE_{ks}$ equals one when an observation is from state k, meaning $s = k$, and is zero otherwise. Observations from California, for example, have $STATE_{CA,s}$ switched on, and all other state dummies switched off.

The state effects, β_k, are the coefficients on the state dummies. For example, the California state effect, β_{CA} is the coefficient on $STATE_{CA,s}$. Every state except the reference state, the one omitted when constructing state dummies, has a state effect in equation (5.5). Because there are so many of these, we use summation notation, $\sum_{k=\text{Alaska}}^{\text{Wyoming}} \beta_k STATE_{ks}$, to save writing them all out. The time effects, γ_t, are similarly coefficients on the year dummies, $YEAR_{jt}$. These switch on when observations in the data come from year j, that is, when $t = j$. We therefore also call them *year effects*. The 1975 year effect, γ_{1975}, is the coefficient on $YEAR_{1975,t}$. Here, too, every year in the sample except the reference year has a year effect, so we use summation notation to write these out compactly.[8]

Our multistate MLDA analysis uses a data set with 14 years and 51 states (including the District of Columbia), for a total of 714 observations. This data structure is called a *state-year panel*. The state effects in equation (5.5) control for fixed differences between states (for example, fatal car accidents are more frequent, on average, in rural states with high average travel speeds). The time (year) effects in this equation control for trends in death rates that are common to all states (due, for example, to national trends in drinking or vehicle safety). Equation (5.5) attributes changes in mortality within states to changes in $LEGAL_{st}$. As we'll see shortly, this causal attribution turns on a common trends assumption, just as in our analysis of Caldwell-induced bank failures in the previous section.

Estimates of δ_{rDD} in equation (5.5) suggest that legal alcohol access caused about 11 additional deaths per 100,000 18–20-year-olds, of which seven or eight deaths were the result of motor vehicle accidents. These results, reported in the first column of Table 5.2, are somewhat larger than but still broadly consistent with the RD estimates reported in Table 4.1 in Chapter 4. The MVA estimates in Table 5.2 are also reasonably precise, with standard errors of about 2.5. Importantly, as with the RD estimates, this regression DD model generates little evidence of an effect of legal drinking on deaths from internal

---

[8] Here's another way to see how the notation works. Consider an observation for $s = NY$. Then we have

$$\sum_{k=\text{Alaska}}^{\text{Wyoming}} \beta_k STATE_{ks} = \beta_{NY},$$

so the sum of all possible state dummies picks up the New York state effect, β_{NY}, when observations are from New York. All the other dummies in the sum are zero. Likewise, if $t = 1980$, then we have

$$\sum_{j=1971}^{1983} \gamma_j YEAR_{jt} = \gamma_{1980},$$

so the sum picks up the 1980 year effect when observations are from 1980.

TABLE 5.2
Regression DD estimates of MLDA effects on death rates

Dependent variable	(1)	(2)	(3)	(4)
All deaths	10.80	8.47	12.41	9.65
	(4.59)	(5.10)	(4.60)	(4.64)
Motor vehicle accidents	7.59	6.64	7.50	6.46
	(2.50)	(2.66)	(2.27)	(2.24)
Suicide	.59	.47	1.49	1.26
	(.59)	(.79)	(.88)	(.89)
All internal causes	1.33	.08	1.89	1.28
	(1.59)	(1.93)	(1.78)	(1.45)
State trends	No	Yes	No	Yes
Weights	No	No	Yes	Yes

Notes: This table reports regression DD estimates of minimum legal drinking age (MLDA) effects on the death rates (per 100,000) of 18–20-year-olds. The table shows coefficients on the proportion of legal drinkers by state and year from models controlling for state and year effects. The models used to construct the estimates in columns (2) and (4) include state-specific linear time trends. Columns (3) and (4) show weighted least squares estimates, weighting by state population. The sample size is 714. Standard errors are reported in parentheses.

causes. The regression DD evidence for an effect on suicide is weaker than the corresponding RD evidence in Table 4.1. At the same time, both strategies suggest any increase in numbers of suicides is smaller than for MVA deaths.

Probing DD Assumptions

Samples that include many states and years allow us to relax the common trends assumption, that is, to introduce a degree of nonparallel evolution in outcomes between states in the absence of a treatment effect. A regression DD model with controls for state-specific trends looks like

$$Y_{st} = \alpha + \delta_{rDD}LEGAL_{st}$$

$$+ \sum_{k=\text{Alaska}}^{\text{Wyoming}} \beta_k STATE_{ks} + \sum_{j=1971}^{1983} \gamma_j YEAR_{jt}$$

$$+ \sum_{k=\text{Alaska}}^{\text{Wyoming}} \theta_k \left(STATE_{ks} \times t\right) + e_{st}. \qquad (5.6)$$

This model presumes that in the absence of a treatment effect, death rates in state k deviate from common year effects by following the linear trend captured by the coefficient θ_k.

Heretofore and hitherto we've been sayin' that DD is all about common trends. How can it be, then, that we're now entertaining models like equation (5.6), which relax the key common trends assumption? To see how such models work, consider a sample of two states: The first, Allatsea, reduced the MLDA to 18 in 1975, while neighboring Alabaster held the line at 21. As a baseline, Figure 5.4 sketches the common trends story. Deaths per 100,000 move in parallel until 1975 (most things got worse in the 1970s, so we show death rates increasing). Death rates also jump above trend in Allatsea in 1975, when that state lowered its MLDA. Given the parallelism and the timing, it seems fair to blame Allatsea's lower MLDA for this jump.

Figure 5.5 sketches a scenario with a steeper trend in Allatsea than in Alabaster. As with the data plotted in the previous figure, simple regression DD estimation in this case generates estimates implicating the MLDA (the post-minus-pre contrast in Allatsea is larger than the post-minus-pre contrast in Alabaster). In this case, however, the resulting DD estimate is spurious: the difference in state trends predates Allatsea's MLDA liberalization and must therefore be unrelated to it.

Luckily, such differences in trend can be captured by the state-specific trend parameters, θ_k, in equation (5.6). In models that control for state-specific trends, evidence for MLDA effects comes from sharp deviations from otherwise smooth trends, even where the trends are not common. Figure 5.6

FIGURE 5.4
An MLDA effect in states with parallel trends

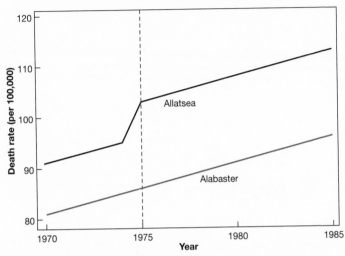

FIGURE 5.5
A spurious MLDA effect in states where trends are not parallel

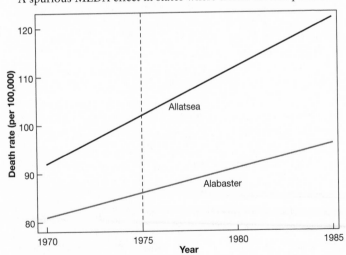

FIGURE 5.6
A real MLDA effect, visible even though trends are not parallel

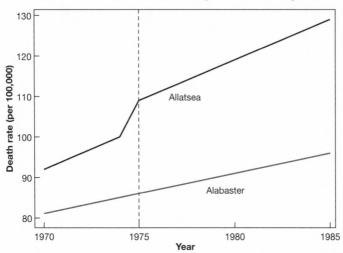

shows how regression DD captures treatment effects in the face
of uncommon trends. Death rates in Allatsea increase more
steeply than in Alabaster throughout the sample period. But
the Allatsea increase is especially steep from 1974 to 1975,
when Allatsea lowered its MLDA. The coefficient on $LEGAL_{st}$
in equation (5.6) picks this up, while the model allows for the
fact that death rates in different states were on different tra-
jectories from the get-go.

Models with state-specific linear trends provide an important check on the causal interpretation of any set of regression
DD estimates using multiperiod data. In practice, however, empirical reality may be considerably mushier and harder to interpret than the stylized examples laid out in Figures 5.4–5.6. The
findings generated by a regression model like equation (5.6) are
often imprecise. The sharper the deviation from trend induced
by a causal effect, the more likely we are to be able to uncover
it. On the other hand, if treatment effects emerge only grad-

ually, estimates of equations like (5.6) may fail to distinguish treatment effects from differential trends, with the end result being an imprecise and therefore inconclusive set of findings.

Happily for a coherent causal DD analysis of MLDA effects, introduction of state-specific trends has little effect on our regression DD estimates. This can be seen in column (2) of Table 5.2, which reports regression DD estimates of MLDA effects from the model described by equation (5.6). The addition of trends increases standard errors a little, but the loss of precision here is modest. The findings in column (2) support a causal interpretation of the more precise MLDA effects reported in column (1) of the table.

State policymaking is a messy business, with frequent changes on many fronts. DD estimates of MLDA effects, with or without state-specific trends, may be biased by contemporaneous policy changes in other areas. An important consideration in research on alcohol, for example, is the price of a drink. Taxes are the most powerful tool the government uses to affect the price of your favorite beverage. Many states levy a heavy tax on beer, which we measure in dollars per gallon of alcohol content. Beer taxes range from just pennies per gallon to more than a dollar per gallon in some Southern states. Beer taxes change from time to time, mostly increasing, much to the dismay of the Beer Institute (with a tax rate of 2 cents per gallon since 1935, Wyoming is beer bliss). It stands to reason that states might raise tax rates at the same time that they increase their MLDA, perhaps as a part of a broader effort to reduce drinking. If so, we should control for time-varying state tax rates when estimating MLDA effects.

Regression DD models that include controls for state beer taxes generate MLDA estimates similar to those without such controls. This can be seen in Table 5.3, which reports both the estimated coefficients on $LEGAL_{st}$ and the estimated coefficients on state beer taxes in models for the four death rates examined in Table 5.2. Columns (1) and (2) of Table 5.3 show beer tax and MLDA effects estimated using a single regression without controls for state-specific trends, while those in columns (3) and (4) come from another regression including controls for state-specific trends. Beer tax effects are estimated

TABLE 5.3
Regression DD estimates of MLDA effects controlling for beer taxes

| Dependent variable | Without trends | | With trends | |
	Fraction legal (1)	Beer tax (2)	Fraction legal (3)	Beer tax (4)
All deaths	10.98 (4.69)	1.51 (9.07)	10.03 (4.92)	−5.52 (32.24)
Motor vehicle accidents	7.59 (2.56)	3.82 (5.40)	6.89 (2.66)	26.88 (20.12)
Suicide	.45 (.60)	−3.05 (1.63)	.38 (.77)	−12.13 (8.82)
Internal causes	1.46 (1.61)	−1.36 (3.07)	.88 (1.81)	−10.31 (11.64)

Notes: This table reports regression DD estimates of minimum legal drinking age (MLDA) effects on the death rates (per 100,000) of 18–20-year-olds, controlling for state beer taxes. The table shows coefficients on the proportion of legal drinkers by state and year and the beer tax by state and year, from models controlling for state and year effects. The fraction legal and beer tax variables are included in a single regression model, estimated without trends to produce the estimates in columns (1) and (2) and estimated with state-specific linear trends to produce the estimates in columns (3) and (4). The sample size is 700. Standard errors are reported in parentheses.

less precisely than MLDA effects, most likely because beer taxes change less often than the MLDA. The beer tax estimates from models that include state trends are especially noisy. Still, the Beer Institute will be pleased to learn that these results don't speak in favor of further beer tax increases. We're likewise pleased to know that our MLDA estimates are robust to the inclusion of a beer tax control; we'll share a beer to celebrate!

What Are You Weighting For?

The estimates of equations (5.5) and (5.6) in columns (1) and (2) of Table 5.2 give all observations equal weight, as if data from each state were equally valuable. States are not created equal, however, in at least one important respect: some, like Texas and California, are bigger than most countries, while others, like Vermont and Wyoming, have populations smaller than those of many American cities. We may prefer estimates that reflect this fact by giving more populous states more weight. The regression procedure that does this is called *weighted least squares* (WLS). The standard OLS estimator fits a line by minimizing the sample average of squared residuals, with each squared residual getting equal weight in the sum.[9] Just as the name suggests, WLS weights each term in the residual sum of squares by population size or some other researcher-chosen weight.

Population weighting has two consequences. First, as noted in Chapter 2, regression models of treatment effects capture a weighted average of effects for the groups or cells represented in our data. In a state-year panel, these groups are states. OLS estimates of models for state-year panels produce estimates of average causal effects that ignore population size, so the resulting estimates are averages over states, not over people. Population weighting generates a people-weighted average, in which causal effects for states like Texas get more weight than those for states like Vermont. People-weighting may sound appealing, but it need not be. The typical citizen is more likely to live in Texas than Vermont, but changes in the Vermont MLDA provide variation that may be just as useful as changes in Texas. You should hope, therefore, that regression estimates from your state-year panel are not highly sensitive to weighting.

Population weighting may also increase the precision of regression estimates. With far fewer drivers in Vermont than in Texas, MVA death rates in Vermont are likely to be more variable from year to year than those in Texas (this reflects the sampling variation discussed in the appendix to Chapter 1). In a statistical sense, the data from Texas are more reliable and therefore, perhaps, worthy of higher weight. Here too,

---

[9] Regression residuals, defined in the appendix to Chapter 2, are the differences between the fitted values generated by the model we're estimating and the dependent variable in this model.

however, the case for weighting is not open and shut. As a matter of econometric theory, masters of 'metrics can claim that weighted estimates are more precise than unweighted estimates only when a number of restrictive technical conditions are met.[10] Once again, the best scenario is a set of findings (that is, estimates and standard errors) that are reasonably insensitive to weighting.

Columns (3) and (4) in Table 5.2 report WLS estimates of equations (5.5) and (5.6). These correspond to the OLS estimates shown in columns (1) and (2) of the table, but the WLS estimator weights each observation by state population aged 18–20. Happily for our understanding of MLDA effects, weighting here matters little. It would seem once again that teetotaling masters have been rewarded for their temperance.

MASTER STEVEFU: Wrap it up for me, Grasshopper.

GRASSHOPPER: Treatment and control groups may differ in the absence of treatment, yet move in parallel. This pattern opens the door to DD estimation of causal effects.

MASTER STEVEFU: Why is DD better than simple two-group comparisons?

GRASSHOPPER: Comparing changes instead of levels, we eliminate fixed differences between groups that might otherwise generate omitted variables bias.

MASTER STEVEFU: How is DD executed with multiple comparison groups and multiple years?

GRASSHOPPER: I have seen the power and flexibility of regression DD, Master. In a state-year panel, for example, with time-varying state policies like the MLDA, we need only control for state and year effects.

---

[10] One requirement is that the underlying CEF be linear. The appendix to Chapter 2 notes, however, that many regression models are only linear approximations to the CEF.

MASTER STEVEFU: On what does the fate of DD estimates turn?

GRASSHOPPER: Parallel trends, the claim that in the absence of treatment, treatment and control group outcomes would indeed move in parallel. DD lives and dies by this. Though we can allow for state-specific linear trends when a panel is long enough, masters hope for results that are unchanged by their inclusion.

Masters of 'Metrics: John Snow

British physician John Snow was one of the fathers of modern epidemiology, the study of how illness moves through a population. Studying an outbreak of cholera in London in 1849, Snow challenged the conventional wisdom that the disease is caused by bad air. He thought cholera might be caused by bad water instead, an idea he first laid out in his 1849 essay *On the Mode of Communication of Cholera*.

A further cholera outbreak in 1853 and 1854 claimed many lives in the London neighborhood of Soho. Snow attributed the Soho epidemic to water from a pump on Broad Street. Not afraid to give a natural experiment a helping hand, he convinced the local parish council to remove the handle of the Broad Street pump. Cholera deaths in Soho subsided soon after, though Snow noted that death rates in his Broad Street treatment zone were already declining, and that this made the data from his natural experiment hard to interpret. DD was as fickle at birth as it is today.

Snow was a meticulous data grubber, setting a standard we still aspire to meet. In an 1855 revision of his essay, Snow reported death rates by district and water source for various parts of London. He noted that many of the high-death-rate districts in South London were supplied by one of two companies, the Southwark and Vauxhall Company or the Lambeth Company. In 1849, both companies drew water from the contaminated Thames in central London. Starting in 1852, however, the Lambeth Company drew from the river at Thames Ditton, an uncontaminated water source upstream. Snow showed that between 1849 and 1854 deaths from cholera fell in the area supplied by the Lambeth Company but rose in that supplied by the Southwark and Vauxhall Company. Our Figure 5.7 reproduces Table 12 from Snow's 1855 essay.[11] This table contains the ingredients for Snow's two-period DD analysis of death rates by water source.

Appendix: Standard Errors for Regression DD

Regression DD is a special case of estimation with panel data. A state-year panel consists of repeated observations on states over time. The repetitive structure of such data sets raises special statistical problems. Economic data of this sort typically exhibit a property called *serial correlation* (that's *serial* as in "murder," not "breakfast"). Serially correlated data are persistent, meaning the values of variables for nearby periods are likely to be similar.

We expect serial correlation in time series data like annual unemployment rates. When a state's unemployment rate is higher than average in one year, it's likely to be higher than average in the next. Because panel data sets combine repeated observations for individual states (in our MLDA example) or regions (in our Mississippi experiment), such data are often serially correlated. When the dependent variable in a regression is serially correlated, the residuals from any regression model explaining this variable are often serially correlated as well. A combination of serially correlated residuals and serially correlated regressors changes the formula required to calculate standard errors.

If we ignore serial correlation and use the simple standard error formula, equation (2.15), the resulting statistical conclusions are likely to be misleading. The penalty for ignoring serial correlation is that you exaggerate the precision of regression estimates. This is because the sampling theory for regression inference laid out in the appendix to Chapter 1 presumes the

---

[11] John Snow, *On the Mode of Communication of Cholera*, John Churchill, second edition, 1855.

FIGURE 5.7
John Snow's DD recipe

TABLE XII.

Sub-Districts.	Deaths from Cholera in 1849.	Deaths from Cholera in 1854.	Water Supply.
St. Saviour, Southwark .	283	371	
St. Olave . . .	157	161	
St. John, Horsleydown .	192	148	
St. James, Bermondsey .	249	362	
St. Mary Magdalen .	259	244	
Leather Market . .	226	237	Southwark & Vaux-
Rotherhithe* . .	352	282	hall Company only.
Wandsworth . . .	97	59	
Battersea . . .	111	171	
Putney	8	9	
Camberwell . . .	235	240	
Peckham . . .	92	174	
Christchurch, Southwark	256	113	
Kent Road . . .	267	174	
Borough Road . .	312	270	
London Road . .	257	93	
Trinity, Newington .	318	210	
St. Peter, Walworth .	446	388	Lambeth Company,
St. Mary, Newington .	143	92	and Southwark and
Waterloo Road (1st) .	193	58	Vauxhall Compy.
Waterloo Road (2nd) .	243	117	
Lambeth Church (1st) .	215	49	
Lambeth Church (2nd).	544	193	
Kennington (1st) . .	187	303	
Kennington (2nd) .	153	142	
Brixton . . .	81	48	
Clapham . . .	114	165	
St. George, Camberwell	176	132	
Norwood . . .	2	10	
Streatham . . .	154	15	Lambeth Company
Dulwich . . .	1	—	only.
Sydenham . . .	5	12	
First 12 sub-districts .	2261	2458	Southwk.& Vauxhall.
Next 16 sub-districts .	3905	2547	Both Companies.
Last 4 sub-districts .	162	37	Lambeth Company.

* A small part of Rotherhithe is now supplied by the Kent Water
Company.

data at hand come from random samples. Serial correlation is a deviation from randomness, with the important consequence that each new observation in a serially correlated time series contains less information than would be the case if the sample were random.

Just as the robust standard errors discussed in the appendix to Chapter 1 correct for heteroskedasticity, there's a modified standard error formula that answers the serial correlation challenge. The appropriate formula in this case is known as a *clustered standard error*. The formula for clustered standard errors is more complicated than the formula for robust standard errors given in equation (2.16); we won't ask you to learn it for the test. The important thing is that clustering (an option in most regression software) allows for correlated data within researcher-defined clusters. In contrast with the assumption that all data are randomly sampled, the formula for clustered standard errors requires only that clusters be sampled randomly, with no random sampling assumption invoked for what's inside them.

In the MLDA example discussed in this chapter, states are clusters. Often, it's individual people who appear in our samples repeatedly. Participants in the RAND HIE contributed up to five annual observations on their health-care use in the sample used to construct Table 1.4, and children appear in two separate grades in the sample used to estimate the peer effects model, equation (4.9). In these examples, we adjust for the fact that repeated outcomes for the same person tend to be correlated by clustering on individual.

In the Mississippi experiment, clusters are Federal Reserve Districts. There are only two of these, an important caution. Serial correlation might not be a problem in the Mississippi experiment, but if it is, we'll need more data before we can say anything conclusive about the effects of liquidity on bank survival. Once you start clustering, the formal theory behind statistical inference presumes you have many clusters instead of (or in addition to) many individual observations within clusters. In practice, "many" might be only a few dozen, as with American states. That's probably OK, but a pair or a handful of clusters may not be enough.[12]

Clustered standard errors are appropriate for a wide variety of settings, not only for panel data. In principle, clustering solves any sort of dependence problem in your data (though you might not like the large standard errors that result). For example, data from achievement tests taken by schoolchildren are likely to be correlated within classrooms if children in the same classes share a teacher and have similar family backgrounds. When reporting estimates of the effects of educational interventions like peer effects in equation (4.6) or the effects of private universities in Chapter 2, masters cluster their standard errors on class, school, or university.

---

[12] For a more detailed discussion of this point, see our book, *Mostly Harmless Econometrics*, Princeton University Press, 2009. In an analysis of hundreds of counties on either side of Federal Reserve District borders, Andrew Jalil adds clusters to the Mississippi experiment. See "Monetary Intervention Really Did Mitigate Banking Panics during the Great Depression: Evidence along the Atlanta Federal Reserve District Border," *Journal of Economic History*, vol. 74, no. 1, March 2014, pages 259–273.

Chapter 6

The Wages of Schooling

Legend tells of a legendary econometrician whose econometric skills were the stuff of legend.

Masters at Work

This chapter completes our exploration of paths from cause to effect with a multifaceted investigation of the causal effect of schooling on wages. Good questions are the foundation of our work, and the question of whether increased education really increases earnings is a classic. Masters have tackled the schooling question with all tools in hand, except, ironically, random assignment. The answers they've fashioned are no less interesting for being incomplete.

6.1 Schooling, Experience, and Earnings

British World War II veteran Bertie Gladwin dropped out of secondary school at age 14, though he still found work as a radio communication engineer in the British intelligence service. In his sixties, Bertie returned to school, completing a BA in psychology. Later, Bertie earned a BSc in microbiology, before embarking on a Master's degree in military intelligence, completed at the age of 91. Bertie has since been considering study for a PhD.[1]

It's never too late to learn something new. Unlike Bertie Gladwin, however, most students complete their studies before establishing a career. College students spend years buried in books and tuition bills, while many of their high school friends who didn't go to college may have started work and gained a measure of financial independence. In return for the

[1] See "'I'm Just a Late Bloomer': Britain's Oldest Student Graduates with a Degree in Military Intelligence Aged 91," *The Daily Mail*, May 21, 2012.

time-consuming toil and expense of college, college graduates hope to be rewarded with higher earnings down the road. Hopes and dreams are one thing; life follows many paths. Are the forgone earnings and tuition costs associated with a college degree worthwhile? That's a million dollar question, and our interest in it is more than personal. Taxpayers subsidize college attendance for students around the world, a policy motivated in part by the view that college is the key to economic success.

Economists call the causal effect of education on earnings the *returns to schooling*. This term evokes the notion that schooling is an investment in human capital, with a monetary payoff similar to that of a financial investment. The financial return to a particular year of schooling compares the earnings that could be had by completing that year with the earnings generated by leaving school a year earlier. Counterfactuals here are multi-faceted: instead of the single contrast, $Y_{1i} - Y_{0i}$, associated with a dichotomous choice, we imagine returns generated by every possible schooling choice (say, $Y_{12,i} - Y_{11,i}$ for the last year of high school or $Y_{25,i} - Y_{24,i}$ for the last year of graduate school). Linear regression models reduce these many possible causal effects to a single coefficient that captures the average causal effect of one additional year of education.

Inspired by the human capital story, generations of masters have estimated the economic returns to schooling. 'Metrics master Jacob Mincer pioneered efforts to quantify the return to schooling using regression.[2] Working with U.S. census data, Mincer ran regressions like

$$\ln Y_i = \alpha + \rho S_i + \beta_1 X_i + \beta_2 X_i^2 + e_i, \qquad (6.1)$$

where $\ln Y_i$ is the log annual earnings of man i, S_i is his schooling (measured as years spent studying), and X_i is his years of work experience. Mincer defined the latter as age minus years of schooling minus 6, a calculation that counts all years since graduation as years of work. Masters call X_i calculated in this way *potential experience*. It's customary to control for a quadratic function of potential experience to allow for the fact

---

[2] Mincer's work is reported in his landmark book, *Schooling, Experience, and Earnings*, Columbia University Press and the National Bureau of Economic Research, 1974.

that, although earnings increase with experience, they do so at a decreasing rate, eventually flattening out in middle age.

Mincer's estimates of equation (6.1) for a sample of about 31,000 nonfarm white men in the 1960 Census look like

$$\ln Y_i = \alpha + \underset{(.002)}{.070} \, S_i + e_i$$

$$\ln Y_i = \alpha + \underset{(.001)}{.107} \, S_i + \underset{(.001)}{.081} \, X_i - \underset{(.00002)}{.0012} \, X_i^2 + e_i. \quad (6.2)$$

With no controls, $\rho = .07$. This estimate comes from a model built with logs, so $\rho = .07$ implies average earnings rise by about 7% with each additional year of schooling (the appendix to Chapter 2 discusses regression models with logs on the left-hand side). With potential experience included as a control variable, the estimated returns increase to about .11.

The model with potential experience controls for the fact that those with more schooling typically have fewer years of work experience, since educated men usually start full-time work later (that is, after their schooling is completed). Because S_i and X_i are negatively correlated, the OVB formula tells us that omitting experience, which has a positive effect on earnings, leads to a lower estimate of the returns to schooling than we can expect in long regressions that include experience controls. Mincer's estimates imply that white men with a given level of experience enjoy an 11% earnings advantage for each additional year of education. It remains to be seen, however, whether this is a causal effect.[3]

Of Singers, Fencers, and PhDs: Ability Bias

Equation (6.1) compares men with more and fewer years of schooling, while holding their years of work experience fixed.

---

[3] The relationship between experience and earnings described by these estimates reflects a gradual decline in earnings growth with age. To see this, suppose we increase X_i from a value x to $x + 1$. The term X_i increases by 1, while X_i^2 increases by

$$(x + 1)^2 - x^2 = 2x + 1.$$

The net effect of a 1-year experience increase is therefore

$$(.081 \times 1) - (.0012 \cdot (2x + 1)) = .08 - .0024x.$$

The first year of experience is therefore estimated to boost earnings by almost 8% while the tenth year of experience increases earnings by only about 5.6%. In fact, the *experience profile*, as this relationship is called, flattens out completely after about 30 years of experience.

Is control for potential experience sufficient for *ceteris* to be *paribus*? In other words, at a given experience level, are more- and less-educated workers equally able and diligent? Do they have the same family connections that might offer a leg up in the labor market? Such claims seem hard to swallow. Like other masters, we're pretty highly educated ourselves. And we're smarter, harder working, and better bred than most of those who didn't stick it out in the schooling department, or so we tell ourselves. The good qualities that we imagine we share with other highly educated workers are also associated with higher earnings, complicating the causal interpretation of regression estimates like those in equation (6.2).

We can hope to improve on these simple regression estimates by controlling for attributes correlated with schooling, variables we'll call A_i (short for "ability"). Ignoring the experience term for now and focusing on other sources of OVB, the resulting long regression can be written as

$$\ln Y_i = \alpha^l + \rho^l S_i + \gamma A_i + e_i. \qquad (6.3)$$

The OVB formula tells us that the short regression slope from a model with no controls, ρ^s, is related to the long regression slope in model (6.3) by the formula

$$\rho^s = \rho^l + \underbrace{\delta_{AS}\gamma}_{\text{ability bias}},$$

where δ_{AS} is the slope from a bivariate regression of A_i on S_i. As always, short (ρ^s) equals long (ρ^l) plus the regression of omitted (from short) on included (δ_{AS}) times the effect of omitted in long (γ). In this context, the difference between short and long is called *ability bias* since the omitted variable is ability.

Which way does ability bias go? We've defined A_i so that γ in the long regression is positive (otherwise, we'd call A_i dis-ability). Surely δ_{AS} is positive as well, implying upward ability bias: we expect the short regression ρ^s to exceed the more controlled ρ^l. After all, our London School of Economics and MIT students tend to be high ability, at least in the sense of having high test scores and good grades in high school. On the other hand, some people cut their schooling short so as to pursue more immediately lucrative activities. Sir Mick Jagger abandoned his pursuit of a degree at the London School of Economics in 1963 to play with an outfit known as the Rolling Stones. Jagger got no satisfaction, and he certainly never graduated from college, but he earned plenty as a singer in a rock and roll band. No less impressive, Swedish épée fencer Johan Harmenberg left MIT after 2 years of study in 1979, winning a gold medal at the 1980 Moscow Olympics, instead of earning an MIT diploma. Harmenberg went on to become a biotech executive and successful researcher. These examples illustrate how people with high ability—musical, athletic, entrepreneurial, or otherwise—may be economically successful without the benefit of an education. This suggests that δ_{AS}, and hence ability bias, can be negative as easily as positive.

The Measure of Men: Controlling Ability

Here's an easy work-around for the ability bias roadblock: collect information on A_i and use it as a control in regressions like equation (6.3). In an effort to tackle OVB in estimates of the returns to schooling, 'metrics master Zvi Griliches used IQ as an ability control.[4] Without IQ in the model, Griliches' estimate of ρ^s in a model controlling for potential experience is .068. Griliches' estimated short regression schooling coefficient is well below Mincer's estimate of about 11%, probably due to differences in samples and dependent variables (Griliches looked at effects on hourly wages instead of annual earnings). Importantly, the addition of an IQ control knocks Griliches' estimate down to $\rho^l = .059$, a consequence of the facts that IQ and schooling are strongly positively correlated and that higher IQ people earn more (so the effect of omitted ability in long is indeed positive).

---

[4] Zvi Griliches, "Estimating the Returns to Schooling—Some Econometric Problems," *Econometrica*, vol. 45, no. 1, January 1977, pages 1–22.

Although intriguing, it's hard to see Griliches' findings as conclusive. IQ doesn't capture Mick Jagger's charisma or Johan Harmenberg's perseverance, dimensions of ability that are rarely measured in statistical samples. The relevant notion of ability here is an individual's *earnings potential*, a concept reminiscent of the potential outcomes we use to describe causal effects throughout the book. The problem with potential outcomes, as always, is that we can never see them all, we see only the one associated with the road taken. For example, we see only the "highly educated" potential outcome in a sample of college graduates. We can't know how such people would have fared if they'd followed Johan and Mick out of college. Attempts to summarize potential earnings with a single test score are probably inadequate. Moreover, for reasons explained in Section 6.2 and detailed further in the appendix to this chapter, when schooling is mismeasured (as we think it often is), estimates with ability controls can be misleadingly small.

Beware Bad Control

Perhaps more controls are the answer. Why not control for occupation, for example? Many data sets that report earnings also classify workers' jobs, such as manager or laborer. Surely occupation is a strong predictor of both schooling and earnings, possibly capturing traits that distinguish Mick and Johan from more average Joes. By the logic of OVB, therefore, we should control for occupation, a matter easily accomplished by including dummy variables to indicate the types of jobs held.

Although occupation is strongly correlated with both schooling and wages, occupation dummies are *bad controls* in regressions meant to capture causal effects of schooling on wages. The fact that Master Joshway works today as a professor and not as a nurse's aide (as he once did) is in part a reward for his extravagant schooling. It's a mistake to eliminate this benefit from our calculation by comparing only professors or nurse's aides when attempting to quantify the economic value of schooling. Even in a world where all professors earn a uniform $1 million a year (may it soon come to pass) and all nurse's aides earn a uniform $10,000, an experiment that randomly assigns schooling would show that schooling raises wages. The channel by which wages are increased in this notional experiment is the shift from lowly nurse's aide to elevated professorness.

There's a second, more subtle, confounding force here: bad controls create selection bias. To illustrate, suppose we're interested in the effects of a college degree and that college completion is randomly assigned. People can work in one of two occupations, white collar and blue collar, and a college degree naturally makes white collar work more likely. Because college changes occupation for some, comparisons of wages by college degree status conditional on occupation are no longer well balanced, even when college degrees are randomly assigned and unconditional comparisons are apples-to-apples.

This troubling phenomenon is a composition effect. By virtue of random assignment, those who do and don't have a college degree are similar in every way, at least on average. Most importantly, they have the same average Y_{0i}, that is, the same average earnings potential. Suppose, however, that we limit the comparison to those who have white collar jobs. The noncollege control group in this case consists entirely of especially bright workers who manage to land a white collar job without the benefit of a college education. But the white collar group that graduates from college includes these always-white-collar guys plus a weaker group that lands a white collar job by virtue of completing college but not otherwise.

We can see the consequences of this compositional difference by imagining three equal-sized groups of workers. The first group works a blue collar job with or without college (Always Blue, or AB). A second group works a white collar job irrespective of their education (Always White, or AW). Members of a third group, Blue White (BW), get a white collar job only with a college degree. These potential occupations are described in the first two columns of Table 6.1, which lists jobs obtained by those in each group in scenarios with and without a college degree.

In spite of the fact that college is randomly assigned, and simple comparisons of college and noncollege workers reveal causal effects, within-occupation comparisons are misleading.

TABLE 6.1
How bad control creates selection bias

Type of worker	Potential occupation		Potential earnings		Average earnings by occupation	
	Without college (1)	With college (2)	Without college (3)	With college (4)	Without college (5)	With college (6)
Always Blue (AB)	Blue	Blue	1,000	1,500	Blue 1,500	Blue 1,500
Blue White (BW)	Blue	White	2,000	2,500		White 3,000
Always White (AW)	White	White	3,000	3,500	White 3,000	

Suppose, for the sake of argument, the value of college is the same $500 per week for all three groups. Although the three types of workers enjoy the same gains from a college education, their potential earnings (that is, their Y_{0i} values) are likely to differ. To be concrete, suppose the AW group earns $3,000 per week without a college degree, the AB group earns only $1,000 per week without a college degree, and the BWs earn something in the middle, say, $2,000 per week without a college degree. Columns (3) and (4) of Table 6.1 summarize these facts.

Limiting the college/noncollege comparison to those who have white collar jobs, the average earnings of college graduates is given by the average of the $3,500 earned by the AWs with a college degree and the $2,500 earned by the BWs, while the average for noncollege graduates is the constant $3,000 earned by the AWs without a college degree. Because the average of $3,500 and $2,500 also equals $3,000, the conditional-on-white-collar comparison by college graduation status is zero, a misleading estimate of the returns to college, which is $500 for everyone. The comparison of earnings by graduation status among blue collar workers is an equally misleading zero. Although random assignment of college ensures equal proportions of apples and oranges (types or groups) in the college and noncollege barrels, conditioning on white collar employment, an outcome determined in part by college graduation, distorts this balance.

The moral of the bad control story is that timing matters. Variables measured before the treatment variable was determined are generally good controls, because they can't be changed by the treatment. By contrast, control variables that are measured later may have been determined in part by the treatment, in which case they aren't controls at all, they are outcomes. Occupation in a regression model for the causal effect of schooling is a case in point. Ability controls (such as test scores) may also have this problem, especially if test scores come from tests taken by those who have completed most of their schooling. (Schooling probably boosts test scores.) This is one more reason to question empirical strategies that rely on test scores to remove ability bias from econometric estimates of the returns to schooling.[5]

6.2   Twins Double the Fun

Twinsburg, Ohio, near Cleveland, was founded as Millsville in the early nineteenth century. Prosperous Millsville businessmen Moses and Aaron Wilcox were identical twins whom few could distinguish. Moses and Aaron were generous to Millsville in their success, a fact recognized when Millsville was renamed Twinsburg in the early nineteenth century. Since 1976, Twinsburg has embraced its zygotic heritage in the form of a summer festival celebrating twins. Millsville's annual Twins Days attract not only twins reveling in their similarities but also researchers looking for well-controlled comparisons.

Twin siblings indeed have much in common: most grow up in the same family at the same time, while identical twins

---

[5] Attentive readers will notice that potential experience, itself a downstream consequence of schooling, also falls under the category of bad control. In principle, the bias here can be removed by using age and its square to instrument potential experience and its square. As in the studies referenced in the rest of this chapter, we might also simply replace the experience control with age, thereby targeting a net schooling effect that does not adjust for differences in potential experience.

even share genes. Twins might therefore be said to have the same ability as well. Perhaps the fact that one twin gets more schooling than his or her twin sibling is due mostly to the sort of serendipitous forces discussed in Chapter 2. The notion that one twin provides a good control for the other motivates a pair of studies by masters Orley Ashenfelter, Alan Krueger, and Cecilia Rouse.[6] The key idea behind this work, as in many other studies using twins, is that if ability is common to a pair of twin siblings, we can remove it from the equation by subtracting one twin's data from the other's and working only with the differences between them.

The long regression that motivates a twins analysis of the returns to schooling can be written as

$$\ln Y_{if} = \alpha^l + \rho^l S_{if} + \lambda A_{if} + e^l_{if}. \qquad (6.4)$$

Here, subscript f stands for family, while subscript $i = 1, 2$ indexes twin siblings, say, Karen and Sharon or Ronald and Donald. When Ronald and Donald have the same ability, we can simplify by writing $A_{if} = A_f$. This in turn implies that we can model their earnings as

$$\ln Y_{1,f} = \alpha^l + \rho^l S_{1,f} + \lambda A_f + e^l_{1,f}$$

$$\ln Y_{2,f} = \alpha^l + \rho^l S_{2,f} + \lambda A_f + e^l_{2,f}.$$

Subtracting the equation for Donald from that for Ronald gives

$$\ln Y_{1,f} - \ln Y_{2,f} = \rho^l \left(S_{1,f} - S_{2,f} \right) + e^l_{1,f} - e^l_{2,f}, \qquad (6.5)$$

an equation from which ability disappears.[7] From this we learn that when ability is constant within twin pairs, a short

---

[6] Orley Ashenfelter and Alan B. Krueger, "Estimates of the Economic Returns to Schooling from a New Sample of Twins," *American Economic Review*, vol. 84, no. 5, December 1994, pages 1157–1173, and Orley Ashenfelter and Cecilia Rouse, "Income, Schooling, and Ability: Evidence from a New Sample of Identical Twins," *Quarterly Journal of Economics*, vol. 113, no. 1, February 1998, pages 253–284.

[7] Estimates of this differenced model can also be obtained by adding a dummy for each family to an undifferenced model fit in a sample that includes both twins. Family dummies are like selectivity-group dummies in equation (2.2) in Chapter 2 and state dummies in equation (5.5) in Section 5.2.

regression of the difference in twins' earnings on the difference in their schooling recovers the long regression coefficient, ρ^l.

Regression estimates constructed without differencing in the twins sample generate a schooling return of about 11%, remarkably similar to Mincer's. This can be seen in the first column of Table 6.2. The model that produces the estimates in column (1) includes age, age squared, a dummy for women, and a dummy for whites. White twins earn less than black twins, an unusual result in the realm of earnings comparisons by race, though the gap here is not significantly different from zero.

The differenced equation (6.5) generates a schooling return of about 6%, a result shown in column (2) of Table 6.2. This is substantially below the short regression estimate in column (1). This decline may reflect ability bias in the short model. Yet, once again, more subtle forces may also be at work.

Twin Reports from Twinsburg

Twins are similar in many ways, including—alas—their schooling. Of 340 twin pairs interviewed for the Twinsburg schooling studies, about half report identical educational attainment. Schooling differences, $S_{1,f} - S_{2,f}$, vary much less than schooling levels, S_{if}. If most twins really have the same schooling, then a fair number of the nonzero differences in reported schooling may reflect mistaken reports by at least one of them. Erroneous reports, called *measurement error,* tend to reduce estimates of ρ^l in equation (6.5), a fact that may account for the decline in the estimated returns to schooling after differencing. A few people reporting their schooling incorrectly sounds unimportant, yet the consequences of such measurement error can be major.

To see why mistakes matter, imagine that twins from the same family always have the same schooling. In this scenario,

---

With only two observations per family, models estimated after differencing across twins within families to produce a single observation per family generate estimates of the returns to schooling identical to those generated by "dummying out" each family in a pooled sample that includes both twins.

TABLE 6.2
Returns to schooling for Twinsburg twins

	Dependent variable			
	Log wage (1)	Difference in log wage (2)	Log wage (3)	Difference in log wage (4)
Years of education	.110 (.010)		.116 (.011)	
Difference in years of education		.062 (.020)		.108 (.034)
Age	.104 (.012)		.104 (.012)	
Age squared/100	−.106 (.015)		−.106 (.015)	
Dummy for female	−.318 (.040)		−.316 (.040)	
Dummy for white	−.100 (.068)		−.098 (.068)	
Instrument education with twin report	No	No	Yes	Yes
Sample size	680	340	680	340

Notes: This table reports estimates of the returns to schooling for Twinsburg twins. Column (1) shows OLS estimates from models estimated in levels. OLS estimates of models for cross-twin differences appear in column (2). Column (3) reports 2SLS estimates of a levels regression using sibling reports as instruments for schooling. Column (4) reports 2SLS estimates using the difference in sibling reports to instrument the cross-twin difference in schooling. Standard errors appear in parentheses.

the only reason $S_{1,f} - S_{2,f}$ isn't zero for everyone is because schooling is sometimes misreported. Suppose such erroneous reports are due to random forgetfulness or inattention rather than something systematic. The coefficient from a regression of earnings differences on schooling differences that are no more than random mistakes should be zero since random mistakes are unrelated to wages. In an intermediate case, where some but not all of the variation in observed schooling is due to misreporting, the coefficient in equation (6.5) is smaller than it would be if schooling were reported correctly. The bias generated by this sort of measurement error in regressors is called *attenuation bias*. The mathematical formula for attenuation bias is derived in the chapter appendix.

Misreported schooling attenuates the levels regression estimates shown in column (1) of Table 6.2, but less so than the differenced estimates in column (2). This difference in the extent of attenuation bias is also illustrated by the hypothetical scenario where all twins share the same schooling but schooling levels differ across families. When twins in the same family really have the same schooling, all variation in within-family differences in reported schooling comes from mistakes. By contrast, most of the cross-family variation in reported schooling reflects real differences in education. Real variation in schooling is related to earnings, a fact that moderates attenuation bias in estimates of the model for levels, equation (6.4). This reflects a general point about the consequences of covariates for models with mismeasured regressors—additional controls make attenuation bias worse—a point detailed in the chapter appendix.

Measurement error raises an important challenge for the Twinsburg analysis, since measurement error alone may explain the pattern of results seen in columns (1) and (2) of Table 6.2. Moving from the levels to the differenced regression accentuates attenuation bias, probably more than a little. The decline in schooling coefficients across columns may therefore have little to do with ability bias. Fortunately, seasoned masters Ashenfelter, Krueger, and Rouse anticipated the attenuation problem. They asked each twin to report not only their own schooling but also that of their sibling. As a result, the Twinsburg data sets contain two measures of schooling for each twin, one self-report and one sibling report. The sibling reports provide leverage to reduce, and perhaps even eliminate, attenuation bias.

The key tool in this case, as with many of the other problems we've encountered, is IV. Karen and Sharon make mistakes when reporting each other's schooling as well as when reporting their own. As long as the mistakes in Karen's report of her sister's schooling are unrelated to mistakes in her sister's self-report, and vice versa, Karen's report of Sharon's schooling can be used as an instrument for Sharon's self-report, and vice versa. IV eliminates attenuation bias in the levels regression as well as in estimates of the differenced model (though the levels regression is still more likely than the differenced regression to suffer from ability bias).

As always, an IV estimate is the ratio of reduced-form estimates to first-stage estimates. When instrumenting the levels equation, the reduced-form estimate is the effect of Karen's report of Sharon's schooling on Sharon's earnings. The corresponding first-stage estimate is the effect of Karen's report of Sharon's schooling on Sharon's self-reported schooling. Reduced-form and first-stage results are still subject to attenuation bias. But when we divide one by the other, these biases cancel out, leaving us with an unattenuated IV estimate.

IV works similarly in the first differenced model. The instrument for within-family differences in schooling is the difference in the cross-sibling reports. Provided that measurement errors in own- and cross-sibling schooling reports are uncorrelated, IV produces the no-OVB, unattenuated long-regression return to schooling, ρ^l, that we set out to obtain. Uncorrelatedness of reporting errors across siblings is a strong assumption, but a natural starting point for any exploration of bias from measurement error.

IV estimates of the levels equation appear in column (3) of Table 6.2 (as always, we execute this IV procedure by running 2SLS, which works no less well with instruments that are not dummy variables). Instrumenting self-reported schooling with cross-sibling reported schooling increases the estimated return to schooling only a little, from .110 to .116. This result is consistent with the notion that there's little measurement error in the level of schooling. By contrast, instrumenting the differenced equation boosts the estimated return to schooling from .062 to .108. This result, reported in column (4) of Table 6.2, points to considerable measurement error in the differenced data. At the same time, the differenced IV estimate of .108 is not far below the cross-sectional estimate of .116, suggesting the problem we set out to solve—ability bias in estimates of the returns to schooling—isn't such a big deal after all.

6.3   Econometricians Are Known by Their . . . Instruments

It's the Law

Economists think people make important choices such as those related to schooling by comparing anticipated costs with expected benefits. The cost of staying in secondary school is determined partly by compulsory schooling laws, which punish those who leave school too soon. Since you avoid punishment by staying in school, compulsory schooling laws make extra schooling seem cheaper relative to the alternative, dropping out. This generates a causal chain reaction leading from compulsory schooling laws to schooling choices to earnings that might reveal the economic returns to schooling. The 'metrics methods behind this idea are those of Chapters 3 and 5: instrumental variables and differences-in-differences.

As always, IV begins with the first stage. One hundred years ago, there were few compulsory attendance laws, while today most American states keep students in school until at least age 16. Many states also forbid school-aged children from working, or require school authorities to give permission for a child to work. Assuming that some students would otherwise drop out if not for such laws, stricter compulsory school requirements should increase average schooling. Provided changes in state compulsory attendance laws are also unrelated to the potential earnings of residents in each state (as determined by things like family background, the states' industrial structure, or other policy changes), these laws create valid instruments for schooling in equations like (6.1).

But compulsory attendance laws probably are related to potential earnings. In the early twentieth century, for example, agricultural Southern states had few compulsory attendance requirements, while compulsory schooling laws were stricter in the more industrial North. Simple comparisons of earnings across U.S. regions typically reveal vast differences in earnings, but these are mostly unrelated to the North's more rigorous schooling requirements. Compulsory schooling requirements also grew stricter over time, but here, too, simple comparisons are misleading. Many features of the American economy changed as the twentieth century progressed; compulsory schooling laws are but a small part of this ever-evolving economic story.

A creative combination of DD and IV offers a possible way around OVB roadblocks in this context. Compulsory schooling requirements expanded and tightened most dramatically in the first half of the twentieth century. Masters Joshway and Daron Acemoglu collected state-by-year information on the compulsory schooling laws applicable to those who might have been in school at this time.[8] These laws include child labor provisions as well as compulsory attendance requirements. Child labor laws that require a certain amount of schooling be completed before children are allowed to work seem to have increased schooling more than attendance requirements. A useful simplification in this context uses the laws in effect in census respondents' states of birth at the time they were 14 years old to identify states and years in which 7, 8, and 9 or more years of schooling were required before work was allowed. The resulting set of instrumental variables consists of dummies for each of these three categories; the omitted category consists of states and years in which 6 or fewer years of schooling were required before work was allowed.

Because child labor instruments vary with both state and year of birth, they can be used to estimate a first-stage equation that controls for possible time effects through the inclusion of year-of-birth dummies, while controlling for state characteristics through the inclusion of state-of-birth dummies. Control for state effects should mitigate bias from regional differences that are correlated with compulsory schooling provisions, while the inclusion of year-of-birth effects should mitigate bias from the fact that earnings differ across birth cohorts for many reasons besides compulsory schooling laws. The resulting first-stage equation looks like the Chapter 5 regression

[8] Daron Acemoglu and Joshua D. Angrist, "How Large Are Human-Capital Externalities? Evidence from Compulsory-Schooling Laws," in Ben S. Bernanke and Kenneth Rogoff (editors), *NBER Macroeconomics Annual 2000*, vol. 15, MIT Press, 2001, pages 9–59.

DD model (described by equation (5.5)) used to estimate the effect of state and year changes in the MLDA on death rates. Here, however, year-of-birth dummies replace dummies for calendar time.

The Acemoglu and Angrist compulsory schooling first-stage equation was estimated with an extract of men in their forties, drawn from each of the U.S. census samples available every decade from 1950 to 1990. Stacking these five censuses produces a single large data set in which different censuses contribute different cohorts. For example, men in their forties observed in the 1950 Census were born from 1900 to 1909 and subject to laws in effect in the 1910s and 1920s, while men in their forties observed in the 1960 Census were born from 1910 to 1919 and subject to laws in effect in the 1920s and 1930s.

The first-stage estimates reported in column (1) of Table 6.3 suggest that child labor laws requiring 7 or 8 years of schooling before work was allowed increased schooling (measured as highest grade completed) by about two-tenths of a year. Laws requiring 9 or more years of schooling before work was allowed had an effect twice as large. A parallel set of reduced-form estimates appear in column (3) of the table. These come from regression models similar to those used to construct the first-stage estimates reported in column (1), with the log weekly wage replacing years of schooling as the dependent variable. Laws requiring 7 or 8 years of schooling before work was allowed appear to have raised wages by about 1%, while laws requiring 9 or more years of schooling before work increased earnings by almost 5%, though only the latter estimate is significant. The 2SLS estimate generated by these estimates is .124 (with an estimated standard error of .036).

A 12% wage gain for each additional year of schooling is impressive, all the more so since the schooling increase in question is involuntary. Stronger compulsory schooling laws appear to raise schooling, and this in turn produces higher wages for the men constrained by these laws (compulsory schooling compliers, in this case). Especially interesting is the fact that the 2SLS estimate of the returns to schooling generated by compulsory schooling instruments exceeds the

Table 6.3
Returns to schooling using child labor law instruments

	Dependent variable			
	Years of schooling		Log weekly wages	
	(1)	(2)	(3)	(4)
A. First-stage and reduced-form estimates				
Child labor law req. 7 years	.166	−.024	.010	−.013
	(.067)	(.048)	(.011)	(.011)
Child labor law req. 8 years	.191	.024	.013	.005
	(.062)	(.051)	(.010)	(.010)
Child labor law req. 9 years or more	.400	.016	.046	.008
	(.098)	(.053)	(.017)	(.014)
B. Second-stage estimates				
Years of education			.124	.399
			(.036)	(.360)
State of birth dummies × linear year of birth trends	No	Yes	No	Yes

Notes: This table shows 2SLS estimates of the returns to schooling using as instruments three dummies indicating the years of schooling required by child labor laws as a condition for employment. Panel A reports first-stage and reduced-form estimates controlling for year and state of birth effects and for census year dummies. Columns (2) and (4) show the results of adding state-specific linear trends to the list of controls. Panel B shows the 2SLS estimates of the returns to schooling generated by the first-stage and reduced-form estimates in panel A. Sample size is 722,343. Standard errors are reported in parentheses.

corresponding OLS estimate of .075. This finding weighs against the notion of upward ability bias in the OLS estimate.

Before declaring mission accomplished, a master looks for threats to validity. The variation in schooling generated by compulsory schooling laws produces a DD-style first stage and reduced form. As discussed in Chapter 5, the principal threat to validity in this context is omitted state-specific trends. Specifically, we must worry that states in which compulsory schooling laws grew stricter simultaneously experienced unusually large wage growth across cohorts for reasons unrelated to schooling. Perhaps wage growth and changes in schooling laws are both driven by some third variable, say, changes in industrial structure.

The case for omitted variables bias in this context grows even stronger once we recognize that most of the action in the compulsory schooling research design comes from comparisons of Northern and Southern states. Southern states saw enormous economic growth in the twentieth century, while at the same time, social legislation in these states proliferated. The relative growth in earnings in Southern states might have been caused in part by more restrictive compulsory attendance provisions. But it might not.

Chapter 5 explains that a simple check for state-specific trends adds a linear time trend for each state to the model of interest. In this case, the relevant time dimension is year of birth, so the model with state-specific trends includes a separate linear year-of-birth variable for each state of birth in the sample (the regression model with year-of-birth trends looks like equation (5.6)).

Columns (2) and (4) in Table 6.3 report the results of this addition. The estimates in these columns offer little evidence that compulsory schooling laws matter for either schooling or wages. First-stage and reduced-form estimates both fall precipitously in the model with trends, and none are significantly different from zero. Importantly, the first-stage estimates in column (2) are more precise (that is, have smaller standard errors) than those estimated without state-specific trends. Lack of statistical significance therefore comes from the fact that the estimates with trends are much smaller and not from reduced precision. The reduced-form estimates in column (4) similarly offer little evidence of a link between compulsory school laws and earnings. The 2SLS estimate generated by columns (2) and (4) comes out at an implausibly large .399, but with a standard error almost as large. Sad to say for Master Joshway, Table 6.3 reveals a failed research design.

To Everything There Is a Season (of Birth)

MASTER OOGWAY: Yesterday is history, tomorrow is a mystery, but today is a gift. That is why it is called the present.
Kung Fu Panda

You get presents on your birthday, but some birth dates are better than others. A birthday that falls near Christmas might reduce your windfall if gift givers try to make one present do double duty. On the other hand, many Americans born late in the year get surprise gifts in the form of higher schooling and higher earnings.

The path leading from late-year births to increased schooling and earnings starts in kindergarten. In most states, children enter kindergarten in the year they turn 5, whether or not they've had a fifth birthday by the time school starts in early September. Jae, born on January 1st, was well on the way toward his sixth birthday when he started school. By contrast, Dante, born on December 1st, was not even 5 when he started. Such birthday-based differences in school-starting age are life changing for some.

The life-changing nature of school-starting age is an unintended consequence of American compulsory attendance laws. By the middle of the twentieth century, most states were allowing students to leave school (that is, to drop out of high school) only after they'd turned 16 (some states require attendance until 17 or 18). Most compulsory attendance laws allow you to quit school once you've reached the dropout age, without finishing the school year. Jae, having started school at the ripe old age of 5 years and 8 months, turned 16 in January ten years later, early in his tenth-grade year. Dante, having started school at the tender age of 4 years and 9 months, turned 16 in December eleven years later, after finishing tenth grade and starting eleventh. Both were itching to leave school as soon as they were allowed, and each dropped out immediately on turning 16. But Dante, having started school younger, was forced by accident of birth to complete one more grade than Jae.

You can't pick your birthday. Even your parents probably found your birthday hard to fix. Ultimately, birth timing has a good deal of randomness to it, mimicking experimental random assignment. By virtue of the partly random nature of birth dates, men like Jae and Dante, born at different times of the year, are likely to have similar family backgrounds and talents, even though they have very different educational attainment. This sounds like a promising scenario for IV, and it is.

Masters Joshway and Alan Krueger used differences in schooling generated by quarter of birth (QOB) to construct IV estimates of the economic returns to compulsory schooling.[9] Angrist and Krueger analyzed large publicly available samples from the 1970 and 1980 U.S. Censuses, samples similar to those used by Acemoglu and Angrist. Somewhat unusually for publicly available data sets, these census files contain information on respondents' QOB.

The QOB first stage for 1980 Census respondents appears in Figure 6.1. This figure plots average schooling by year and QOB for men born in the 1930s. Most men in these cohorts finished high school, so their average highest grade completed ranges from 12 to 13 years. Figure 6.1 exhibits a surprising sawtooth pattern: Men born earlier in the year tend to have lower average schooling than those born later. The teeth of the saw have an amplitude of about .15. This may not seem like much, but it's consistent with the story of Jae and Dante. Among men born in the 1930s, about 20% left school in grade 10 or sooner. Late-quarter births impose about .75 of a grade's worth of extra schooling on this 20%. The calculation $.2 \times .75 = .15$ accounts for the ups and downs in Figure 6.1.

As always, IV is the ratio of the reduced form to the corresponding first stage. The QOB reduced form is plotted in Figure 6.2. The flatness of earnings from year to year seen in this figure isn't surprising. Earnings initially increase sharply with age, but the age-earnings profile tends to flatten out for

[9] Joshua D. Angrist and Alan B. Krueger, "Does Compulsory School Attendance Affect Schooling and Earnings?" *Quarterly Journal of Economics*, vol. 106, no. 4, November 1991, pages 979–1014.

FIGURE 6.1
The quarter of birth first stage

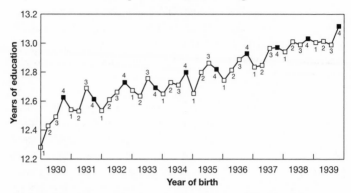

Notes: This figure plots average schooling by quarter of birth for men born in 1930–1939 in the 1980 U.S. Census. Quarters are labeled 1–4, and symbols for the fourth quarter are filled in.

FIGURE 6.2
The quarter of birth reduced form

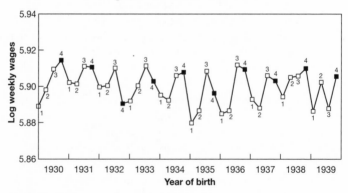

Notes: This figure plots average log weekly wages by quarter of birth for men born in 1930–1939 in the 1980 U.S. Census. Quarters are labeled 1–4, and symbols for the fourth quarter are filled in.

men in their forties. Importantly, however, the QOB saw-tooth in schooling is paralleled by a similar QOB sawtooth in average earnings. Men born later in the year not only get more schooling than those born earlier, they have higher earnings as well. IV logic attributes the sawtooth pattern in average earnings by QOB to the sawtooth pattern in average schooling by QOB.

A simple QOB-based IV estimate compares the schooling and earnings of men born in the fourth quarter to the schooling and earnings of men born in earlier quarters. Table 6.4 organizes the ingredients for this IV recipe using the same sample as was used to construct Figure 6.1. Men born in the fourth quarter earn a little more than those born earlier, a difference of about .7%. Fourth-quarter births also have higher average educational attainment; here, the difference is about .09 years. Dividing the first difference by the second, we have

Effect of schooling on wages

$$= \frac{\{Effect \ of \ QOB \ on \ wages\}}{\{Effect \ of \ QOB \ on \ schooling\}}$$

$$= \frac{.0068}{.0092} = .074.$$

TABLE 6.4
IV recipe for an estimate of the returns to schooling using a single quarter of birth instrument

	Born in quarters 1–3	Born in quarter 4	Difference
Log weekly wage	5.8983	5.9051	.0068 (.0027)
Years of education	12.7473	12.8394	.0921 (.0132)
IV estimate of the returns to schooling			.074 (.028)

Notes: Sample size is 329,509. Standard errors are reported in parentheses.

TABLE 6.5
Returns to schooling using alternative quarter of birth instruments

	OLS (1)	2SLS (2)	OLS (3)	2SLS (4)	2SLS (5)
Years of education	.071 (.0004)	.074 (.028)	.071 (.0004)	.075 (.028)	.105 (.020)
First-stage F-statistic		48		47	33
Instruments	None	Quarter 4	None	Quarter 4	3 quarter dummies
Year of birth controls	No	No	Yes	Yes	Yes

Notes: This table reports OLS and 2SLS estimates of the returns to schooling using quarter of birth instruments. The estimates in columns (3)–(5) are from models controlling for year of birth. Columns (1) and (3) show OLS estimates. Columns (2), (4), and (5) show 2SLS estimates using the instruments indicated in the third row of the table. F-tests for the joint significance of the instruments in the corresponding first-stage regression are reported in the second row. Sample size is 329,509. Standard errors are reported in parentheses.

By way of comparison, the bivariate regression of log weekly wages on schooling comes out remarkably close, at .071. These simple OLS and IV estimates are repeated in the first two columns of Table 6.5. The columns containing IV estimates are labeled "2SLS" because, as always, that's how we do IV.

As with the IV estimates of the effects of family size discussed in Chapter 3, we can use 2SLS to add covariates and additional instruments to the QOB IV story. OLS and 2SLS estimates of models including year of birth dummies (a control for age in our 1980 cross section) appear in columns (3) and (4) of Table 6.5. These results are almost indistinguishable from those in columns (1) and (2). Adding dummies for first and second quarters of birth to the instrument list, however, leads to a noteworthy gain in precision. The three-instrument estimate, reported in column (5), is larger than single-instrument estimates reported in columns (2) and (4), with a standard error that falls from .028 to .020.

What's required for 2SLS estimates using QOB instruments to capture the causal effect of education on earnings? First, the instruments must predict the regressor of interest (in this case, schooling). Second, the instruments should be as good as randomly assigned in the sense of being independent of omitted variables (in this case, variables like family background and ability). Finally, QOB should affect outcomes solely through the channel we've chosen as the variable to be instrumented (in this case, schooling). Other channels must be excluded. It's worth asking how QOB instruments measure up to these first-stage, independence, and exclusion restriction requirements.

We've seen that QOB produces a clear sawtooth pattern in highest grade completed. This is a compelling visual representation of a strong first stage, confirmed by the large F-statistics in Table 6.5. As discussed in the appendix to Chapter 3, a large first-stage F-statistic suggests bias from weak instruments is unlikely to be a problem in this context.

Is QOB independent of maternal characteristics? Birthdays aren't literally randomly assigned, of course. Researchers have long documented season of birth patterns in mothers' socio-economic background. A recent study by Kasey Buckles and Daniel Hungerman explores these patterns further.[10] Buckles and Hungerman find that maternal schooling—a good measure of family background—peaks for mothers who give birth in the second quarter. This suggests that family background cannot account for the seasonal pattern in schooling and wages seen in Figures 6.1 and 6.2, both of which exhibit third- and fourth-quarter peaks. In fact, average maternal schooling by QOB is slightly negatively correlated with average offspring schooling by QOB. Not surprisingly, therefore, control for average maternal characteristics moderately increases IV estimates of schooling returns using QOB instruments. Season of birth variation in family background, though not zero, does

---

[10] Kasey Buckles and Daniel M. Hungerman, "Season of Birth and Later Outcomes: Old Questions, New Answers," NBER Working Paper 14573, National Bureau of Economic Research, December 2008. See also John Bound, David A. Jaeger, and Regina M. Baker, who were the first to caution that IV estimates using QOB instruments might not have a causal interpretation in "Problems with Instrumental Variables Estimation When the Correlation between the Instruments and the Endogeneous Explanatory Variable Is Weak," *Journal of the American Statistical Association*, vol. 90, no. 430, June 1995, pages 443–450.

not follow a pattern that changes QOB-based 2SLS estimates substantially.

Finally, what of exclusion? The QOB first stage is generated by the fact that later-born students enter school younger than those born earlier in the year, and therefore complete more schooling before they're allowed to drop out. But what if school-starting age itself matters? The most commonly told entry-age story is that the youngest children in a first-grade class are at a disadvantage, while children who are a little older than their classmates tend to do better. Here too, the circumstantial evidence for QOB instruments is encouraging. The crux of the QOB-compulsory schooling story is that younger entrants ultimately come out ahead, and this is what the data show.[11]

Empirical strategies are never perfect. Weak nails bend, but the house of 'metrics needn't collapse. We can't prove that a particular IV strategy satisfies the assumptions required for a causal interpretation. The econometrician's position is necessarily defensive. As we've seen, however, key assumptions can be probed and checked in a variety of ways, and so they must be. Masters routinely check their own work and assumptions, while carefully evaluating results reported by others.

On the substantive side, IV estimates using QOB instruments come out similar to or larger than the corresponding OLS estimates of the economic return to schooling. Modest measurement error in the schooling variable might explain the gap between 2SLS and OLS estimates, much as in the twins data. These results suggest downward bias from mismeasured schooling matters as much or more than any ability bias that causes us to overestimate the economic value of education. The earnings gain generated by an additional grade completed seems to be about 7–10%. Bertie Gladwin might have accomplished even more had he finished his schooling sooner.

[11] For more on this point, see Joshua D. Angrist and Alan B. Krueger, "The Effect of Age at School Entry on Educational Attainment: An Application of Instrumental Variables with Moments from Two Samples," *Journal of the American Statistical Association*, vol. 87, no. 418, June 1992, pages 328–336.

6.4   Rustling Sheepskin in the Lone Star State

Schooling means many things, and every educational experience is different. But economists look at diverse educational experiences and see them all as creating human capital: a costly investment in skills from which we also expect to see a return. Some students, like Bertie Gladwin, enjoy school for its own sake and show little interest in economic returns. But many more probably see their schooling as stressful, tiring, and expensive. In addition to tuition costs, time spent in school could have been spent working. Many college students spend relatively little on tuition, but all full-time students pay an opportunity cost. This notion—that a large part of the costs of acquiring an education comes in the form of forgone earnings—leads us to expect each year of additional schooling to generate about the same economic return, whether it's the tenth, twelfth, or twentieth year at the books. The simple human capital view of schooling embodies this idea.

Of course, people who have not had the benefit of economics training probably don't think about education like this. Most measure their educational attainment in terms of degrees instead of years. Few job applicants describe themselves as having completed "17 years of schooling." Rather, applicants list the schools from which they graduated and the dates of degrees received. To an economist, however, degrees are just pieces of paper that should have little or no real value. Master Stevefu is a case in point: though he spent many years in college, attending Susquehanna University in central Pennsylvania (among other fine institutions) he has yet to earn his bachelor's degree. Reflecting this dismissive view of the value of certification, economists refer to the hypothesis that degrees matter as "sheepskin effects," after the material on which diplomas were originally inscribed.

The search for sheepskin effects led Masters Damon Clark and Paco Martorell to a clever fuzzy RD research design.[12]

---

[12] Damon Clark and Paco Martorell, "The Signaling Value of a High School Diploma," *Journal of Political Economy*, vol. 122, no. 2, April 2014, pages 282–318.

They exploit the fact that in Texas, as in many other states, receipt of a high school diploma is conditional on satisfactory completion of an exit exam in addition to state-required coursework. Students first take this exam in tenth or eleventh grade, with retests scheduled periodically for those who fail. A last-chance exit exam for those who have failed previously is administered at the end of twelfth grade. In truth this isn't the last chance for a Texas senior to earn a diploma; it's possible to try again later. Still, for many who take it, the last-chance exam is decisive.

The decisive nature of the last-chance exit exam for many Texas high school seniors is documented in Figure 6.3, which plots the probability of diploma receipt against last-chance exam scores, centered at the passing threshold. The figure, which plots averages conditional on each score value along with fitted values from a fourth-order polynomial estimated separately on either side of the passing cutoff, shows diploma award rates close to .5 for students who miss the cutoff. For those whose scores clear the cutoff, however, diploma award rates jump above 90%. This change is discontinuous and un-ambiguous: Figure 6.3 documents a fuzzy RD first stage of nearly .5 for the effects of exit exam passage on diploma receipt.

Many of those who earn a diploma go on to college, in which case their earnings stay low until this additional schooling is also completed. It's therefore important to look far enough down the road for any sheepskin effect in earnings to emerge. Clark and Martorell used data from the Texas unemployment insurance system, which records longitudinal information on the earnings of most workers in the state, to follow the earnings of those taking the last-chance exam for up to 11 years.

Earnings data for a period ranging from 7–11 years after students sat for their last-chance exit exam show no evidence of sheepskin effects. This can be seen in Figure 6.4, which plots average annual earnings against exam scores in a format paralleling that of Figure 6.3 (earnings here are in dollars and not in logs, and the averages include zeros for people who aren't working). Figure 6.4 is a picture of the reduced form in a fuzzy RD design that uses a dummy for passing the exit exam

FIGURE 6.3
Last-chance exam scores and Texas sheepskin

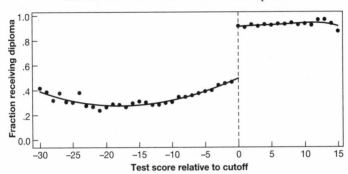

Notes: Last-chance exam scores are normalized relative to passing thresholds. Dots show average diploma receipt conditional on each score value. The solid lines are fitted values from a fourth-order polynomial, estimated separately on either side of the passing cutoff (indicated by the vertical dashed line).

FIGURE 6.4
The effect of last-chance exam scores on earnings

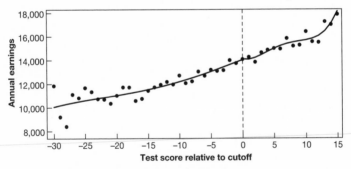

Notes: Last-chance exam scores are normalized relative to passing thresholds. Dots show average earnings conditional on each score value, including zeros for nonworkers. The solid lines are fitted values from a fourth-order polynomial, estimated separately on either side of the passing cutoff (indicated by the vertical dashed line).

as an instrumental variable for the effect of diploma receipt on earnings. As always, when the reduced form is zero—in this case, no jump appears in Figure 6.4—we know that the corresponding 2SLS estimate is zero as well.

The 2SLS estimates generated by dividing the first-stage and reduced-form discontinuities seen in Figures 6.3 and 6.4 show a diploma effect of $52 (with a standard error of about $630). This amounts to less than half a percent of average earnings, which are about $13,000. These are small effects indeed, weighing against the sheepskin hypothesis. On the other hand, the associated confidence intervals also include earnings effects of nearly 10%.

Large standard errors leave us with the possibility of some sheepskin effects, so the search for evidence on this point will surely continue. Masters know the search for econometric truth never ends, and that what is good today will be bettered tomorrow. Our students teach us this.

MASTER STEVEFU: Time for you to leave, Grasshopper. You must continue your journey alone. Remember, when you follow the 'metrics path, anything is possible.

MASTER JOSHWAY: Anything is *possible*, Grasshopper. Even so, always take the measure of the evidence.

Appendix: Bias from Measurement Error

You've dreamed of running the regression

$$Y_i = \alpha + \beta S_i^* + e_i, \tag{6.6}$$

but data on S_i^*, the regressor of your dreams, are unavailable. You see only a mismeasured version, S_i. Write the relationship between observed and desired regressors as

$$S_i = S_i^* + m_i, \tag{6.7}$$

where m_i is the measurement error in S_i. To simplify, assume errors average to zero and are uncorrelated with S_i^* and the residual, e_i. Then we have

$$E[m_i] = 0$$
$$C(S_i^*, m_i) = C(e_i, m_i) = 0.$$

These assumptions describe *classical measurement error* (jazzier forms of measurement error may rock your regression coefficients even more).

The regression coefficient you're after, β in equation (6.6), is given by

$$\beta = \frac{C(Y_i, S_i^*)}{V(S_i^*)}.$$

Using the mismeasured regressor, S_i, instead of S_i^*, you get

$$\beta_b = \frac{C(Y_i, S_i)}{V(S_i)}, \tag{6.8}$$

where β_b has a subscript "b" as a reminder that this coefficient is biased.

To see why β_b is a biased version of the coefficient you're after, use equations (6.6) and (6.7) to substitute for Y_i and S_i in the numerator of equation (6.8):

$$\beta_b = \frac{C(Y_i, S_i)}{V(S_i)}$$

$$= \frac{C(\alpha + \beta S_i^* + e_i, S_i^* + m_i)}{V(S_i)}$$

$$= \frac{C(\alpha + \beta S_i^* + e_i, S_i^*)}{V(S_i)} = \beta \frac{V(S_i^*)}{V(S_i)}.$$

The next-to-last equals sign here uses the assumption that measurement error, m_i, is uncorrelated with S_i^* and e_i; the last equals sign uses the fact that S_i^* is uncorrelated with a constant and with e_i, since the latter is a residual from a regression on S_i^*. We've also used the fact that the covariance of S_i^* with itself is its variance (see the appendix to Chapter 2 for an explanation of these and related properties of variance and covariance).

We've assumed that m_i is uncorrelated with S_i^*. Because the variance of the sum of uncorrelated variables is the sum of their variances, this implies

$$V(S_i) = V(S_i^*) + V(m_i),$$

which means we can write

$$\beta_b = r\beta, \tag{6.9}$$

where

$$r = \frac{V(S_i^*)}{V(S_i)} = \frac{V(S_i^*)}{V(S_i^*) + V(m_i)}$$

is a number between zero and one.

The fraction r describes the proportion of variation in S_i that is unrelated to mistakes and is called the *reliability* of S_i. Reliability determines the extent to which measurement error attenuates β_b. The attenuation bias in β_b is

$$\beta_b - \beta = -(1 - r)\beta,$$

so that β_b is smaller than (a positive) β unless $r = 1$, and there's no measurement error after all.

Adding Covariates

In Section 6.1, we noted that the addition of covariates to a model with mismeasured regressors tends to exacerbate attenuation bias. The Twinsburg story told in Section 6.2 is a special case of this, where the covariates are dummies for families in samples of twins. To see why covariates increase attenuation bias, suppose the regression of interest is

$$Y_i = \alpha + \beta S_i^* + \gamma X_i + e_i, \tag{6.10}$$

where X_i is a control variable, perhaps IQ or another test score. We know from regression anatomy that the coefficient on S_i^* in this model is given by

$$\beta = \frac{C(Y_i, \tilde{S}_i^*)}{V(\tilde{S}_i^*)},$$

where $\tilde{S}_i^*$ is the residual from a regression of S_i^* on X_i. Likewise, replacing S_i^* with S_i, the coefficient on S_i becomes

$$\beta_b = \frac{C(Y_i, \tilde{S}_i)}{V(\tilde{S}_i)},$$

where $\tilde{S}_i$ is the residual from a regression of S_i on X_i.

Add the (classical) assumption that measurement error, m_i, is uncorrelated with the covariate, X_i. Then the coefficient from a regression of mismeasured S_i on X_i is the same as the coefficient from a regression of S_i^* on X_i (use the properties of covariance and the definition of a regression coefficient to see this). This in turn implies that

$$\tilde{S}_i = \tilde{S}_i^* + m_i,$$

where m_i and $\tilde{S}_i^*$ are uncorrelated. We therefore have

$$V(\tilde{S}_i) = V(\tilde{S}_i^*) + V(m_i).$$

Applying the logic used to establish equation (6.9), we get

$$\beta_b = \frac{C(Y_i, \tilde{S}_i)}{V(\tilde{S}_i)}$$

$$= \frac{V(\tilde{S}_i^*)}{V(\tilde{S}_i^*) + V(m_i)}\beta = \tilde{r}\beta, \qquad (6.11)$$

where

$$\tilde{r} = \frac{V(\tilde{S}_i^*)}{V(\tilde{S}_i^*) + V(m_i)}.$$

Like r, this lies between zero and one.

What's new here? The variance of $\tilde{S}_i^*$ is necessarily reduced relative to that of S_i^*, because the variance of $\tilde{S}_i^*$ is the variance of a residual from a regression model in which S_i^* is the dependent variable. Since $V(\tilde{S}_i^*) < V(S_i^*)$, we also have

$$\tilde{r} = \frac{V(\tilde{S}_i^*)}{V(\tilde{S}_i^*) + V(m_i)} < \frac{V(S_i^*)}{V(S_i^*) + V(m_i)} = r.$$

This explains why adding covariates to a model with mismeasured schooling aggravates attenuation bias in estimates of the returns to schooling. Intuitively, this aggravation is a consequence of the fact that covariates are correlated with accurately measured schooling while being unrelated to mistakes. The regression-anatomy operation that removes the influence of covariates therefore reduces the information content of a mismeasured regressor while leaving the noise component—the mistakes—unchanged (test your understanding of the formal argument here by deriving equation (6.11)). This argument carries over to the differencing operation used to purge ability from equation (6.4): differencing across twins removes some of the signal in schooling, while leaving the variance of the noise unchanged.

IV Clears Our Path

Without covariates, the IV formula for the coefficient on S_i in a bivariate regression is

$$\beta_{IV} = \frac{C(Y_i, Z_i)}{C(S_i, Z_i)}, \qquad (6.12)$$

where Z_i is the instrument. In Section 6.2, for example, we used cross-sibling reports to instrument for possibly mismeasured self-reported schooling. Provided the instrument is uncorrelated with the measurement error and the residual, e_i, in equations like (6.6), IV eliminates the bias due to mismeasured S_i.

To see why IV works in this context, use equations (6.6) and (6.7) to substitute for Y_i and S_i in equation (6.12):

$$\beta_{IV} = \frac{C(Y_i, Z_i)}{C(S_i, Z_i)} = \frac{C(\alpha + \beta S_i^* + e_i, Z_i)}{C(S_i^* + m_i, Z_i)}$$

$$= \frac{\beta C(S_i^*, Z_i) + C(e_i, Z_i)}{C(S_i^*, Z_i) + C(m_i, Z_i)}.$$

Our discussion of the mistakes in Karen and Sharon's reports of one another's schooling assumes that $C(e_i, Z_i) = C(m_i, Z_i) = 0$. This in turn implies that

$$\beta_{IV} = \beta \frac{C(S_i^*, Z_i)}{C(S_i^*, Z_i)} = \beta.$$

This happy conclusion comes from our assumption that the only reason Z_i is correlated with wages is because it's correlated with S_i^*. Since $S_i = S_i^* + m_i$, and m_i is unrelated to Z_i, the usual IV miracle goes through.

> Po: That is severely cool.
> *Kung Fu Panda 2*

ABBREVIATIONS AND ACRONYMS

Abbreviations and acronyms are introduced on the page indicated in parentheses.

2SLS two-stage least squares, an instrumental variables estimator that replaces the regressor being instrumented with fitted values from the first stage (p. 132)

ALS a study by Joshua D. Angrist, Victor Lavy, and Analia Schlosser on the causal link between quantity and quality of children in Israeli families (p. 127)

BLS Boston Latin School, the top school in the Boston exam school hierarchy (p. 164)

C&B College and Beyond, a data set (p. 52)

CEF conditional expectation function, the population average of Y_i with X_i held fixed (p. 82)

CLT Central Limit Theorem, a theorem which says that almost any sample average is approximately normally distributed, with the accuracy of the approximation increasing as the sample size increases (p. 39)

DD differences-in-differences, an econometric tool that compares changes over time in treatment and control groups (p. 178)

HIE Health Insurance Experiment, a large randomized trial conducted by the RAND Corporation that provided treated families with different types of health insurance coverage (p. 16)

ITT intention-to-treat effect, the average causal effect of an offer of treatment (p. 119)

IV   instrumental variables, an econometric tool used to eliminate omitted variables bias or attenuation bias due to measurement error (p. 98)

JTPA   Job Training Partnership Act, an American training program that included a randomized evaluation (p. 122)

KIPP   Knowledge Is Power Program, a network of charter schools in the United States (p. 99)

LATE   local average treatment effect, the average causal effect of treatment on compliers (p. 109)

LIML   limited information maximum likelihood estimator, an alternative to two-stage least squares with less bias (p. 145)

LLN   Law of Large Numbers, a statistical law according to which sample averages approach the corresponding population average (expectation) as the sample size grows (p. 13)

MDVE   Minneapolis Domestic Violence Experiment, a randomized evaluation of policing strategies to combat domestic violence (p. 116)

MLDA   minimum legal drinking age (p. 148)

MVA   motor vehicle accidents (p. 159)

NHIS   National Health Interview Survey, a data set (p. 3)

OHP   Oregon Health Plan, the Oregon version of Medicaid, for which eligibility was partly determined by a lottery (p. 25)

OLS   ordinary least squares, the sample analog of population regression coefficients; we use OLS to estimate regression models (p. 58)

OVB   omitted variables bias, the relationship between regression coefficients in models with different sets of covariates (p. 69)

QOB   quarter of birth (p. 229)

RD   regression discontinuity design, an econometric tool used when treatment, the probability of treatment, or average treatment intensity is a known, discontinuous function of a covariate (p. 147)

RSS   residual sum of squares, the expected (population average of) squared residuals in regression analysis (p. 86)

TOT   treatment effect on the treated, the average causal effect of treatment in the treated population (p. 114)

WLS   weighted least squares, a regression estimator that weights observations summed in the RSS (p. 202)

EMPIRICAL NOTES

Tables

Table 1.1 Health and demographic characteristics of insured and uninsured couples in the NHIS

Data source. The 2009 NHIS data are from the Integrated Health Interview Series (IHIS) and are available at www.ihis.us/ihis/.

Sample. The sample used to construct this table consists of husbands and wives aged 26–59, with at least one spouse working.

Variable definitions. Insurance status is determined by the IHIS variable UNINSURED. The health index is on a five-point scale, where 1 = poor, 2 = fair, 3 = good, 4 = very good, 5 = excellent; this comes from the variable HEALTH. Education is constructed from the variable EDUC and measures completed years of schooling. High school graduates and GED holders are assigned 12 years of schooling. People with some college but no degree, and those with an associate's degree, are assigned 14 years of schooling. Bachelor's degree holders are assigned 16 years of schooling, and holders of higher degrees are assigned 18 years of schooling. Employed individuals are those "working for pay" or "with job but not at work" as indicated by the variable EMPSTAT.

Family income is constructed by assigning to each bracket of the IHIS income variable (INCFAM07ON) the average household income for that bracket based on data from the 2010 Current Population Survey (CPS) March supplement (using the CPS variable FTOTVAL). The CPS sample used for this purpose omits observations with nonpositive household income as well as observations with negative weights. CPS income is censored at the 98th percentile; values above the 98th percentile are assigned 1.5 times the 98th percentile value.

Additional table notes.   All calculations are weighted using the variable PERWEIGHT. Robust standard errors are shown in parentheses.

Table 1.3   Demographic characteristics and baseline health in the RAND HIE

Data source.   The RAND HIE data are from Joseph P. Newhouse, "RAND Health Insurance Experiment [in Metropolitan and Non-Metropolitan Areas of the United States], 1974–1982," ICPSR06439-v1, Inter-University Consortium for Political and Social Research, 1999. This data set is available at http://doi.org/10.3886/ICPSR06439.v1.

Sample.   The sample used to construct this table consists of adult participants (14 years old and older) with valid enrollment, expenditure, and study exit data.

Variable definitions.   The demographic variables in panel A and the health characteristics in panel B are measured at the experimental baseline. The general health index rates the participant's perception of his or her general health at the time of enrollment. Higher values indicate more favorable self-ratings of health; less health-related worry; and greater perceived resistance to illness. The mental health index rates the participant's mental health, combining measures of anxiety, depression, and psychological well-being. Higher values indicate better mental health. The education variable measures number of years of completed education and is only defined for individuals 16 years and older. Family income is in constant 1991 dollars.

Additional table notes.   Standard errors in parentheses are clustered at the family level.

Table 1.4   Health expenditure and health outcomes in the RAND HIE

Data source.   See note for Table 1.3.

Sample. See note for Table 1.3. The panel A sample contains multiple observations for the same person from a different follow-up year.

Variable definitions. See notes for Table 1.3. Variables in panel A are constructed from administrative claims data for each year, and variables in panel B are measured upon exit from the experiment. Face-to-face visits counts the number of face-to-face visits with health professionals that were covered by insurance (excluding dental, psychotherapy, and radiology/anaesthesiology/pathology-only visits). Hospital admissions indicates the total number of covered participant hospitalizations, including admissions for reasons of mental health. The expenditure variables are in constant 1991 dollars.

Additional table notes. Standard errors in parentheses are clustered at the family level.

Table 1.5 OHP effects on insurance coverage and health-care use

Sources. The numbers in columns (1) and (2) are from Amy N. Finkelstein et al., "The Oregon Health Insurance Experiment: Evidence from the First Year," *Quarterly Journal of Economics,* vol. 127, no. 3, August 2012, pages 1057–1106. Our numbers come from the original as follows:

- row (1) in panel A from row (1), columns (1) and (2) in Table III;
- row (2) in panel A from row (1), columns (1) and (2) in Table IV;
- row (1) in panel B from row (2), columns (5) and (6) in Table V; and
- row (2) in panel B from row (1), columns (1) and (2) in Table V.

The numbers reported in columns (3) and (4) are from Sarah L. Taubman et al., "Medicaid Increases Emergency-Department Use: Evidence from Oregon's Health Insurance Experiment," *Science,* vol. 343, no. 6168, January 17,

2014, pages 263–268. Our numbers come from the original as follows:

- row (1) from row (1), columns (1) and (2) in Table S7;
- row (3) from row (1), columns (3) and (4) in Table S2;
- row (4) from row (1), columns (7) and (8) in Table S2.

Samples. Columns (1) and (2) in panel A use the full sample analyzed in the hospital discharge and mortality data in Finkelstein et al. (2012). Columns (3) and (4) in panel A are drawn from the emergency department records of 12 Portland area emergency departments for visits occurring between March 10, 2008 and September 30, 2009. Panel B uses the follow-up survey data analyzed in Finkelstein et al. (2012).

Variable definitions. The variable in row (1) in panel A is a dummy for Medicaid enrollment in the study period (from lottery notification through the end of September 2009), obtained from Medicaid administrative data. The variable in row (2) in panel A is a dummy equal to 1 if the respondent had a non-childbirth hospitalization from notification until the end of August 2009. The variables in rows (3) and (4) in panel A indicate any emergency department visit and count the number of such visits. The variable in row (1) in panel B measures the number of non-childbirth-related outpatient visits in the past 6 months. The variable in row (2) in panel B is a dummy for whether the patient had a prescription drug at the time of the survey.

Additional table notes. Standard errors in parentheses are clustered at the household level.

Table 1.6 OHP effects on health indicators and financial health

Sources. See notes for Table 1.5. The numbers in row (1) in panel A in this table are obtained from row (2), columns (1) and (2) in Table IX in Finkelstein et al. (2012). The numbers reported in columns (3) and (4) are from Katherine Baicker et al., "The Oregon Experiment—Effects of Medicaid on Clinical Outcomes," *New England Journal of Medicine,* vol. 368, no. 18, May 2, 2013, pages 1713–1722.

The numbers in columns (3) and (4) come from columns (1) and (2) in the original as follows:

- row (2) in panel A from row (3) in Table S2;
- row (3) in panel A from row (2) in Table S2;
- row (4) in panel A from row (6) in Table S1;
- row (5) in panel A from row (1) in Table S1;
- row (1) in panel B from row (3) in Table S3; and
- row (2) in panel B from row (4) in Table S3.

We thank Amy Finkelstein and Allyson Barnett for providing unpublished standard errors for estimates from Baicker et al. (2013).

Samples. Columns (1) and (2) use the sample from the (first) follow-up survey analyzed in Finkelstein et al. (2012). Columns (3) and (4) use the sample from the (second) follow-up survey analyzed in Baicker et al. (2013).

Variable definitions. The variable in row (1) in panel A is a dummy for whether the respondent rated his or her health as good, very good, or excellent (as compared to fair or poor). Rows (2) and (3) in panel A contain the SF-8 physical and mental component scores. Higher SF-8 scores indicate better health. The scale is normalized to have a mean of 50 and standard deviation of 10 in the U.S. population; the range is 0 to 100. See pages 14–16 of the appendix of Baicker et al. (2013) for descriptions of the subjective and clinical measures of health used in rows (2)–(5). The variable in row (1) in panel B is a dummy for whether health expenditures surpassed 30% of total income in the past 12 months. The variable in row (2) in panel B is a dummy for whether the respondent had any medical debt at the time of the survey.

Additional table notes. Standard errors in parentheses are clustered at the household level.

Table 2.2 Private school effects: Barron's matches

Data sources. The data used to construct this table are described in Stacy Berg Dale and Alan B. Krueger, "Estimating the Payoff to Attending a More Selective College: An Application of Selection on Observables and Unobservables," *Quarterly Journal of Economics*, vol. 117, no. 4, November 2002, pages 1491–1527.

These data are from the College and Beyond (C&B) survey linked to a survey administered by Mathematica Policy Research, Inc., in 1995–1997 and to files provided by the College Entrance Examination Board and the Higher Education Research Institute (HERI) at the University of California, Los Angeles. The college selectivity category is as determined by *Barron's Profiles of American Colleges 1978,* Barron's Educational Series, 1978.

Sample. The sample consists of people from the 1976 college entering cohort who appear in the C&B survey and who were full-time workers in 1995. The analysis excludes students from historically black universities (Howard University, Morehouse College, Spellman College, and Xavier University; see pages 1500–1501 in Dale and Krueger (2002) for details). The sample is further restricted to applicant selectivity groups containing some students who attended public universities and some students who attended private universities.

Variable definitions. The dependent variable is the log of pre-tax annual earnings in 1995. The question in the C&B survey has 10 income brackets; see footnote 8 on pages 1501–1502 in Dale and Krueger (2002) for exact construction of the earnings variable. The applicant group variable is formed by matching students according to the list of categories of schools where they applied and were accepted or rejected (from the C&B survey), where school categories are based on the Barron's college selectivity measure (see pages 1502–1503 in Dale and Krueger (2002) for more on this). The variable own SAT score/100 measures the respondent's SAT score divided by 100. See page 1508 in Dale and Krueger (2002) for the definition of the parental income variable (this is imputed using parental occupation and schooling). Variables female, black, Hispanic, Asian, other/missing race, high school top 10%, high school rank missing, and athlete are dummies.

Additional table notes. Regressions are weighted to make the sample representative of the population of students at C&B institutions (see page 1501 in Dale and Krueger (2002) for details). Standard errors in parentheses are clustered at the level of school attended.

Table 2.3 Private school effects: Average SAT score controls

Data sources. See notes for Table 2.2.

Sample. See notes for Table 2.2. The sample used to construct this table contains all C&B students and not just those with Barron's selectivity group matches.

Variable definitions. See notes for Table 2.2. The variable average SAT score of schools applied to/100 is constructed as follows: the average SAT score (divided by 100) is computed for each university using HERI data and then averaged over the universities where each respondent applied.

Additional table notes. Regressions are weighted to make the sample representative of the population of students at C&B institutions. Standard errors in parentheses are clustered at the university level.

Table 2.4 School selectivity effects: Average SAT score controls

Data sources. See notes for Table 2.2.

Sample. See notes for Table 2.3.

Variable definitions. See notes for Table 2.3. The variable school average SAT score/100 is the average SAT score (divided by 100) of the students at the school the respondent attended.

Additional table notes. See notes for Table 2.3.

Table 2.5 Private school effects: Omitted variables bias

Data sources. See notes for Table 2.2.

Sample, variable definitions, and additional table notes. See notes for Table 2.3.

Table 3.1   Analysis of KIPP lotteries

Data sources.   Demographic information on students in Lynn public schools is from the Massachusetts Student Information Management System. Demographic and lottery information for KIPP applicants is from KIPP Lynn school records. Scores are from the Massachusetts Comprehensive Assessment System (MCAS) tests in math and English language arts. For details, see Joshua D. Angrist et al., "Who Benefits from KIPP?" *Journal of Policy Analysis and Management,* vol. 31, no. 4, Fall 2012, pages 837–860.

Sample.   The sample in column (1) contains students who attended fifth grade in Lynn public schools between fall 2005 and spring 2008. The samples in columns (2)–(5) are drawn from the set of KIPP Lynn applicants for fifth- and sixth-grade entry in the same period. Applicants with siblings already enrolled in KIPP or who went directly onto the waiting list are excluded (see footnote 14 in Angrist et al. (2012)). Lottery comparisons are limited to the 371 applicants with follow-up data.

Variable definitions.   Hispanic, black, female, free/reduced-price lunch, and enrolled at KIPP are dummy variables. The math and verbal scores for students in a given grade are standardized with respect to the reference population of all students in Massachusetts in that grade. Baseline scores are from fourth-grade tests. Outcome scores are from the grades following the application grade, specifically, fifth-grade scores for those who applied to KIPP when they were in fourth grade and sixth grade scores for those who applied to KIPP while in fifth.

Additional table notes.   Robust standard errors are reported in parentheses.

Table 3.3   Assigned and delivered treatments in the MDVE

Data sources.   The numbers reported in this table are from Table 1 in Lawrence W. Sherman and Richard A. Berk, "The

Specific Deterrent Effects of Arrest for Domestic Assault," *American Sociological Review,* vol. 49, no. 2, April 1984, pages 261–272.

Table 3.4 Quantity-quality first stages

Data sources. The data used to construct this table are from the 20% public-use microdata samples from the 1983 and 1995 Israeli Censuses, linked with nonpublic information on parents and siblings from the population registry. For details, see Joshua D. Angrist, Victor Lavy, and Analia Schlosser, "Multiple Experiments for the Causal Link between the Quantity and Quality of Children," *Journal of Labor Economics,* vol. 28, no. 4, October 2010, pages 773–824.

Sample. The sample includes Jewish, first-born non-twins aged 18–60. The sample is restricted to individuals whose mothers were born after 1930 and who had their first birth between the ages of 15 and 45.

Variable definitions. The twins instrument (second-born twins) is a dummy variable equal to 1 in families where the second birth produces twins. The sex-mix instrument (same sex) is a dummy variable equal to 1 if the second and first born are same-sex.

Additional table notes. In addition to a dummy for males, additional covariates are dummies for census year, parents' ethnicities (Asian or African origin, from the former Soviet Union, from Europe or America), and missing month of birth; age, mother's age, mother's age at first birth, and mother's age at immigration (where relevant). The first stages in this table go with the second-stage estimates in the first two rows of Table 3.5. Robust standard errors are reported in parentheses.

Table 3.5 OLS and 2SLS estimates of the quantity-quality trade-off

Data sources. See notes for Table 3.4.

Sample. See notes for Table 3.4. Estimates in the third and fourth rows of the table are limited to subjects aged 24–60

at the time of the census. The college graduation outcome has a few additional missing values.

Variable definitions. See notes for Table 3.4. The dependent variables in the second, third, and fourth rows are dummy variables.

Additional table notes. Covariates are listed in the notes for Table 3.4.

Table 4.1 Sharp RD estimates of MLDA effects on mortality

Data sources. Mortality data are from the National Center for Health Statistics (NCHS) confidential mortality detail files for 1997–2004. These data are derived from death certificates and cover all deaths in the United States in the study period. Population estimates in the denominator are from the 1970–1990 U.S. Censuses. For details, see pages 166–169 of Christopher Carpenter and Carlos Dobkin, "The Effect of Alcohol Consumption on Mortality: Regression Discontinuity Evidence from the Minimum Drinking Age," *American Economic Journal—Applied Economics,* vol. 1, no. 1, January 2009, pages 164–182.

Sample. The sample is restricted to fatalities of young adults aged 19–22. The data used here consist of averages in 48 cells defined by age in 30-day intervals.

Variable definitions. Cause of death is reported on death certificates in the NCHS data. Causes are divided into internal and external, with the latter split into mutually exclusive subcategories: homicide, suicide, motor vehicle accidents, and other external causes. A separate category for alcohol-related causes covers all deaths for which alcohol was mentioned on the death certificate. Outcomes are mortality rates per 100,000, where the denominator comes from census population estimates.

Additional table notes. Robust standard errors are reported in parentheses.

Table 5.1   Wholesale firm failures and sales in 1929 and 1933

Source.   Numbers in this table are from Table 8 (page 1066) in Gary Richardson and William Troost, "Monetary Intervention Mitigated Banking Panics during the Great Depression: Quasi-Experimental Evidence from a Federal Reserve District Border, 1929–1933," *Journal of Political Economy,* vol. 117, no. 6, December 2009, pages 1031–1073.

Data sources.   Data are from the 1935 Census of American Business, as compiled by Richardson and Troost (2009).

Table 5.2   Regression DD estimates of MLDA effects on death rates

Data sources.   MLDA provisions by state and year are from "Minimum Purchase Age by State and Beverage, 1933–Present," DISCUS (Distilled Spirits Council of the US), 1996; Alexander C. Wagenaar, "Legal Minimum Drinking Age Changes in the United States: 1970–1981," *Alcohol Health and Research World,* vol. 6, no. 2, Winter 1981–1982, pages 21–26; and William Du Mouchel, Allan F. Williams, and Paul Zador, "Raising the Alcohol Purchase Age: Its Effects on Fatal Motor Vehicle Crashes in Twenty-Six States," *Journal of Legal Studies,* vol. 16, no. 1, January 1987, pages 249–266. We follow the coding of these laws implemented in Karen E. Norberg, Laura J. Bierut, and Richard A. Grucza, "Long-Term Effects of Minimum Drinking Age Laws on Past-Year Alcohol and Drug Use Disorders," *Alcoholism: Clinical and Experimental Research,* vol. 33, no. 12, September 2009, pages 2180–2190, correcting minor coding errors.

   Mortality information comes from the Multiple Cause-of-Death Mortality Data available from the National Vital Statistics System of the National Center for Health Statistics, obtained from www.nber.org/data/mortality-data .html. Population data are from the U.S. Census Bureau's intercensal population estimates available online. See:

- http://www.census.gov/popest/data/state/asrh/ pre-1980/tables/e7080sta.txt;

- http://www.census.gov/popest/data/state/asrh/ 1980s/80s_st_age_sex.html; and
- http://www.census.gov/popest/data/state/asrh/ 1990s/st_age_sex.html.

Sample. The data set used to construct these estimates contains death rates of 18–20-year-olds between 1970 and 1983 by state and year.

Variable definitions. The mortality rate measures the number of 18–20-year-olds who died in a given state and year (per 100,000), by cause of death (all deaths, motor vehicle accidents, suicide, and all internal causes). The MLDA regressor measures the fraction of 18–20-year-olds who are legal drinkers in a given state and year. This fraction is calculated using MLDA change dates in each state and accounts for grandfathering clauses. The calculation assumes that births are distributed uniformly throughout the year.

Additional table notes. Regressions in columns (3) and (4) are weighted by state population aged 18–20. Standard errors in parentheses are clustered at the state level.

Table 5.3 Regression DD estimates of MLDA effects controlling for beer taxes

Data sources. See notes for Table 5.2. Beer tax data are from Norberg et al., "Long-Term Effects," *Alcoholism: Clinical and Experimental Research,* 2009.

Sample. See notes for Table 5.2.

Variable definitions. See notes for Table 5.2. The beer tax is measured in constant 1982 dollars per gallon.

Additional table notes. See notes for Table 5.2.

Table 6.2 Returns to schooling for Twinsburg twins

Data sources. The twins data are detailed in Orley Ashenfelter and Cecilia Rouse, "Income, Schooling, and Ability: Evidence from a New Sample of Identical Twins," *Quarterly Journal of Economics,* vol. 113, no. 1, February 1998,

pages 253–284. These data are available at http://dataspace
.princeton.edu/jspui/handle/88435/dsp01xg94hp567. This
includes data used in Orley Ashenfelter and Alan B. Krueger,
"Estimates of the Economic Returns to Schooling from
a New Sample of Twins," *American Economic Review,*
vol. 84, no. 5, December 1994, pages 1157–1173.

Sample. The sample consists of 680 twins who were interviewed at the Twinsburg Twins Festival in 1991, 1992, and
1993. The sample is restricted to U.S.-resident twins who
have been employed in the 2 years preceding the interview.

Variable definitions. Estimates in this table were constructed
using self-reported years of education and sibling reports,
defined as an individual's report of the number of years of
education attained by his or her twin sibling.

Additional table notes. Robust standard errors are reported in
parentheses.

Table 6.3 Returns to schooling using child labor law instruments

Data sources. The data used to construct this table are de-
tailed in Daron Acemoglu and Joshua D. Angrist, "How
Large Are Human-Capital Externalities? Evidence from
Compulsory-Schooling Laws," in Ben S. Bernanke and
Kenneth Rogoff (editors), *NBER Macroeconomics Annual
2000,* vol. 15, MIT Press, 2001, pages 9–59.

Sample. The sample consists of U.S.-born white men aged 40–
49, interviewed in U.S. censuses from 1950 through 1990.
The sample was drawn from the integrated public use micro
data samples (IPUMS) for these censuses.

Variable definitions. The dependent variable is the log weekly
wage. The schooling variable is top-coded at 17. The 1990
Census schooling variable is partly imputed using categorical means from other sources. The child labor law instruments are dummies indicating the schooling required before
work was allowed in the respondent's state of birth, according to laws in place at the time the respondent was 14 years

old. For details, see pages 22–28 and Appendix B in Acemoglu and Angrist (2001).

Additional table notes. All regressions are weighted using the IPUMS weighting variable. Standard errors in parentheses are clustered at the state level.

Table 6.4 IV recipe for an estimate of the returns to schooling using a single quarter of birth instrument

Data sources. The data used to construct this table are detailed in Joshua D. Angrist and Alan B. Krueger, "Does Compulsory School Attendance Affect Schooling and Earnings?" *Quarterly Journal of Economics,* vol. 106, no. 4, November 1991, pages 979–1014.

Sample. The sample consists of men born between 1930 and 1939 in the 1980 U.S. Census 5% public use sample. Observations with allocated values were excluded from the analysis, as were respondents who reported no wage income or no weeks worked in 1979. See pages 1011–1012 in Appendix 1 in Angrist and Krueger (1991).

Variable definitions. Log weekly wages in 1979 are computed by dividing annual earnings by weeks worked. The schooling variable is the highest grade completed.

Additional table notes. Robust standard errors are reported in parentheses.

Table 6.5 Returns to schooling using alternative quarter of birth instruments

Data sources, sample, variable definitions, and additional table notes. See notes for Table 6.4.

Figures

Figure 2.1 The CEF and the regression line

Source. This is Figure 3.1.2 on page 39 in Joshua D. Angrist and Jörn-Steffen Pischke, *Mostly Harmless Econo-*

metrics: An Empiricist's Companion, Princeton University Press, 2009.

Sample. See notes for Table 6.4.

Variable definitions. The dependent variable is the log weekly wage. The schooling variable is the highest grade completed.

Figure 3.1 Application and enrollment data from KIPP Lynn lotteries

Data sources. See notes for Table 3.1.

Sample. The KIPP data set analyzed here contains first-time applicants for fifth- and sixth-grade seats in 2005–2008. This sample contains 446 applicants and includes some applicants without follow-up data.

Figure 3.2 IV in school: the effect of KIPP attendance on math scores

Data sources. See notes for Table 3.1.

Sample. The sample here matches that in column (3) of Table 3.1.

Figure 4.1 Birthdays and funerals

Source. This figure is from Appendix A of Christopher Carpenter and Carlos Dobkin, "The Effect of Alcohol Consumption on Mortality: Regression Discontinuity Evidence from the Minimum Drinking Age," *American Economic Journal—Applied Economics,* vol. 1, no. 1, January 2009, pages 164–182.

Additional figure notes. The figure plots the number of deaths in the United States between 1997 and 2003 by age in days measured relative to birthdays.

Figure 4.2 A sharp RD estimate of MLDA mortality effects

Data sources and sample. See notes for Table 4.1.

Variable definitions. See notes for Table 4.1. The Y-axis measures mortality (per 100,000) from all causes. Averages in the figure are for 48 cells defined by age in 30-day intervals.

Figure 4.4   Quadratic control in an RD design

Data sources, sample, and variable definitions. See notes for Table 4.1.

Additional figure notes. See notes for Figure 4.2.

Figure 4.5   RD estimates of MLDA effects on mortality by cause of death

Data sources and sample. See notes for Table 4.1.

Variable definitions. See notes for Table 4.1. The Y-axis measures mortality rates per 100,000 population by cause of death. These are averages for 48 cells defined by age in 30-day intervals.

Additional figure notes. See notes for Figure 4.2.

Figure 4.6   Enrollment at BLS

Data sources. This figure uses Boston Public Schools (BPS) data on exam school applications, including information on Independent School Entrance Exam (ISEE) scores, school enrollment status between 1999 and 2008, and MCAS scores from school years 1999/2000 through 2008/2009. For details, see pages 142–143 and appendix C in the supplement to Atila Abdulkadiroglu, Joshua D. Angrist, and Parag Pathak, "The Elite Illusion: Achievement Effects at Boston and New York Exam Schools," *Econometrica,* vol. 81, no. 1, January 2014, pages 137–196. The supplement is available at http://www.econometricsociety.org/ ecta/supmat/10266_data_description.pdf.

Sample. The sample includes BPS-enrolled students who applied to Boston Latin School (BLS) for seventh grade seats from 1999 to 2008. The sample is restricted to students for whom BLS is either a first choice or a top choice after eliminating schools where the student didn't qualify.

Variable definitions. The running variable, labeled "entrance exam score" in the figure, is a weighted average of applicants' ISEE total score and GPA. Exam school enrollment is measured using data from the school year following application.

Additional figure notes. Running variable values in the figure were normalized by subtracting the lowest score offered a seat at BLS in a given year, so that the cutoff for each year is 0. The smoothed lines in the figures are fitted values from regression models estimated with data near each point. These models regress the dependent variable on the running variable for observations with values inside a nonparametric bandwidth. See Abdulkadiroglu et al. (2014) for details.

Figure 4.7 Enrollment at any Boston exam school

Data sources, sample, and additional figure notes. See notes for Figure 4.6.

Variable definitions. See notes for Figure 4.6. Enrollment at any exam school indicates whether an applicant enrolled at Boston Latin School, Boston Latin Academy, or the John D. O'Bryant High School of Mathematics and Science.

Figure 4.8 Peer quality around the BLS cutoff

Data sources, sample, and additional figure notes. See notes for Figure 4.6.

Variable definitions. See notes for Figure 4.6. For each exam school applicant, peer quality is the average of the fourth-grade MCAS math scores of his or her schoolmates in seventh grade, at any school he or she attended in that grade.

Figure 4.9 Math scores around the BLS cutoff

Data sources, sample, and additional figure notes. See notes for Figure 4.6.

Variable definitions. See notes for Figure 4.6. The variable on the Y-axis here is the average of seventh- and eighth-grade MCAS math scores.

Figure 4.10   Thistlethwaite and Campbell's Visual RD

Source. This is Figure 3 in Donald L. Thistlethwaite and Donald T. Campbell, "Regression-Discontinuity Analysis: An Alternative to the ex post facto Experiment," *Journal of Educational Psychology*, vol. 51, no. 6, December 1960, pages 309–317.

Sample. The sample contains 5,126 near winners and 2,848 near losers of a Certificate of Merit in the 1957 National Merit Scholarship competition. The running variable is the score on the College Entrance Examination Board's Scholarship Qualifying Test, now known as the PSAT. The two outcome measures come from a survey administered to all students in the sample approximately 6 months after awards were announced.

Variable definitions. The two outcome variables are dummies for whether a student plans to do 3 or more years of graduate study (plotted as line I–I′), and whether a student plans to be a college teacher or a scientific researcher (plotted as line J–J′).

Figure 5.1   Bank failures in the Sixth and Eighth Federal Reserve Districts

Data sources. Daily data on the number of banks operating in Mississippi were compiled by Gary Richardson and William Troost and are described on pages 1034–1038 of Gary Richardson and William Troost, "Monetary Intervention Mitigated Banking Panics during the Great Depression: Quasi-Experimental Evidence from a Federal Reserve District Border, 1929–1933," *Journal of Political Economy*, vol. 117, no. 6, December 2009, pages 1031–1073.

Sample. The bank operations data count all national and state chartered banks in Mississippi, summed within Federal Reserve Districts and in operation on July 1, 1930, and July 1, 1931.

Variable definitions. The Y-axis shows the number of banks open for business on July 1 of a given year in a given district.

Figure 5.2 Trends in bank failures in the Sixth and Eighth Federal Reserve Districts

Data sources. See notes for Figure 5.1.

Sample. The bank operations data count all national and state chartered banks in Mississippi, summed within Federal Reserve Districts, in operation between July 1929 and July 1934.

Variable definitions. See notes for Figure 5.1.

Figure 5.3 Trends in bank failures in the Sixth and Eighth Federal Reserve Districts, and the Sixth District's DD counterfactual

Data sources and variable definitions. See notes for Figure 5.1.

Sample. See notes for Figure 5.2.

Figure 5.7 John Snow's DD recipe

Source. This is Table XII (on page 90) in John Snow, *On the Mode of Communication of Cholera,* second edition, John Churchill, 1855.

Figure 6.1 The quarter of birth first stage

Data sources, sample, and variable definitions. See notes for Table 6.4.

Figure 6.2 The quarter of birth reduced form

Data sources, sample, and variable definitions. See notes for Table 6.4.

Figure 6.3 Last-chance exam scores and Texas sheepskin

Data sources. This figure was constructed using a data set linking administrative high school records, administrative post-secondary schooling records, and unemployment insurance earnings records from Texas. These data are detailed on pages 288–289 of Damon Clark and Paco Martorell, "The Signaling Value of a High School Diploma," *Journal of Political Economy*, vol. 122, no. 2, April 2014, pages 282–318.

Sample.   The sample consists of five cohorts of seniors taking their last-chance high school exit exam in spring 1993–1997. Earnings data are available through 2004, namely, for a period running from 7 to 11 years after the time of the last-chance exam.

Variable definitions.   The running variable on the *X*-axis measures the score on the last-chance exam, centered around the passing score. Because the exit exam tests multiple subjects and students must pass all to graduate, scores are normalized relative to passing thresholds and the running variable is given by the minimum of these normalized scores. The *Y*-axis plots the probability of diploma receipt conditional on each score value.

Figure 6.4   The effect of last-chance exam scores on earnings

Data sources and sample.   See notes for Figure 6.3.

Variable definitions.   The running variable on the *X*-axis is as in Figure 6.3. The *Y*-axis measures average annual earnings including zeros for those not working conditional on each score value.

ACKNOWLEDGMENTS

Georg Graetz, Kyle Greenberg, Christian Perez, Miikka Rokkanen, Daisy Sun, Chris Walters, and Alicia Xiong provided expert research assistance. Noam Angrist, A. J. Bostian, Stephanie Cheng, Don Cox, Dan Fetter, Yi Jie Gwee, Samuel Huang, Ayrat Maksyutov, Thomas Pischke, and Melvyn Weeks gave us detailed readings and written comments. Special thanks go to Gabriel Kreindler, who painstakingly compiled and drafted the empirical appendix, and to Mayara Silva for insightful proofreading and invaluable organization of the final manuscript. The empirical applications were developed with the assistance of indulgent masters Kitt Carpenter, Damon Clark, Stacy Dale, Carlos Dobkin, Amy Finkelstein, Karen Norberg, Gary Richardson, and Analia Schlosser, whom we thank for their help as well as their data. Grateful thanks also go to our editor, Seth Ditchik at Princeton University Press, for encouraging and guiding this project; to our skilled and disciplined production editors, Princeton Editorial Associates and Terri O'Prey at the Press; and to Garrett Scafani and Yeti Technologies for awesome original artwork.

In this endeavor as elsewhere, those we love light our path.

INDEX

Page numbers for entries occurring in figures are followed by an *f*; those for entries in notes, by an *n*; and those for entries in tables, by a *t*.